Success or Failure?

Learning and the Language Minority Student

HENRY T. TRUEBA, Editor

University of California, Santa Barbara

NEWBURY HOUSE PUBLISHERS, Cambridge
A division of Harper & Row, Publishers, Inc.
New York, Philadelphia, San Francisco, Washington, D.C.,
London, Mexico City, São Paulo, Singapore, Sydney

Library of Congress Cataloging-in-Publication Data

Success or failure? Learning and the language minority student

  Bibliography: p.
  1. English language—Study and teaching—Foreign
speakers. I. Trueba, Henry T.
PE1128.A2S88 1987   428'.007   86-28473
ISBN 0-06-632547-1

Cover Design: Sally Carson Design
Production: Kewal K. Sharma
Compositor: ComCom Division of Haddon Craftsmen, Inc.
Printer and Binder: McNaughton & Gunn

Success or Failure?
Learning and the Language Minority Student

NEWBURY HOUSE PUBLISHERS
A division of Harper & Row, Publishers, Inc.

Language Science
Language Teaching
Language Learning

CAMBRIDGE, MASSACHUSETTS

Printed in the U.S.A.   First printing: April 1987

63-25476   2 4 6 8 10 9 7 5 3 1

Contents

Preface

We can no longer assume that the knowledge and skills that mainstream children bring to our schools are readily transferable to language minority children by means of regular schooling. The language, culture, and values acquired in the home environment have a direct impact on children's school learning activities and successful adaptation.

For language minority children who have acquired English through another culture in their home, opportunities to learn in U.S. schools are not equal, neither at the point of entry in school, nor at any time thereafter, even if both mainstream and language minority children are exposed to the same instructional process. The social and cognitive skills needed to learn effectively in school are often acquired prior to coming to school, and their continued development requires strong and constant support from the home environment.

Children's ability to participate meaningfully in school learning activities is intimately linked to higher-order cognitive and social skills that presuppose specific and substantial cultural and linguistic knowledge. Most children acquire this knowledge in the home environment. Those who lack this knowledge stand out as low achievers in the early school years. There are many reasons for which language minority children do not acquire this knowledge in the home. These children are often uprooted and isolated. They must move with their parents in search of employment. Their feeling of displacement is often matched by economic and emotional insecurity. Their loss of close personal relationships with adults who help them learn is compounded by drastic changes in the home language and culture.

This book looks at some of the phases of the struggle of language minority children, in contrast with mainstream children, to participate meaningfully in school learning activities and why learning in school seems often to be difficult and unrewarding for them. More than that, the book outlines specific contexts in which learning can be rewarding and successful. The contributors to this book are particularly sensitive to the contrast between language minority and mainstream children, and some of the authors are language minority persons themselves. They know cross-cultural educational research, particularly with the ethnography of schooling. Their writings are diverse, but they focus clearly on the central issue of bringing about a better understanding of why and under what conditions children can learn effectively in schools. There is a clear attempt on the part of the contributors to link learning both to (1) broader sociological, economic, and political factors and to (2) interactional, context-specific learning activities. The authors and editor of this volume hope that the reader will examine critically the problems, potential, and significance of language minority education. Not only does this nation's future economic and scientific superiority depend on the success of minority education, but so does its survival as a democratic nation. It is most likely that by the second decade of the next century, minorities will constitute a very significant part of the work force, and minority children may encompass over 50 percent of the school-age population. Learning about minority children, in contrast with mainstream children, can help us understand all children in a cross-cultural perspective.

This book is indeed optimistic. Children's learning is viewed as an interplay of the close relationships between linguistic, cultural, and cognitive abilities that are acquired in school and in the home through social interaction. While the authors recognize the broader sociological factors affecting school achievement by language minority and low-income children, they offer an optimistic prospect for the development of children's skills.

ACKNOWLEDGMENTS

I would like to thank all of the contributors for their ideas, cooperation, and friendship. I would like to express my profound gratitude to Mary Kimber and Carole MacKenzie for their careful and detailed editing, and to Vincent S. DeYoung and Mary McConkey for their valuable assistance in typing and checking references, and for their help in the various stages of manuscript preparation. I am also thankful to the anonymous reviewers who contributed to the quality of the volume with their constructive criticisms and positive insights. I am deeply grateful to many of my colleagues who have, with their published work, stimulated the production of this volume. My thanks to Fred Erickson, Bud Mehan, John Ogbu, George DeVos, Ray McDermott and, especially, to George and Louise Spindler.

Finally, and most important, to the children who inspired this volume by letting my colleagues and me work with them in school—especially to those children who continue to search for knowledge in spite of many difficulties—I offer my sincere affection and profound gratitude. I hope that these pages can bring greater access to knowledge and academic success for *all* children.

HENRY T. TRUEBA

INTRODUCTION

The Ethnography of Schooling

Henry T. Trueba

In the 1800s ethnography was viewed as the purely descriptive task of recording observed behavioral events. As the following generations became engaged in ethnographic research, they also began to question the work of their masters and to search for a deeper understanding of the cultures under study and for a more rigorous methodology. Anthropologists have been concerned with cultural transmission in the context of the processes of socialization and acculturation. In the 1950s George Spindler applied the concept of cultural transmission to education (1955) and both George and Louise Spindler sponsored a series of publications on anthropology and education which is internationally renowned. George Spindler followed theoretical and methodological developments and produced two publications (1974, 1982) that have become classic textbooks on the ethnography of schooling.

In the Spindlers' ethnographic tradition, this volume attempts to guide the reader through the basic steps that students from diverse linguistic and cultural backgrounds must follow in order to acquire knowledge, both of how to act and of how to manipulate concepts, in other words "learning to learn." Comparing and contrasting the normal academic performance of mainstream children with the low performance of culturally different or language minority students is an exercise that is frequently conducted by school districts. This exercise, however, does not help us to understand the reasons for the continued existence of this disparity. We must explain why the minority student cannot understand, structure, analyze, synthesize, retain, or manipulate the concepts, concept relationships, and conceptual packages required for "learning to learn."

In an attempt to shed some light on the academic problems of minority students, this book touches on the communicative competence and conceptual skills needed to explore or to negotiate for meaning in the classroom context; to classify, to store, and to retrieve information; and to express academic concepts orally as well as in written form. The book also touches on problems of enforcing standards, or gatekeeping, primarily via tests, on the part of school personnel; on problems of isolation, marginality, adaptation to school or to classroom politics; and on the problem of alienation on the part of minority students. Additional considerations pointing to the need for a supportive home environment and for

1

a linkage between school and community highlight the difficulties of achieving success for a language minority student.

Educators and social scientists have made some progress in understanding and remedying the academic failure of linguistic and ethnic minority students in this country. Still, the task seems to be of such magnitude that we feel urged to move faster. In some instances the rapid increase in absolute numbers of minority students and their relative concentration in certain school districts have made it virtually impossible to engage in long-range planning. Indeed, some school districts seem to have lost hope and have adopted laissez-faire policies. Warehousing children in run-down schools for several years, without being able to find teachers who speak their language, has obviously resulted in a great deal of frustration, resentment, and failure. Some of these children, who continue to be monolingual and have not moved up the academic ladder, are now classified as mentally retarded and are moved out to different, but permanent, warehouses.

Whether or not we want to or can accept it, in two or three decades the technological and cultural future of this country will be primarily in the hands of young adults who come from ethnolinguistic minority cultures. American traditions, economic productivity, industrial power, and even national security will depend on their ability to learn in our schools and to operate effectively, using English text in a variety of contexts. If our school districts find it either impossible or irrelevant to deal with the problem of student alienation, they will by default create an irreparable vacuum.

It seems that most minority children are happy and competent in their home environments. Most of them learn everything they need to know in order to operate effectively in their social environment. As they move from home to school, however, the problems begin to become apparent for many of them; school experiences can become highly stressful, unrewarding, and undesirable. For many, school is viewed as a way to escape from their home culture and become invisible in mainstream America. Often however, their skin color, phonetic patterns, physical appearance, kinetic behavioral characteristics, and many other subtle cultural markers will denounce them as "ethnic." For all who have come to the United States, nevertheless, going from home to school is a one-way cultural and linguistic journey that is traumatic and wrought with profound personal and social consequences. One of the consequences is that the child must integrate his or her learning modes acquired in the home with those acquired in school. Learning how this is done and under what conditions it can be done effectively and painlessly, is of enormous importance for long-term academic achievement and successful adaptation to this country.

During the process of adaptation, ethnolinguistic minority students have the need to continue to learn at the level at which they were operating before they migrated to this country. If the lack of English forces them to stop learning at that level, or if these children are treated as incompetent, stupid, or underachieving, their perception of their own academic ability and personal worth will suffer irreparable damage. These minority students will never have confidence in themselves, feel competent enough to do their school work, or knowledgeable enough to compete with their mainstream peers.

Convinced as we are of the significance of this theme and the importance of the studies presented in this volume, we think it is necessary to present a cohesive theoretical view in order to place each contribution in its appropriate perspective. In the following pages we attempt to share with the reader some basic understanding about the theoretical assumptions common to all of the contributors, the nature of underachievement, and the explanations offered regarding underachievement and alienation, and a summary of what we have learned in the last few years about the best ways to attack these problems.

SOCIALIZATION FOR SCHOOL ACHIEVEMENT

We all continue to ask questions about the nature of differential achievement in ethnolinguistic minority students and the relationship between literacy and successful academic efforts. We have discovered that there are some basic and natural social units, such as the family, the church, and peer groups, in which a child learns to behave in socially acceptable ways and learns to inquire, to search for meaning, to participate in social interactions, and to act independently. The child has no problem acquiring the knowledge needed to operate competently in these natural units that surround the early preschool years when and if there exists some degree of stability.

Without being consulted or even comprehending its full meaning, many children are uprooted and transplanted to a new setting where they stand out as strange and incompetent. The social sciences study these personal traumas as part of the ongoing rapid sociocultural change that often results in disenfranchised populations. Rapid social change seems to involve a total reorganization of the cognitive categories, sociocultural values, and perception of self that developed in the home.

Minority children sometimes have to leave their country of origin, culture, and language. What they experience, however, is not simply a language change; it is a change of the basic social unit in which children live: the family, the peer group, the church. These changes affect not just some aspects of their personal life, but rather *all* aspects. While attempting to acquire English as their new language, these minority children realize that they are not dealing with changes in sound units, syntactic forms, or the meaning of words and sentences. They discover that they are dealing with an entirely different world conception, which classifies behavioral phenomena and expresses emotions in different ways. At that point they are confronted with the challenge of acquiring an entirely different culture, which they often view as being in conflict with their own.

While most social sciences recognize the significance of the process of socialization in the family as the natural unit for cognitive and linguistic growth, anthropology emphasizes the common characteristics of this process across cultures:

1. The socialization process takes a relatively long time in humans and is carried on within the nuclear and extended family by adults and peers within a predictable distribution of activities.
2. The process stresses knowledge, skills, and strategies necessary for survival in the local environment.
3. The process consists of rewards and penalties associated with the acquisition of knowledge, skills, and strategies, and with the expected behavior for each age and sex group.
4. Most frequently, emphasis will be placed on the acquisition of knowledge needed to operate appropriately in the family and community rather than on the cognitive skills required to understand, classify, and retrieve abstract information about matters not directly relevant to survival, distribution of labor, and appropriate behavior.
5. In all cultures there is a certain amount of language use to teach children appropriate behaviors, but there are marked differences within and across cultures regarding the emphasis placed on the actual teaching of the language and the reward system associated with its appropriate use.

An additional reason to reexamine the process of socialization across cultures in the context of minority education and differential school achievement is that school work requires skills and knowledge learned at home. Some children, particularly those from mainstream middle- and upper-class families, are better prepared to face school tasks than are those from rural, low-income, non-Western, minority families. Thus, a minority child's very start in school is marked by clear disadvantages, regardless of any linguistic differences.

Having stressed the importance of the family and the socialization process within the family, we think that it is important to express our conceptual position regarding the nature of the linguistic, cognitive, and cultural knowledge expected in ethnolinguistic minority students, as well as the nature of their frequent "failure" in school.

MODERN ETHNOGRAPHY IN EDUCATIONAL RESEARCH

Modern ethnography adopted the use of linguistic research methods to obtain and analyze data. This led to the so-called "emic" approach, in contrast with the "etic" approach. "Emic" was understood as the perspective of the members of a cultural and linguistic group, that is, the insiders' view of phenomena; and "etic" was understood as the outsiders' view, that is, in the context of cross-cultural comparisons (Pike 1954:8–10).

The teaching of ethnographic methods has developed rapidly and has become highly diversified in the social sciences. Researchers have emerged in two distinct clusters with theoretical and methodological preferences: (1) macro-ethnographers, who deal with large population sets, economic structures, decision making, and broad sociological and cultural processes; and (2) micro-ethnographers, who deal with clearly focused interactional issues of child growth and development, early childhood, transfer of information, inferencing, intra- and inter-ethnic communication, and cognitive processes. These clusters parallel the two approaches discussed earlier.

School ethnographers from both clusters have called for increased rigor in the analysis of observed behavior and the need to ground inferences. Ethnographers using the context-specific approach have placed enormous importance on language, based on the assumption that people interpret their world of experience and build their code of behavior from the way they talk about it. Frake, for example, discusses how this code "is construed as knowledge in people's heads" (1964:132).

Thus, while some ethnographers discussed below, taking a broader sociological perspective, view school experiences as determined by social, economic and political macro-societal forces, others, advocating a context-specific approach, view school experiences as determined by interaction patterns and the immediate social-psychological characteristics of the learning environment. The theoretical foundation for the latter approach is taken from the ethnography of communication as developed primarily by Gumperz and Hymes (1964), and from Vygotsky's theory of development of higher psychological functions (1978). The pre-eminent role of language and communicative competence for the development of higher psychological functions is, according to Vygotsky (1978) and his followers (Scribner and Cole 1981; Griffin, Newman, and Cole 1981; Cole and D'Andrade 1982; Cole and Griffin 1983; Wertsch 1985), intimately related to the teachers' ability to help children understand symbols and symbolic systems, which are presumed to mediate between the mind and outside reality. Symbols can be understood if they are culturally and linguistically meaningful. In the ultimate analysis, development consists of an increased ability to manipulate symbols and to use them in inter- and intra-psychological operations.

Central to the specific use of ethnographic methods in this study was Vygotsky's assessment of differential learning potential in children, via the use of the *Zone of Proximal Development* (ZPD) defined as ". . . the distance between the actual developmental level as determined by independent problem solving and the level of potential development as determined through problem solving under adult guidance or in collaboration with more capable peers" (Vygotsky 1978:86).

Vygotsky's sociohistorical school of psychology has departed substantially from traditional Western psychology in that it requires an active role on the part of the child in determining his or her level of activity. Activity is understood as an intellectual engagement composed of action and operations, which can be inter-psychological (social, i.e., carried out in interaction with others), or intra-psychological (carried out inside of the individual). For the child to play an active role and work effectively within his or her ZPD, he or she must continuously go from the social to the intra-psychological and back to the social. In effect, every developmental step is mediated by social situations and inter-psychological activities (Griffin, Newman, and Cole 1981:8).

Failure, in this theoretical perspective, is not an attribute of the individual, but rather a social phenomenon, a *systemic failure,* understandable only in its own historical context. Although it may exist in the classroom, it also exists in the home, workplace, community, and society at large. In order to overcome systemic failures, one has to change or impact the entire system. One can only begin by appropriately socializing minority students for academic success (Cole and Griffin 1983:71).

In Vygotsky's perspective one of the most conspicuous systemic failures occurs in the identification and treatment of handicapped children. These children's inability to handle symbolic systems (language, text, and other communicative instruments) often indicates a societal failure in that these children have not had a chance to gain control of the mediating symbols that translate outside reality into culturally appropriate and meaningful entities. One must look for ways to help handicapped children acquire control of these symbols.

New Vygotskians feel that clinical definitions of learning-handicapped or learning-disabled students are to be suspected of political opportunism and cultural ethnocentrism. A close look at the categories used to classify linguistic minority children's problems shows them to be essentially inconsistent, arbitrary, inappropriate, and developed in response to pragmatic concerns and not in accordance with the knowledge gathered in cognitive research (Brown, Campione, Cole, Griffin, Mehan, and Riel 1982:43). Cole and D'Andrade indicate that concept formation is deeply impacted by formal schooling. Thus, in tasks that required the clear grasping of taxonomic systems and the ability to process knowledge, schooled populations cognitively outperformed nonschooled populations (Cole and D'Andrade 1982:19).

From the perspective of the socio-historical school of psychology led by Vygotsky, cognitive development is manifested in higher-order mental functions that are rooted in social interaction. This is called a "culturally or socially based notion of cognitive development," and it means that social competence and mental competence are inseparable. This approach has important implications for the ethnographic analysis of instructional events and for the study of children's adjustment to a school whose culture is different from the home culture.

Data collection and analysis in most of the book's chapters has followed the steps used by Hymes (1981), Gumperz (1981, 1982), Erickson (1979, 1982, 1984), Au (1980), Erickson and Shultz (1982), Au and Jordan (1981), and Gilmore and Glatthorn (1982), among others, and has often consisted of participant observation in classroom and playground activities as well as interviews with children, with their teachers, and with their families.

THEORETICAL APPROACHES TO STUDY MINORITY EDUCATION

Current theoretical models have not sufficiently emphasized the intimate relationship between language, culture and, cognition during the home socialization process and early stages of academic socialization. Furthermore, the symbiotic relationship of the linguistic, cultural, and cognitive skills needed by pupils must be matched by the teacher's ability to recognize differential degrees of student participation during instruction and to understand how these are related to the students' skill levels.

Linguistic, cultural, and cognitive skills are necessary to operate competently in the home. Children's correct use of grammar and discourse is taught along with cultural norms in the context of actual communication in social situations. There are strong reasons to believe that the child develops his or her cognitive skills and language proficiency at the same time that he or she learns social and cultural norms. Thus, academic achievement requires social and cultural knowledge. To acquire the language skills needed to establish relationships between concepts and the oral or written forms of that language, it is also necessary to understand social and cultural norms, values, and premises. We speak of low achievement as the presumed lack of ability to do the following:

1. Grasp concepts
2. Establish relationships between concepts or information sets
3. Analyze, synthesize, classify, store and retrieve information sets and packages
4. Articulate the information processed in oral and written form

Naturally, the grasping of concepts assumes some general notion of how a given concept fits into one's own experience and cognitive map. For example, it is common knowledge that Alaskan children have a rich linguistic repertoire to describe types of snow. Anthropologists have also reported that Mayan children recognize a large variety of medicinal plants important to their physical survival. Undoubtedly, North American children are familiar with types and characteristics of electronic games rather unknown to rural children in developing countries.

Concept formation, therefore, is intimately related to the previous personal or vicarious experiences of children. So also are the relationships between concepts (classes of objects, sets and subsets, types and subtypes of things—inanimate objects, plants, animals, persons, etc.). The more instruction moves from concepts to information sets and packages, as well as from simple concepts to complex cognitive operations (e.g., analysis, synthesis, classification, retrieval, etc.), the more children require coaching and training through the process of socialization.

School achievement greatly depends on literacy. Making sense of text is not difficult in and of itself. It becomes difficult only when the message is meaningless vis-à-vis the lack of social and cultural information essential to make sense of the text. Lack of information regarding the symbols is at the heart of the initial difficulty in reading: for example, the ambiguity of the same written symbol (e.g., "th") that corresponds to two entirely different sound units, or the ambiguity of the sound unit that has two totally different meanings ("green house" and "green-house") or even that has the same sound but different spellings and meanings (e.g., "night" and "knight," or "sew" and "so"). Theoretically, at one level of difficulty, that is, at the level of coding or decoding written symbols, most children presumably encounter similar difficulties, regardless of sociocultural and linguistic differences, because all children have to acquire the correspondence of written to spoken linguistic symbols. In fact, some children become quite familiar with letters and sets of letters long before they become interested in their meaning or translation into spoken language.

When the level of difficulty examined goes beyond the graphic symbols, the experience of children becomes critical for the understanding of text and for making sense of larger segments and their relationships. Thus, beyond word recognition and meaning identification of words and sentences, important cognitive and metacognitive skills are required to quickly establish the potential meaning of a sentence and to exclude alternative meanings. The choices available to the reader cannot exceed his or her personal or vicarious experience. Thus, for example, in order to fictionalize an event and one's own role as reader, one must have an accumulation of cultural cues based on the relatively common experiences of readers for whom the text was intended. It is not surprising, therefore, that immigrant children can at times be very poor readers in English and excellent readers in their own language, or that they can, upon learning cultural clues, advance rapidly in reading comprehension in English. By the same token, recent research seems to indicate that minority youth can rapidly acquire writing skills in English, provided the subject is culturally meaningful and applicable to real-life situations (Trueba, Moll, Diaz, and Diaz 1984).

SOCIOCULTURAL FACTORS OF MINORITY ACHIEVEMENT

To argue that blacks, Hispanics and other minority groups achieve less in school because of their genetic endowment is unscientific and unfounded. Evidence of high achievement in minority individuals contradicts those pseudotheories, which do not deserve further attention and have been sufficiently refuted (see Ogbu 1978:54–65).

There are two main theoretical approaches currently exploring the sociocultural factors of minority achievement that are presented in social science literature: (1) the cultural-ecological approach, based on broad sociological, historical, and economic factors, and (2) the context-specific approach, focused on the organization of teaching and learning activities. These approaches can be complementary and represent two different and important conceptual avenues for interpreting the same social phenomena and accomplishing similar goals.

The first approach is best represented in the work of Ogbu and his associates (Ogbu 1974, 1978, 1982; Ogbu and Matute-Bianchi 1986; Suarez-Orozco 1986); the second approach is best represented by the work of Vygotsky as interpreted by Cole, D'Andrade, Diaz, Moll, Mehan, and other members of the Laboratory of Comparative Human Cognition (Cole and Griffin 1983; D'Andrade 1984; Cole and D'Andrade 1982; Erickson 1984; Wertsch 1985).

Ogbu and his associates distinguish three types of minority groups (Ogbu 1978; Ogbu and Matute-Bianchi 1986):

1. *Autonomous:* those groups that "may be victims of prejudice, but not of subordination in a system of rigid stratification" (Ogbu and Matute-Bianchi, 1986), such as the Amish, Jews, and Mormons in the United States

2. *Immigrant:* those groups that moved "more or less *voluntarily,*" for economic, social, or political reasons to the United States, such as Cuban-Americans, Chinese-Americans, Japanese-Americans, and West Indians (Ogbu and Matute-Bianchi, 1986:87).

3. *Castelike minorities:* those groups that "have become *incorporated* into a society more or less *involuntarily* through slavery, conquest, or colonization, and then relegated to menial status," such as blacks, Mexican-Americans, and Native Americans (Ogbu and Matute-Bianchi, 1986:92–96).

According to these authors, the denigrating ideology and treatment of minorities on the part of the dominant society applies to all three types but affects mainly the castelike group members on account of "their own rationalization or explanation of the existing social order and their place in it . . ." (Ogbu and Matute-Bianchi 1986:93).

Castelike minorities develop a collective sociocultural identity in opposition to that of the dominant group. They respond with "cultural inversion," that is, with a mechanism whereby symbols, behaviors, and meanings of mainstream society are viewed as inappropriate for the caste-like group (Ogbu and Matute-Bianchi 1986:98).

What does constitute the caste-like status is not clear. The question remains as to whether it is a personal, psychological attribute or a social, collective one. When does a caste-like person or group stop being such? If this status is rooted in historical and economic experiences beyond the reach of current groups and individuals, then is it not a permanent and irreversible status? Are blacks, Chicanos, and Native Americans truly comparable? Is the sociological and organizational impact of those institutions comparable beyond the broad historical comparability of slavery, conquest, and colonization? Are we not ignoring historically documented differences in interbreeding patterns between Europeans and members of these three groups? More important, are we not also ignoring current social, cultural, and political realities that are creating significant intra- and intergroup differences?

We know that Chicanos have maintained systematic cultural and linguistic contact with Mexicans across the border. Chicanos have developed a truly binational social structure with well-defined economic, social, political, and cultural organizations—as well as flexible boundaries. Scholars have also recognized the impact of immigration policies on the mental health and achievement of many Mexican-American children whose parents are undocumented workers. The "Migra" raids are only too frequent and well known to thousands of Hispanics in the Southwest.

Perhaps the strongest argument against this view is the abundant empirical evidence and personal experiences of academic mobility among blacks, Chicanos, and Native Americans in response to well-planned and culturally meaningful educational activities on their behalf. While the social phenomenon of underachievement looks permanent with the ever-increasing number of newcomers, the success of many individuals, families, and communities is also undeniable.

While the perspective of Ogbu and his associates has brought about significant attention to historical, cultural and sociological factors affecting differential school achievement in minority populations, the question still stands: Is it true that current behavior can be patterned primarily by historical experiences far removed from today's life of minority individuals and groups? What can teachers do with this "theory" of underachievement? The only logical alternative is to stop doing anything with castelike children.

Some authors are attempting to reconcile the cultural-ecological approach with the context-specific approach. See for example Cortes (1986), who presents a panoramic historical and legal view of minority educational experiences in the United States, particularly in California, and outlines demographic, economic, and educational reform trends. Sue and Padilla (1986) discuss the differential academic performance of blacks, Hispanics, American Indians, Asians, and mainstream whites in California. Others, such as Heath (1986), argue for linkage between home and school in order to create more adequate learning experiences for minority children.

The proponents of the context-specific view, discussed below, ask this question: If all children exhibit similar linguitic and cognitive capabilities required for literacy and school achievement in the home environment, why do they exhibit vast differences in ability and academic performance in school? This approach attributes particular significance to the study of communicative interaction in problem solving.

This approach, having recognized the impact of broad sociological and economic factors, attempts to explain why individual differences in achievement still remain. The context-specific approach emphasizes the description of teaching and learning events with contexts constructed by interaction participants, analyzed from a Vygotskian perspective. In this perspective, the Zone of Proximal Development and the notion of teacher–peer mediation are central to the understanding of effective knowledge acquisition and the development of cognitive skills needed for academic achievement (Diaz, Moll, and Mehan 1986).

In contrast to the previous one, this approach shifts the responsibility for children's academic failure from the child and his or her group's sociohistorical, economic, and political experiences of the past to the present social and pedagogical organizations responsible for the process of academic socialization. The emphasis is on obtaining full participation in the learning process. These authors look for ways in which the organizational structure of the teaching and learning processes and the overall social organization of the school is made responsive to students' cultural and cognitive needs, regardless of the students' historical background or socioeconomic and immigrant status. Far from imputing to them lack of motivation or will to learn, it recognizes the intrinsic rewards of learning.

The context-specific approach cannot be seen as a myopic and trivial microscopic approach to minority underachievement if it is judged from the vantage point of the nature of culture and its role in knowledge acquisition, as discussed in current literature (see Shweder and LeVine 1984; Cummins 1986:23–35; and especially D'Andrade 1984.89–100). Initial formulations of culture as knowledge overemphasized codes of behavior shared by a group of individuals. Subsequently, social scientists began to contrast "codes of behavior" with binding norms to direct action. Issues about the nature of culture are closely related to questions "about the degree to which culture is shared and how culture is distinguished from social structure" (D'Andrade 1984:109). D'Andrade's significant insight is that "the concept of social structure appears to refer to the systems of meanings." (109) Therefore, the context-specific approach, by means of interactional analysis, is providing important information about the differential sharing patterns of culture as a system of meanings, that is, as a binding knowledge. It is precisely through interactional analysis and the study of single events that we discover the social structure and the linkages between macrosociological variables (unemployment, economic and political oppression, etc.) and participant structures of individuals. Ultimately, the degree of participation of minority students and their differential success in schools is comprehensible only when we can understand those linkages.

In brief, the context-specific approach views the psychological reality of knowledge acquisition in its cultural and social context. Learning is stimulated by complex cultural meaning systems with representational, constructive, directive, and evocative functions. It is precisely through these functions that minority students are empowered to perform competently in school. The substantial literature on the relationships between interactional contexts and macrosociological factors is quite convincing. Theories are needed now that open the door to our understanding of how children can increase their knowledge.

The present volume presents chapters that employ both approaches, the cultural-ecological approach and the context-specific approach. Some authors, for example, Walker, Suarez-Orozco, Richards, and Sinclair and Ghory, may perhaps reflect some preference for the former, while others, like Shultz and

Theophano, Cheng, Deyhle, Delgado-Gaitan, and Rueda, may find the latter more suitable for their analytical purposes. The reader will see how the authors integrate different views and philosophies. It is important, however, to view both approaches as deeply rooted in the ethnograpic research tradition, which has enjoyed long-standing and well-deserved respect from all social scientists.

THE STUDIES PRESENTED HERE

Chapter 1, by Walker, provides contextual information about the Spanish-speaking minorities in this country, their growth, and their social, economic, and educational problems. Chapter 2, by Shultz and Theophano, offers an ethnographic account of three-year-old children in a day-care center as they attempt to protect their own sitting places through verbal strategies and thus exercise their social competence in manipulating abstract concepts of time. Chapter 3, by Cheng, presents case studies that describe the difficulty of speech clinicians in dealing with language-impaired minority children and the need to use qualitative research methods to assess children's abilities. Chapter 4, by Willett, is the study of two preschool girls, one Korean and the other Brazilian, who demonstrate contrasting responses to similar English language exposure. Chapter 5, by Deyhle, points to the problems involved in testing Navajo children and the efforts of some teachers to protect their students. Chapter 6, by Richards, describes the Guatemalan Spanish-dominant environment in which Mayan children are placed and their subsequent failure to learn Spanish. Chapter 7, by Delgado-Gaitan, describes the home environment and the role of parents as supporters of children's academic development. Chapter 8, by Suarez-Orozco, looks at the differential school adaptation of Central Americans in contrast to Mexican-Americans. Chapter 9, by Sinclair and Ghory, describes the various stages and patterns exhibited by marginal learners. Finally, chapter 10, by Rueda, discusses issues of bilingualism, cognition, and learning handicaps.

The introductory and last chapters attempt to discuss learning problems and relationships between language, culture, and cognition in the cohesive theoretical framework of Vygotsky's sociohistorical school psychology. The volume begins and ends with chapters focusing on the learning problems of minorities in the United States, with special emphasis on the Spanish-speaking population. Other chapters include studies of North American (Shultz and Theophano, and Sinclair and Ghory), Korean and Brazilian (Willett), Indochinese (Cheng), Native American (Deyhle) and Mayan (Richards) populations. The problems of Mexican-Americans and Native Americans in acquiring English can be compared with those of Mayan children acquiring Spanish, the dominant language in Guatemala. These problems can be relatively manageable and transitional (Willett, Cheng, Delgado-Gaitan), or they can result in handicaps presumed permanent (Rueda). The volume includes studies of preschool-age children (Shultz and Theophano, Willett, and Cheng) and elementary school-age children (Deyhle, Richards), and it concludes with studies of adolescent and adult populations (Sinclair and Ghory, and Delgado-Gaitan).

Most of the chapters are the result of participant observation methods and field intensive studies. They attempt to study children's behavior in their actual interactional context—the social and cultural milieu that influence their learning. Various chapters do shed some light on why minority students fail. Classroom behavior, as studied by Shultz and Theophano, Willett, Deyhle, Richards, and Suarez-Orozco is not just a mirror of the social environment but is also an arena where micro-political processes count towards success or failure. Home language and learning environment is seen as greatly influencing school work, and harmony between home and school interactional strategies is presented as being crucial by Cheng, Willett, Deyhle, Delgado-Gaitan, and Sinclair and Ghory. Cheng and Deyhle recognize the importance of helping minority children deal with text. Delgado-Gaitan, Cheng, and Sinclair and Ghory look at achievement differences not as a "terminal condition," but rather as something that can be changed through intervention.

This book is intended to offer hope and understanding to those teachers who have come to realize that traditional concepts and practices of teacher training fail as we face a student population with a language, culture, and world view profoundly different from mainstream persons. The insights presented by the contributors to this volume should persuade teachers that they have a unique role in the future of this nation. Effective teaching of linguistic minority students implies a teacher's ability to communicate with the students and to engage them in learning interactions in such a way that their participation determines the teacher's communicative strategies. Viewing teaching as a two way communicative process forces us to revise our assumptions about teacher preparation and the need for cooperative partnerships of schools, community, and institutions of higher education.

Hispanic Achievement: Old Views and New Perspectives

Constance L. Walker

If we were to examine in detail the phenomenon of Hispanic students in American public schools over the last fifty years we would see much of interest, and not a little that would astound and shame us. Evidence of low achievement and attainment, overage students, and high dropout rates would permeate our information. We would search widely to find information from the early part of the twentieth century that could tell us about students of Spanish-language heritage in our schools. Later on we would find that not until the 1960s did this population begin to become more visible on a national level (indeed, many writings during that period spoke of the "invisible Mexican population of the United States"). Only after serious study began of the American black population in the wake of the War on Poverty and the Civil Rights Movement did attention also focus on the Mexican-American, Puerto Rican, and Cuban populations of the United States. Not until census studies were prepared in 1960 and 1970 did the federal government even begin to consider the complexity of defining and describing this component of our national population.

During the 1970s and 1980s we see a significant increase in both the quantity and the quality of research on Hispanic students and their school experiences. The totality of information available on the experiences of the Hispanic student at school would be impossible to compile—indeed, (and fortunately) its variety and complexity renders such a task overwhelming. But if one were to examine the focus, the flavor, the thrust of such research, the results might prove indicative of our collective wisdom at certain periods concerning the issue of language minority students and school. Such is the purpose of this study—to examine the extent and nature of Hispanic underachievement while at the same time to trace how this underachievement has been examined and explained. How have researchers and practitioners described the failure of minority students, particularly Hispanic students? How have they examined the relationship between Hispanic students and academic achievement? What kinds of questions have been asked? This article attempts to trace the development of questions raised concerning Hispanic student achievement in order to identify patterns of research. Trends in research are examined here in order for the reader to see the groundwork on which our knowledge of Hispanic student achievement has been built. Certainly, old theories laid the foundation for years of research and hypotheses concerning minority student achievement. More important, a look at the evolution of research in this area gives us perspective on the tremendous departures in recent years—from simple, child-culture focused study to more complex interactionist research that considers multiple contributors to achievement.

Finally, brief references to patterns of current research studies serve to underscore a most important thesis offered here: that the complexity of student achievement, particularly for minority students attending school in a majority culture, cannot be underestimated.

A QUESTION OF DEFINITION

The use of the term *Hispanic* requires discussion. It is an umbrella term that may have originally been brought into use at the federal level, and its limitations as a sole defining term must be stressed. The term Hispanic has evolved from efforts to arrive at an acceptable definition of persons of Spanish language or cultural heritage, or both, in order to measure with relatively consistent enumeration their demographic and social characteristics. Brown, Rosen, Hill, and Olivas (1980) describe the two operational procedures in current use for identifying Hispanics: (1) self identification and (2) visual identification. In the majority of instances where the term Hispanic is currently used, emphasis has been placed on the use of data that have stressed self-identification. In 1970 the inclusion of census questions concerning ethnic heritage resulted in data on "persons of Spanish heritage." The Census Bureau required in 1980 that respondents select their origin or descent from a list of possible origins. Categorized as "persons of Spanish origin" were those individuals who selected to describe themselves with the terms Mexican, Puerto Rican, Cuban, Central or South American, or other Spanish origin.

More recently, federal agencies seem to have crystallized the term *Hispanic* through repeated use, often using it simultaneously with the term "persons of Spanish origin." A large-scale compilation of demographic trends defines Hispanics as those individuals "self identified as persons who trace their heritage to Spanish-speaking countries" (Davis, Haub, and Willette 1983). One agency, the Federal Interagency Committee on Education of what was then the Department of Health, Education, and Welfare, defined a Hispanic as "a person of Mexican, Puerto Rican, Cuban, Central or South American, or other Spanish culture or origin" (Brown et al. 1980). Articles in the popular press now use the term Hispanic, with those in national periodicals stressing the variety and variability of persons considered Hispanic ("It's Your Turn in the Sun" *Time* 1978; Morgan 1983). Hispanic seems to be used as a convenient term: "Broadly, Hispanic may be taken to mean Latin American brown, like European white, African black, and Asian yellow. But such connotations only make life simpler for demographers" (Morgan 1983: 51).

Indeed, difficulties with the term Hispanic arise from what it hides rather than from what it describes for the term in fact obscures ethnic differences, racial differences, national origin, cultural background, geographic separation, language usage, and more. A white Brazilian immigrant of German heritage may call him or herself Hispanic. A black Puerto Rican would also be considered Hispanic, as might a third-generation Mexican-American with no Spanish-language skills whatsoever. The caution imperative here is that any discussion of a Hispanic group must describe the parameters of the group and its subpopulation characteristics. Interpretation of results of studies of Hispanic populations must always consider the variety and nature of their subpopulations and respond accordingly. Such interpretations must rely on either the stated or implicit characteristics of the sample studied and should, to every extent possible, attempt to break down subpopulation data rather than aggregate them.

Clearly, the difficulty of describing the American Hispanic population is substantial. Where this varied and complex component of our national population is concerned, demographic researchers continue to wrestle with the issues surrounding ethnic identification (Hernandez, Estrada, and Alvirez 1973; Smith 1980; Alvirez 1981). The term Hispanic will be used here as a global term, referring to the aggregate Hispanic subpopulations as a group. Individual studies will be cited for their specific reference to subpopulations.

Discussion of research on Hispanic student achievement is divided into three major parts. Part One, Hispanic Demographics and School Achievement, contains data concerning what we know at this time about the numbers and school achievement of Hispanic-American students. Part Two, Focus on the Learner, examines traditional views of Hispanic student achievement by exploring research that sought to examine specific contributors to underachievement: language, socioeconomic status, and affective and cognitive factors. Finally, Part Three explores New Perspectives on Hispanic Achievement, the way in which more recent research has expanded and seems to have moved in two separate but complementary directions—focus on larger questions (macroanalytical foci) as well as on smaller questions (microanalytical foci).

In examining the trends in viewing Hispanic student achievement, several research studies will be cited. While they are not examined in depth, introduction of such studies will acquaint the reader with both the volume and variety of work directed to unlocking the nature of minority student achievement, particularly Hispanic achievement. It is hoped that such information may shed light on the complexity of interrelated factors that contribute to school success or failure.

HISPANIC DEMOGRAPHICS AND SCHOOL ACHIEVEMENT

The 1980 United States Census identified 13.2 million individuals of Spanish-language background, from 6 to 7 percent of the total national population. Estimates that include uncounted and undocumented workers raise that number to 14.6 million (U.S. Bureau of the Census 1981). While the general population grew a total of 11 percent between 1970 and 1980, the Hispanic population grew by 61 percent. Almost one-third of the Hispanic population is under the age of fifteen, while that age cohort for the general population is one-fifth.

In 1976 there were 3 million Hispanic children enrolled in elementary and secondary school programs, 6 percent of the total school-age population. Of this group, 63 percent (approximately two-thirds) are Mexican-American, 15 percent are Puerto Rican, 5 percent are Cuban, and 16 percent are of other Hispanic background—Central or South American or other Spanish-language background. (National Center for Education Statistics 1976). Two-thirds of Hispanic students attend schools composed predominantly of minority students. Data on the numbers of Hispanic students who may come from a non-English-speaking home background or may be limited in their English proficiency are difficult to determine and provide many perplexing problems to researchers and educators (O'Malley 1981; Ulibarri 1982). It is impossible to ascribe exact figures without extensive discussion of the criteria used, as well as discussion about how language-status classification is dependent upon the goals of instructional services.

The underachievement of minority students has long been documented (Manuel 1930, 1965; Coleman, Campbell, Hobson, Partland, Mood, Weinfeld, and York 1966; Jencks, Smith, Aclard, Bane, Cohen, Gintis, Heyrs, and Michaelson 1972; U.S. Congress 1976; Ogbu 1978; Durán 1983). A cursory examination of several areas of underachievement brings to light a picture of continued failure at school for Hispanic students. The overage phenomenon (being older than the usual grade-age) is significant for Hispanic high school seniors (Nielsen and Fernandez 1981)—one out of four Mexican-American and Puerto Rican students is two years or more behind classmates in academic achievement. Grade retention was a significant factor in treatment of language minority students in the past, and while efforts have been made to eliminate low grade placement, evidence still remains that underachievement and overage are a damaging combination in terms of school progress and motivation.

At the secondary level, tracking plays a significant role in the types of school programs offered and resultant achievement experienced by Hispanic students. Seventy percent of Hispanic students are enrolled in general education or vocational education programs in high schools, 30 percent in academic programs. This contrasts with the 54 percent of non-Hispanic whites enrolled in general education or vocational programs and 45 percent enrolled in academic programs (NCES 1975). Tracking most certainly eliminates opportunities and options for Hispanic students, reinforces minority student stereotypes, and reduces self-expectations for performance. More directly, it affects general achievement and high school completion. Hispanics aged fourteen to nineteen are twice as likely as whites not to have completed high school (Brown et al. 1980). Hispanic adolescents and adults from ages fourteen to thirty, with a non-English-language background in particular, are expected to drop out two and one-half times more than do white students.

Students of Hispanic background complete fewer median years of schooling (10.3) than do whites (12.5) or blacks (11.9) (National Council of La Raza 1982). Puerto Rican students in the mainland United States on the average complete 8.7 years of schooling. In 1981, an analysis of eighteen-to-nineteen-year-old Hispanics found that 36 percent were high school dropouts—more than double the national figure (Steinberg, Blinde, and Chan, 1984). Among Hispanics aged fourteen to twenty-five, 40 percent leave or have left school before the tenth grade (Hirano-Nakanishi n.d.). One must caution here that studies that have compared high school and college achievement and retainment of Hispanic subpopulations find strong differences between Cuban students and Mexican-American or Puerto Rican students (NCES 1982). Perhaps related to a number of parental and socioeconomic reasons, Cubans demonstrate higher achievement at the secondary level than do their other Hispanic peers, and they also give evidence about more positive attitudes concerning educational attainment. Of comparative high school student groups asked whether they expect to achieve a college degree, Mexican-Americans, Puerto Ricans, and other Latin American students have the lowest college expectations when compared with white and black students. Cubans appear to have extremely high college aspirations, even higher than those of non-Hispanic white students. Blacks have aspirations similar to those of whites. Again, caution is required here when considering such aggregate data without attention to socioeconomic status, language use and proficiency, or recency of immigration. Such factors would be expected to influence expectations for attending college. More recent studies (NCES 1982) have attempted to develop a model of educational achievement for Hispanic subpopulations, which will consider the myriad of factors that are at play as we try to study this problem.

Patterns of underachievement at elementary and secondary levels are duly reflected in enrollment and achievement patterns in postsecondary education. Durán (1983) documents extensively that those factors influencing and inhibiting achievement at the high school level contribute to achievement in college as well. Enrollment in and completion of college for Hispanics is low in comparison with their representation in the general population. Brown and Stent (1977) predicted that during the period 1976–1986 Hispanic enrollment in college would remain steady at approximately 1.5 percent. Many minority students begin college life with poor academic preparation from high school, and the aforementioned difficulties with achievement in school generally are manifested in the small numbers of students enrolling in college and completing degree programs. (For an extensive discussion of the nature of Hispanic preparation for college, see Robinson, Gerace and Mestre 1980; Durán 1983, 1985.) Hispanic graduates obtain very small proportions of the scientific degrees granted (Burns, Gerace, Mestre, and Robinson 1982): 2.2 percent of undergraduate majors in biological sciences; .8 percent of physical science majors; 2.4 percent of engineering majors. Where advanced degrees are concerned, the numbers are even smaller: 1 percent of master's degrees in biological sciences, physical sciences, and mathematics are awarded to Hispanics (NCES 1975; Brown and Stent 1977).

When employment and income data are considered, Hispanics are under-represented in every area of professional development, most particularly in the areas of science, engineering, and technology. Hispanic science doctorates account for less than 1 percent of the total science doctorates awarded (Rodriguez and Gallegos 1981). Where Puerto Ricans are concerned, much of the statistical data available on education comes from community groups and agencies that have made compiled data available for congressional hearings and commissions that are exploring the particular needs of the Puerto Rican community or from federal documents that have compiled national data (U.S. Bureau of the Census 1973; ASPIRA 1976; U.S. Congress 1976).

FOCUS ON THE LEARNER—TRADITIONAL VIEWS OF MINORITY ACHIEVEMENT

Early documentation of the treatment of Hispanic students in the English-only school system was presented by George I. Sanchez (1932) in his examination of Mexican-American student enrollment in the Southwest. As a result of decades of segregation that separated primarily Hispanic schools from white schools in the Southwest and saw the isolation of community schools in the Northeast, there was little official interest at either local or national levels in the academic achievement of minority children in general, or of Hispanic students in particular. While there existed individuals who were calling attention to Hispanic student underachievement from an early period, (Manuel 1930; Sanchez 1932), little action was taken that would more clearly examine the extent of the problem until the birth of compensatory education programs of the 1960s. Community agencies and government hearings that explored issues of Hispanic economic conditions, employment, and health, often mentioned their educational characteristics and needs (U.S. Department of Labor 1970; National Puerto Rican Forum 1970). The development of compensatory education was based on several premises concerning the nature of schooling and learning. First, the inherent value and correctness of the existing school programs and curricula were accepted without question. Second, the nature of achievement was described in terms specific to an English-speaking middle-class white culture in a way that developed one-dimensional standards for achieving behaviors. Third, and most important, was the focus of compensatory models of schooling. In comparing the linguistic, cultural, social, and familial characteristics of some learners to the standard developed as part of the successful achievement model, the deficit (or deviation, or disadvantage) was attributed to the learner. Historical support for this view began with the testing and classification of early immigrants to the United States, thought to be of inferior intellectual capability due to ethnic and linguistic characteristics. Continued intelligence testing and comparison of early immigrants and Caucasian Americans reflected ingrained prejudices that stressed the immutability and permanence of intelligence. When such prejudices were applied to ethnic communities, gross misinterpretations were the result. The long-range influence of such ideas cannot be underestimated, for we have yet to clarify the issues of heredity versus environment, and much subsequent research has continued to stress a person-centered approach. We have not entirely escaped the days when individual intelligence and achievement were seen in isolation from social, economic, linguistic, and cultural factors.

The increased focus on the minority learner as having difficulties in school was supported by research concerning factors thought to contribute to poor school achievement: genetic deficiencies (Jensen 1971), beliefs about the inherent lack or deficiencies of language in minority children (Deutsch 1963), and family and culture characteristics (Moynihan 1967). These stereotypes placed the blame for school failure on the child and his or her cultural group rather than on the school environment. Such a one-dimensional perspective of learning and schooling also contributed to the later evolution of the "culturally different" perspective —a view that some believe still retains a somewhat negative connotation of children handicapped by their language, culture, and background. While more enlightened than beliefs concerning social, cultural, and cognitive disadvantage, the "difference" view still holds as a standard of comparison the achievement, school adjustment characteristics, and behavior of white middle-class students. Often the inability to match mainstream school characteristics carries the risk of being regarded as a student lacking ability.

Today our schools seek to individualize instruction and "to meet the needs of the learner." To that end we find increased classification of students for particular funded instruction, ability grouping, or special-needs instruction (bilingual education, gifted and talented, learning disabilities). For the Hispanic child, the social and political issues that determine attention paid to his or her learning are not without cost. Meeting his or her needs may still mean that such needs are seen as handicaps and that the elimination of such handicaps through specialized instruction and remediation will "solve the problem." Vestiges of the child-culture-centered views of underachievement are not entirely gone, and in fact are alive and well in many colleges, administrative offices, and classrooms.

Language—A Major Focus

Perhaps the greatest concentration of energy in the analysis and attention paid to issues of Hispanic achievement has been in the domain of language. Early views considered other than English language background and bilingualism to be the handicap precluding success in school. But later theories considered language in a different light. Linguistic mismatch hypotheses offered the premise that the lack of congruence between the language of the child and that of the school produced a situation in which achievement was difficult at best, impossible at worst (Cardenas and Cardenas 1972). The first districts to offer services for bilingual students based such instruction upon the premise that lack of English language proficiency was the primary cause of low achievement of language minority students. Submersion in the English language curriculum or in English as a Second Language instruction were considered remedies, with the firm belief that remedy of the language "problem" would result in success at school. The early development of bilingual education programs (within the compensatory education model) were a result of the need for concerned parents and educators to subvert their goals for truly bilingual and bicultural programs to the prevailing political reality. The focus on language as the primary determinant of Hispanic underachievement meant that questions concerning student achievement rarely were without a discussion of how such achievement was related to bilingualism, Spanish affinity, or lack of English proficiency. Language proficiency measures were developed to assess the English language proficiency of bilingual students, with the objective of determining eligibility for remedial or bilingual education programs. More recently, the focus on language has widened to encompass more complex variables such as cognition, learning, and bilingualism. Studies have shown that English language proficiency is not sufficient to ensure achievement at school (DeAvila, Cervantes, and Duncan 1978). Moreover, researchers have determined that bilingualism may have cognitive benefits as yet not fully determined (DeAvila and Duncan 1981) and in fact offer evidence that lack of adequate first language development may contribute to poor school achievement in the second language (Cummins 1976, 1981, and 1985; Skutnabb-Kangas 1981.) It is this last focus, the interrelationship between first and second language development and cognition, that has received increased attention. Cummins and Skutnabb-Kangas argue that the development of bilingualism does not occur in a linguistic or social vacuum and that it must be examined in relationship to the societal conditions that determine bilingualism. By nature their theories are complex and thought-provoking. Their influence on our treatment of minority student achievement as a language issue has been significant, and it offers an important new direction in the examination of Hispanic student achievement.

Studies that ascertain language use and proficiency and can relate them to school achievement are emerging. Analyses of the *High School and Beyond* study (NCES 1982), with a focus on Hispanic students in the sample, has found that proficiency in English and proficiency in Spanish are positively related to achievement. In fact, the study finds that Cuban students, with the highest degree of retention of Spanish within the population (thought to be due to recency of immigration and social and educational status of the population) have the highest level of achievement. Mexican-Americans, on the other hand, who have less retention of Spanish across the population (indicating linguistic assimilation) might be expected, if traditional views concerning the primacy of English proficiency are considered, to be higher achievers in school. This was not borne out. An interesting result of the inclusion of both language use and proficiency in this study involved the relationship of each to achievement. Students highest in Spanish proficiency were high achievers, but those highest in the daily use of Spanish were lowest achievers. The NCES study indicates that it is tempting to speculate concerning the influence of socioeconomic level and immigrant status on the language-achievement data for Cuban students: perhaps the effect of higher socio-economic status may be sufficient to compensate for loyalty to Spanish and recent immigration. They also hypothesize that the particular characteristics of the Cuban immigration of the 1960s may be part of academic achievement.

The nature of attention paid to language in the focus on Hispanic student achievement has been far from purely linguistic. While educators and linguists struggle to ask and answer the most important questions concerning bilingualism and schooling, the politics of language use continues to influence decisions made concerning the education of language minority students. Social and educational perspectives of language use and the appropriate language of instruction for language minority students strongly influence opportunities for Hispanic student achievement. Such perspectives, often at the local level, result in a variety of avenues through which bilingual students learn—remedial instruction, English as a Second Language instruction, bilingual education programs. The language assessment process itself, the determination of language proficiency for placement and instructional purposes, continues to serve as a sorting mechanism that has significant impact on the ultimate school success of Hispanic students (McCollum and Walker, in press). Decisions based on language assessment often result in ability grouping at the elementary school level and tracking in academic or vocational education programs at the secondary school level. Clearly, the language of instruction has significant effects on the achievement of language minority students, and studies in this area are currently in progress as part of research funded through the National Institute of Education as Subpart C of the Title VII Bilingual Education Act, U. S. Department of Education, Office of Bilingual Education and Minority Languages Affairs (OBEMLA).

The inclination to view Hispanic achievement as an issue of language fails to consider not only the complexity of both societal and school influences, but falls flat when the numbers of *English-speaking* Hispanic students who are low achievers are considered. As the sophistication of research on bilingualism, language use, and language proficiency increases, our knowledge of the implications of language differences in a monolingual school system will also grow. Years of misconceptions concerning the nature of bilingualism and its effects on school achievement are only now beginning to be challenged. As will be discussed later, sociocultural perspectives and ethnographic research into the language, lives, and school achievement of bilingual children has begun to identify more clearly the complexity of the schooling experience itself and the variety of factors that impinge upon a child's success at school.

Socioeconomic Issues

When cultural deprivation and cultural disadvantage were used to explain minority children's school failure, a focus on the family and its socioeconomic resources produced several satellite views of the causality of school failure. Poverty and a supposed social deprivation projected on black and Hispanic populations was cause for several generalizations about minority populations. Some have suggested that such simplistic stereotyping actually can determine directions of school achievement as a result of expectations on the part of teachers (Rist 1970).

It is generally accepted that socioeconomic status (SES) is significantly related to school achievement, and that minority children usually come from home backgrounds of lower economic means. While data concerning income and employment document lower incomes among minority families, larger percentages of poverty level incomes, and so forth, attention to economic issues exclusive of the psychological, sociolinguistic, and sociocultural factors serves to simplify an extremely complex issue. In addition, this focus on SES reflects an explanation for school failure that does not account for the all-consuming nature and influence of the school curriculum. This curriculum has been shown to require a knowledge of the social interactive skills and behaviors that are supported by and in fact are taught by white middle-class culture. A child coming to school without such prior knowledge is required to compete in a system perhaps only tangentially related to his or her social, behavioral, and cognitive environment. Differences in test scores on standardized measures seem to be due to a variety of factors, not the least of which are factors related to the nature of school curriculum and testing. Such factors cannot be so easily ignored in favor of explanations citing generic socioeconomic status. While social and environmental factors seem to be major contributors in the academic performance and achievement of Hispanic students (Carter and Segura 1979), the onus cannot be cast on socioeconomic factors alone. Most important, the effect of socioeconomic status is so intricately tied to other group characteristics for Hispanic populations, as well as to issues of teacher expectation and treatment, that the interaction of SES with other such variables would be an important requirement in studies of achievement.

Affective and Cognitive Factors

A long-held belief concerning Hispanic and black students asserted that minority children had negative self-concepts and low motivation, which contributed to their failure at school. The existence of low achievement and negative self-concept have been traditionally reported as characteristic of Mexican-American children (Bloom, Davis, and Hess 1965; Gordon and Wilkerson 1966; Jensen 1971; Madsen 1964). The belief that Spanish-speaking children see themselves negatively was fairly common, stemming from the questionable assumption that anyone who is poor sees him- or herself as a failure and thus has a negative self-perception.

While there is conflicting evidence concerning differences in cultural orientation in the affective domain (Carter and Segura 1979), several studies have sought to refute the view of minority student negative self-concept, arguing that some students may have less consideration for the feedback they receive from school performance in their concept of self. Other work has shown that motivation factors such as attitudes and attributions are not specifically related to achievement patterns with Hispanic students (Kagan and Buriel 1977; Walker 1980; Rakow and Walker 1985; and Walker and Rakow 1985). Such studies substantiate the fact that underachievement is not necessarily related to self-perceptions of failure or negative attitudes toward school or school subjects.

Issues of cognitive style have been part of the study of achieving behaviors of Hispanic children. Ramirez and Castañeda (1974) developed a controversial and widely disseminated theory of cognitive style that they contended supports the dissonance between Mexican-American culture and the schools. Initially, they analyzed particular values (identification with family and community, personalization of interpersonal relationships, status and role definition of the family, and prevalent Mexican Catholic ideology) thought to be cultural characteristics forming the foundation of the socialization of Mexican-American children. Based on perceptual differences in individuals thought to be "field sensitive" and "field independent," Ramirez and Castañeda generated the theory of bicognitive ability. Theirs and other studies (Holtzman, Diaz-Guerrero, and Swartz 1975) argued that cultural values and socialization practices of Mexican-Americans corresponded with a field dependent (field sensitive) cognitive style. Criticism of the Ramirez and Castañeda work has been substantial.

Some researchers suggest that more comprehensive and meaningful cognitive data can be examined for Hispanic students through application of cognitive developmental stages (Piaget 1930) in the analysis of Hispanic student learning behaviors (DeAvila 1976; DeAvila and Havassy 1974). They suggest that a failure to find differences between Anglo-and Mexican-American children on neo-Piagetian measures indicates that Mexican-American children develop cognitively at basically the same rates and in the same manner as do Anglo-American children. Evidence of strong differences in traditional test scores between the two groups and differences in academic achievement cannot thus be explained by differences in cognitive ability. Such intriguing avenues of research argue strongly for the exploration of school-related influences on Hispanic student achievement.

It is important to note here that a consistent theme in earlier examinations of achievement orientation with Hispanics has been the continued focus on Hispanic culture and family life and on the relationship between certain achievement behaviors and sociocultural behaviors in different ethnic groups. Early beliefs concerning the generally rural nature of Hispanics and the monolithic cultural characteristics of Hispanic groups have been altered due to both changes in Hispanic settlement and residential patterns and changes in research foci. More complete counting of Hispanics in the general population has resulted in documentation of urban settlement patterns. As was discussed earlier in this study, the complexity of Hispanic cultures has been examined, and it has been found that the variability across region and social class as well as differences in Hispanic subcultures is substantial (Southern California's Latino Community 1983).

Thus, affective and cognitive factors affecting Hispanic student achievement cannot be viewed from a single perspective. The complexity of learning requires attention to a variety of interrelated variables that contribute to a successful predisposition for learning to take place. Research that has sought to illuminate the areas of affective and cognitive influences on achievement where Hispanic students are concerned is discussed in the next section.

NEW PERSPECTIVES ON HISPANIC ACHIEVEMENT

Research in the area of Hispanic students' performance in school has moved in new directions, all of which will contribute to a more complete picture of the relationship between the minority child and school. What characterizes these new directions and what do they say about our evolving beliefs concerning the Hispanic student at school? How are such studies contributing to a larger, more complete picture of Hispanic student achievement? This section examines several research studies that can be considered reflective of change and growth in research thought where Hispanic students are concerned. Such studies can be viewed within two frameworks that categorize their perspectives as well as summarize the variables they study. First, macroanalysis of minority student achievement consists of general demographic–achievement analyses of Hispanics, social structure theories of minority underachievement, and social reproduction theories that focus on the existence and perpetuation of low achievement and attainment, thus examining schooling in a social context. Studies in this category have been refined in a way that asks large-scale questions concerning the nature of Hispanic minority student achievement and what such achievement might mean in a social context. What factors relate to Hispanic student achievement at school and what do they mean? Second, microanalyses of minority student achievement consist of the analysis of human behavior and interaction in school settings that may contribute to minority student failure, examinations of home socialization and interaction patterns that are thought to contribute to success at school, and research that examines bias in testing and curriculum that affects minority achievement. Such studies consider smaller, more intricate, more individualized foci—what about the nature of teacher-student interaction in school that might affect achievement? How might school success be a function of parent-child relationships? How might Hispanic student achievement be related to the nature of instructional practices?

Macroanalytical Focus

General documentation of Hispanic underachievement.   The proliferation of information concerning the existence and achievement of Hispanic students in the nation's schools has been extensive in the past five years. Studies authorized by government agencies and undertaken by private foundations have begun to identify the magnitude of the underachievement of Hispanic individuals in the general population. Reports such as *The Condition of Education for Hispanic Americans* (Brown et al. 1980), *Children's Languages and Services Studies* (O'Malley 1981), *Hispanic Students in American High Schools: Background Characteristics and Achievement* (NCES 1982), *Make Something Happen: Hispanics and Urban High School Reform* (National Commission on Secondary Schooling for Hispanics 1984), *Hispanics' Education and Background: Predictors of College Achievement* (Durán 1983), *Symposium on School Dropouts* (Hispanic Administrators for Quality Education 1984), and *Hispanics: Challenges and Opportunities* (Ford Foundation 1984) have begun to identify the demographic, economic, and educational characteristics of Hispanics today.

During the 1970s the documentation of the nature of Hispanic underachievement was limited to reports by the U.S. Commission on Civil Rights, the *Mexican American Education Study* (1972), and *Puerto Ricans in the Continental United States: An Uncertain Future* (1976). Several educators wrote consistently concerning the need for systematic examination of the achievement and educational practices related to Spanish-speaking students (Samora 1963; Guerra 1970; Carter 1970; Johnson and Hernandez 1970; Trueba 1974), yet there was little official attention devoted to the documentation of Hispanic underachievement and its specifics: academic failure, grade retention, and dropout rates. The increase in information concerning Hispanics has been due to several factors, not the least of which has been political activism on the part of Hispanic individuals and communities as well as increased representation in areas of policy development and research. In addition, increased population growth and political impact of Hispanic voters has also resulted in attention to the status and needs of Hispanics in several American communities (Southern California's Latino Community 1983). The recent appearance of several large-scale studies of Hispanics must be seen as an optimistic sign that there is increasing concern for issues that affect the Hispanic community. In addition, the larger studies have begun to examine complex variables in large data sets. To examine patterns of achievement, studies such as the *High School and Beyond* (NCES 1982) and *Hispanics' Education and Background: Predictors of College Achievement* (Durán 1983) have sought to synthesize bodies of data and ask "relationship" questions that go beyond simple demographic reporting. We are seeing more complex questions at the forefront of research on Hispanic student achievement: "How might Hispanic ethnic origin, language use, recency of immigration and residency, socioeconomic status, and so forth affect the achievement of Hispanic students?"

Social structure and social reproduction theories of minority underachievement. Another type of macroanalytical examination of minority underachievement involves theories that seek to explain such underachievement in a social context. These theories view schooling within a larger context, and the particular nature of minority-group underachievement is seen as part of a larger agenda for schooling. Departing from concentration on the unique sociocultural back-grounds of individual cultures, these theories hold that schools mirror the power relationships that exist in society among groups and perform a social-sorting function that corresponds to the highly stratified work force of the capitalist system.

Approaching the examination of minority achievement from just such a social and economic perspective, John Ogbu (1977, 1978) has put forth an intriguing theory concerning minority student underachievement. In his work he considers the extent to which generations of exclusion and segregation as well as social structure and economics contribute to the underachievement of minority students. He sees particular stratifying of student achievement along racial and class lines, considering blacks and Hispanics to be "caste-like" minorities. This perspective sees minority school performance as a kind of adaptation to the low educational skills required by their ascribed social and economic roles in the community. Since role allocation and social mobility are dependent upon formal education, students relate to school based upon perceptions of and expectations for future roles. Ogbu believes that black students' observation of community and family members' allocation to certain roles gives them a clear indication of the lack of reward for completion of formal education.

Bowles and Gintis (1976) advance a theory in *Schooling in Capitalist America* that posits that schools in capitalist countries produce workers who are destined to occupy positions in a highly stratified job market. While the manifest curriculum offers a predictable program of study, the hidden curriculum inculcates students with a class consciousness that prepares them to occupy positions within the system. Some students, usually middle class or above, achieve, and eventually occupy high social and employment positions. Others, usually minorities and students of low socioeconomic status, do less well and eventually are relegated to jobs and status similar to that of their parents. Thus, schools are seen as the main agent responsible for reproducing the existing social order. Adherents to perspectives of social reproduction (Apple 1982) believe that schools themselves (as part of a larger social system) construct the reality of underachievement and provide the mechanisms for its existence. Since schools are a vehicle for producing workers for the system, they are in fact social-sorting mechanisms that determine the market, property, and power relationships within the economic system.

As discussed earlier, Skutnabb-Kangas (1981) and Cummins (1981, and 1985) offer the conclusion that the nature of classroom interaction between minority student and teacher takes place within a broader context of relationships between schools and minority communities. These relationships are determined by the power relationships among groups as a whole. Both researchers focus on the nature of language minority achievement in schools, considering that lack of appropriate educational treatment and environments may contribute to the "disabling" of students. Cummins argues in his most recent work (1986) that four structural elements in the organization of schooling contribute to student empowerment or disablement: cultural and linguistic incorporation, community participation, pedagogy, and assessment. He strongly argues that the extent to which these components provide for effective involvement in the instructional process will largely affect achievement in school.

Researchers exploring issues of social structure and social reproduction as it relates to minority student achievement are offering a larger frame on which to formulate our picture of Hispanic student achievement. They argue that the intricacies of student achievement can no longer be examined within the microcosm of the school.

A Microanalytical Focus

Testing and curriculum bias studies.   The contributions of several researchers interested in issues of test and curriculum bias have expanded our knowledge of Hispanic children at school. Movement away from the focus on the persistent failure of the child and his or her culture has resulted in more detailed examination of the nature of the culture of schools and their effect on students of varying cultural and linguistic backgrounds. Mercer (1974) identified several areas of institutional discrimination in the labeling and sorting of minority students into special education categories. Whereas tests had traditionally determined and reinforced perceptions of minority student inadequacy, several researchers began to question the efficacy of such testing procedures. More important, the intellectual development of Spanish-speaking children was examined by comparing the use of standardized measures and neo-Piagetian developmental measures. DeAvila, Havassy and Pascual-Leone (1976) found no difference between Mexican-American and Anglo-American children on developmental measures but pointed out significant differences in their performance on traditional IQ and achievement measures. Test bias with respect to Hispanic students is not a new area of exploration, but the nature of tests, testing procedures, and interrelationships among tests are receiving more thorough scrutiny than ever before (Ulibarri, Spencer, and Rivas 1981). Work by Cazden (1986) and Cazden and Leggett (1981) found that skills learned in a specific situation, in particular language skills used out of context (without an understanding of meaning) are common in tests and curricula found in schools. Minority students, who may not have been socialized in majority culture, that prepared them for the culture of schools, are often unsuccessful test takers (DeAvila 1984). Decisions made in testing more often than not arbitrarily categorize and sort students along lines developed for administrative and instructional purposes (Madaus 1985).

Research that is now beginning to probe the effects of testing and curricula on minority student achievement provides for a more complete picture of the interactive process that occurs between the child and school. The fact that there are components to student learning besides the student underscores the complexity of school failure. Attention to the contributions of curriculum and assessment to school failure can only clarify the picture.

School interaction, home socialization studies. The increase in research focused on Hispanic students and school and home socialization is encouraging. Several intriguing studies have attempted to identify the nature of child-school interaction by the use of ethnographic methods (Wilcox 1982). Studies of classroom settings and the nature of teacher and student perceptions has contributed to our knowledge of the ways in which teachers and students construct meaning in school. McDermott (1974) considers classrooms themselves to be social systems and has identified the particular interaction patterns that create a teacher's perception of a student.

Erickson (1977, 1982), Mehan (1978), and colleagues are building on the knowledge of the construction of meaning in classrooms by observing several different classrooms while asking a number of important questions concerning teacher-student interaction. One area of current research for Erickson's group examines the social construction of problem-student status in classrooms and the decisions teachers make concerning student traits and characteristics. Other studies within this "micro" perspective that examine the learning behaviors of bilingual students have tried to look at the language skills and achievement strategies that are required of students at particular grade levels in an English-speaking classroom. Cazden (1986) and Wong-Fillmore (1976) have both studied student language-use patterns in classrooms to ascertain the kinds of language required for successful functioning at school. Most important, they have identified the nature of the sociolinguistic skills needed for comprehension of teacher, texts, and materials. Certainly an analysis of the kinds of language skills required by limited English proficient students in order to achieve in the English-only class setting is a major step in the determination of where we must go with second language instruction in our school programs. McCollum (1981) explored the attention-getting strategies of Puerto Rican students in both the United States and Puerto Rico and compared them with a same-age Anglo peer in order to ascertain whether particular behavior patterns within the social construct of three different classrooms might spell trouble for a student moving between cultures. Studies of this type seek to explore the nature of teacher-student interaction, with special attention to one particular area of behavior.

Somewhat related to school-effectiveness research that has risen in significance in the past two years, the Mexican-American Advisory Committee to Wilson Riles (1981) sought to examine the characteristics of schools where Hispanic children are successful. Using a sample of California schools meeting specific characteristics of Hispanic student population and achievement, they used descriptive case studies of schools to identify school-related factors that might affect the achievement of Mexican-American students. Results identified several characteristics—among them, student background, teacher and staff characteristics, instructional qualities, and community-school relations that are related to positive student outcomes. It must be noted that the significant feature of this study is its focus on the qualities of schools where Hispanic children *are* successful—a welcome change from continued focus on schools where children fail and on students themselves as the initiators and determiners of their own failure. New directions in research have begun to examine the particular influences of family life and socialization patterns on minority student achievement. Laosa (1978a, 1978b, 1981, 1982) has examined extensively the nature of parent teaching strategies in the home in an attempt to identify patterns of social behavior between parent and child, and, with particular attention to Chicano families, has explored the impact of schooling on the parent-child relationship. He found that ethnic group differences in parent teaching behavior may be the result of differences in average schooling attainment of parents. His results underscore the gap between the Chicano child's home environment and the school environment. Clark (1983) examined in depth the interaction that occurs in black families in Chicago, using qualitative methodology to ascertain and describe characteristics of family life in high-achieving and low-achieving black student homes. According to Clark,

> Perhaps the principal difficulty in solving learning problems in urban schools
> has been the general misunderstanding about how schools teach children and
> how home and community settings work together to influence children's
> school behavior. (Clark 1983: 211)

SUMMARY

This study has attempted to examine the movement of Hispanic achievement research over the past several decades and to explore the kinds of directions of that research from a holistic perspective. It seems clear that early information on minority students in school was most certainly colored by the nature of research questions asked—"Why do Mexican-American children fail in school?" is a qualitatively different question from "What factors underlie the opportunities of Mexican-American students to achieve in school?"

The new directions in research are encouraging. First, they give evidence of an increased focus on the needs of minority students in school, in particular the needs of Hispanic learners. Second, they signal a change in focus or theme, away from child-and culture-centered pejorative analyses of Hispanic achievement, toward both larger and smaller foci on the issue. Macro studies seek to provide answers concerning school in a societal context—What is the nature of the relationship between Hispanics and school, and what part does the social and economic structure of our society play in that relationship? Micro studies are examining more closely the fine points of human interaction in school and home settings. In what way does human communication and interaction, in conjunction with other contributing factors, affect the school behaviors of minority or Hispanic students?

Finally, the evolution of research in this field tells us two fundamental things about the research process itself. First, so complex are the questions that need to be asked and the issues that need resolution that only by a mosaic method of research can we begin to see a complete picture. The gathering of small pieces of information, answers to intriguing questions concerning student learning and student-school interaction will help us to build an accurate composite of Hispanic student achievement. Whether we examine the achieving behaviors of one child or of three million children, we must consider the nature of interacting variables that affect the quality and representativeness of data that will be obtained. These interacting variables—home, school, general societal influences, socioeconomic influences, individual personal characteristics, language, culture—only begin to provide pieces for the complex puzzle of learning. Second, whether our studies examine issues that are macroanalytical or microanalytical in nature, they must use and build upon both quantitative and qualitative data to construct a more complete picture of the relationship of the child with home, school, or social environment. Research cited here, indeed studies included in this volume, build upon the best information that both qualitative and quantitive methodology has obtained.

An integrated analysis of the ways in which our society has considered Hispanic students in the educational setting may serve us well in the future. Attention to the true complexities of the learning process and its attendant variables for students with particular learning characteristics or unique linguistic and cultural strengths will enrich our knowledge of learning itself. More important, and certainly our common goal as educators, will be to see that what we learn from the questions we ask and the answers we receive has a positive effect on us as teachers, researchers, and learners.

CHAPTER 2

Saving Place and Marking Time: Some Aspects of the Social Lives of Three-Year-Old Children

Jeffrey Shultz and Janet Schwarz Theophano

INTRODUCTION

In studying how children become full-fledged members of a group, anthropologists and sociologists have often portrayed them as non-cultural and asocial. In this view, children are seen as incomplete beings who, through processes variously labeled "socialization," "enculturation," or "cultural transmission" are transformed through contact with their elders into competent culture-bearing adults (McKay 1974; Bauman 1982).

Bauman has labeled this perspective "adultocentric". In his view, many studies of children are guilty of the ethnocentrism that anthropologists are quick to condemn when frames of reference are imposed on cultural groups for whom those frames do not apply. That is, children are rarely studied on their own terms, but rather are judged with regard to the ways in which they either measure up to or more frequently do not measure up to adult standards for appropriate conduct, while at the same time, they are not expected to act as adults. What are derived from these studies are not views of who and what children are at a given time, but rather what they are not but will presumably be at a later time.

Children's play, then, is often described in terms of how it allows children to learn adult roles (Schwartzman 1976). Similarly, children's folklore has been viewed as a vehicle for enculturation. Bauman, however, presents a quite different picture:

> Remember here, though, that children's folklore is uniquely the expression of children in the peer group, and the peer group, although situated within the society as a whole, undeniably has its own social structure, and, I would

argue, its own distinctive culture. Perhaps subculture would be a better term, but in either case, a way of life and a way of perceiving, comprehending and operating in a world that is not the same as that of adult members of a society. (1982: 174)

By assuming that children have their own culture, which is different from that of adults, adult-child interaction might be seen as an instance of cross-cultural contact (McKay 1974). Importantly, in this view, children are described as "beings who interpret the world as adults do" (184). The picture of children that emerges, then, is one in which children have the ability to interpret and understand the world around them and are competent in terms of their interaction with others.

Using the analogy of cross-cultural contact, it follows that if the two cultures are continually affecting and influencing one another, then we need to know about both groups individually before we can know more about what happens when they come together. As Bauman (1982) argues, studying children's culture on its own terms should logically precede the study of how children become competent adults. Although he focuses specifically on children's folklore, he also asserts that the same argument could be made regarding other aspects of children's culture.

Although their world view may be different from that of adults, we assume that children are already competent members of society who act on and make sense of the world in much the same way as other members do. In interaction between adults and children, each is continually affecting and influencing the ways in which the other is viewing the world. This interactional approach assumes that culture is continually in a state of flux and that the world views and perspectives of children are continually both influencing and being influenced by the world view and perceptions of adults as well as other children. In terms of learning and the acquisition and transmission of culture, this implies that the culture that the children grow into will be different from the culture of the adults from whom the children are presumably learning.

In this study, we will focus on the ways in which a group of three-year-old children in a day care center obtain a place in an activity and protect membership rights and access to the activity once they are engaged in it. In particular, we will focus on a verbal routine that the children developed in order to protect their own place in the group and to exclude others. We suggest that the children's use of such a verbal routine demonstrates their social competence and their ability to manipulate a complex and abstract conception of time for their own purposes.

STUDIES OF CHILDREN'S GROUPS

A great deal has been written by folklorists and anthropologists regarding the ways in which children form alliances with one another to the exclusion of adults. Bauman (1982) and Roemer (1983) provide excellent reviews of the research on children's folklore. Both reviews focus on verbal routines and forms of speech play used by children for the purpose of interacting with their peers. A key feature of children's folklore is that it is transmitted within the peer group, and as such, it is something that belongs to them and from which adults are purposely excluded. These routines, through their use of features that have been characterized as "aggressive, obscene, scatalogical, anti-authoritarian, and inversive" (Bauman 1982: 173) are used by children to gain the approval of their peers. At the same time, they are often frowned upon and disapproved of by adults, which only adds to the feeling of solidarity among the children.

A good example of the kind of work discussed above is contained in Gilmore's (1983) research on the choreographed chanting rhymes of black girls, called "steps." Because of their allegedly "indecent" and suggestive elements, these routines were disapproved of and condemned by adults. However, the girls performed them to demonstrate not only their alignment with the peer culture, but also their skill in using language. Unfortunately, the verbal skills demonstrated in a performance of "steps" were not the ones that were valued in school (1983: 37). Because of this, the performance of the routine gained the girls the approval of their peers, while at the same time bringing down on them the scorn of the adult members of their community.

Although it has not been studied extensively, research on the ways in which children gain access to groups and form allegiances with one another *to the exclusion of their peers* has received some attention in the sociological and psychological literature. Corsaro's (1979) work, in particular, deserves to be mentioned in this regard.

In studying two groups of children ranging in age from two to four in a nursery school, Corsaro focused on the strategies they used in gaining access to and withdrawing from engagement in activities with others. Specifically, he found that the children had developed quite complex verbal and nonverbal routines for becoming involved in activities that other children were already engaged in. In fact, indirect nonverbal approaches appeared to be more successful than more overt verbal requests to be included. In contrast, he found that children did not seem to be as concerned with withdrawal, as evidenced by the fact that strategies for leaving an activity did not appear to be as fully developed. He sums up his conclusions as follows:

> Still, the findings are in line with recent research that demonstrates that *kids are competent* and that young children actively develop and use communicative skills to produce socially-ordered events in everyday interaction with adults and peers. (1979: 335; emphasis in original)

Garvey (1984) discussed the ways in which children engaged in an activity define themselves as a group and exclude others:

> In voluntarily formed groups, particularly, and in those where adult supervision is minimal, the basis of the temporary cohesion is likely to be a shared activity to which the members are committed. Members form a "we" and are protective of their psychological and physical interactive space and possessive of the objects involved in their mutually defined activity. (162).

In particular, she described the tactics used by children involved in such activities to exclude others who want to join. In contrast, she discussed the use of first-person plural pronouns (we and our) to show solidarity and allegiance among those children who were engaged in the activity. Shultz (1984) reported the same use of pronouns among the children who are the focus of this study. Garvey also examined the ways in which children repeated part of each other's utterances as a mechanism for showing agreement and mutual involvement.

Finally, in a study of a kindergarten classroom, Garnica (1981) found that children who rank low on a social dominance scale were systematically excluded from interaction with their peers. These children, whom Garnica labeled "Omega children," were treated differently from others by being verbally ignored and neglected, and by being taunted when they attempted to become part of a group. In particular, Garnica noted the ways in which these children's bids for particular items, such as marking pens, were ignored, as were their attempts to claim a "save" on an object they wanted that someone else was using at that time (Garnica 1981: 244–245).

These studies show that children have mechanisms for becoming part of ongoing groups and for verbally marking their solidarity with their peers and their exclusion of others. In this study, we examine the ways in which a group of three-year-old children obtained a place in an activity and the verbal routine they developed to ensure their continued participation in that activity. The next section contains a summary of the study from which this analysis was derived.

THE STUDY

The Setting and the Participants

The study was conducted in a day care center serving a middle-sized metropolitan area in the Midwest. It consisted of three classrooms: one each for three-, four-, and five-year-old children. In all, approximately forty children were enrolled in the center, including a small group of school-aged children who came in the morning and afternoon before and after attending a local public school.

The classroom for the three year olds had anywhere from eight to ten children at different points during the duration of the study. At the beginning, in January 1984, there were ten students enrolled, ranging in age from two years, ten months through three years, five months. Seven were boys and three were girls; six were white and four were black. During the course of the study, one of the boys and two of the girls were transferred to the classroom for four year olds. They were replaced by two boys, leaving a composition of eight boys and one girl when the participant observation phase of the study ended in May of the same year.

The teacher was twenty-two years old at the time, a graduate of a two-year early childhood certification program. From January through March, she was joined in the classroom by a student teacher from a local university. When the study began, the teacher had had approximately one and a half years of teaching experience.

The classroom was a rectangular room, approximately fifteen feet wide by thirty feet long. It was divided into activity areas that would change from week to week or month to month. Sometimes one area would be a restaurant; at other times it might be a shoe store or a grocery. Other areas had an easel to paint on, a mattress and bookshelf, and large and small blocks.

One area was called the group area, and it was where the class would gather at the beginning of the day, during what was called "group time" or simply "group." This occurred sometime between nine-thirty and ten in the morning and would last anywhere from ten to twenty minutes.

Following group, the students would scatter around the room and engage in some activity, alone, with other children, or with one of the teachers. This time, called "free play" by the teacher, usually lasted from approximately nine forty-five until eleven-fifteen. During this time, the children could play with or use any of the permanent materials such as books or blocks; they could play in one of the special areas, such as the grocery or restaurant; or they could do one of the special activities the teachers had planned for that particular day. These included things like finger painting, gluing activities, and coloring Easter eggs. All of the teacher-planned activities had a limit regarding the number of children who could participate in them at any given time, as did many of the areas of the room. For the most part, these limits ranged from one to four children. On most days, there were one or two activities that were more popular than the others, and these often had "waiting lists" of children who wanted to do them when a place became available.

Following free play, the children would either be taken outside or upstairs to a gym to play until lunch, which was served in the classroom between eleven-thirty and eleven forty-five. After lunch, they would nap until two, after which they played until their parents arrived to pick them up.

Methods and Procedures

The primary method used was participant observation. An observer (Shultz) was in the classroom an average of three to four half days a week. He conducted numerous informal and formal interviews with the teacher and the director of the center, in addition to using informal discussions with the children to clarify and illuminate something that had just happened. Also, four hours of videotape were collected, which eventually will be used to do fine-grained analyses of the interactions among the children. The data and examples used in this study are derived from the field notes taken during the observation periods.

Most of the observations were conducted during the "free play" period in the morning. This time afforded the best opportunity to observe what essentially amounted to unsupervised activities among the children. Although the teacher, sometimes a student teacher, and sometimes the director were always in the room, there were many times during this segment of the day when the children were playing on their own.

One of the things that became apparent from observing during this time is that the children developed specific strategies for obtaining and then maintaining a place in one of the space-limited activities described earlier. In particular, this was an issue for the activities that became popular on any given day. For those activities, there was sometimes a "waiting list," which was kept by the teacher to keep track of who had had a turn and who was to go next. On other days, the teacher or other adults were not at all involved in making those decisions, except occasionally to mediate a dispute that arose regarding whose turn it was to participate in the activity. For the most part, the children negotiated the turnover problems themselves, and they also developed strategies for discouraging others from attempting to get their place.

In what follows, we will discuss briefly the ways in which the children managed to get a place in one of these activities. We will focus, however, on a particular verbal routine that was developed by the children themselves that served to both establish their claim on a place in the activity and also to discourage others from attempting to take their place.

ON SAVING PLACE AND MARKING TIME

Saving Place[1]

(1)   David got up and Joel took his place on the shelf. When David came back and found Joel sitting there he said: "Get out of my place. I was coming back." (4/30/84)

The above exchange was a typical occurrence in the classroom. Given that many of the activity areas of the room and many of the actual activities that the children participated in had limits regarding the number of participants who could be involved at any given time, children often made claims on their "place," which they expected others to honor. This limitation on participants engendered a high value on rights to participate in the most desirable activities, which the children conceptualized as "having a place."

For the most part, these claims were respected by the other children. Rarely, if ever, did a dispute occur in which one child contested the right of another who was participating in an activity. The only time any questions regarding whose place it was arose was when one child left the activity and then returned, only to find that another child was in the place. This can be seen in example (1).

When a child had to leave a particular activity at some time and was expecting to return, he or she would often ask another child or sometimes one of the adults (teacher, student teacher, director, or observer) who was nearby to save a place. At other times, even when the child had not asked, other children present would make the claim in his or her absence, as is demonstrated in the following example:

(2)   Another thing that struck me was when Tammy and Joel were at table 5 eating peanuts, which was the featured teacher activity of the day. They had an argument after Tammy reached over for Joel's peanuts and called each other names. Teacher mediated. Shortly thereafter, within five minutes, Tammy left the table and Adam sat down in her place. Joel said "No, no, that's Tammy's place." Teacher then told him that Tammy had left that table and was not coming back. (3/17/84)

What is particularly striking in this example is that Tammy and Joel had just finished having an argument regarding the peanuts. In spite of that, when Tammy left the table, Joel was very quick to defend her claim to the place that Adam was attempting to take. The value of protecting a place for a fellow participant seems to have taken precedence over any minor internal squabbles that might have occurred.

Another thing to note from the previous example is that the teacher, and sometimes other adults including the student teacher, the director of the center, and the participant observer, were very much aware of the claims the children made regarding place. On occasion, on seeing a child get up and leave a popular activity, an adult would ask the child if he or she was intending to come back and therefore if the place should be saved. In addition, in mediating disputes among the children, one of the first things that an adult would ascertain was whose place it was and whether any of the disputants was making an illegitimate claim to that place.

In a conversation with the director of the center, we were told that she and her teaching staff did this consciously in order to teach the children to be responsible and to help in the mediating of disputes. What is important to us in this study, though, is not the origin of the importance of saving place, but rather the ways in which the children adopted and adapted it in using it for their own ends. In particular, we are concerned with the ways in which children obtained a place when ostensibly none was available, and the ways in which they maintained their claim to the place once it was obtained.

Obtaining a Place

(3)   When we go back to group area, teacher is disbanding the group and they are
dispersing throughout the room. The popular activity for the day is the
"restaurant," which is a table placed where the mattress used to be (it is now
in block area) and surrounding shelves which have menus, plastic food, and
cups and containers from fast food restaurants. Joel, Tammy, Kenny and
Nicholas go there and there is a waiting list for the remaining four students
who are present (David, Francie, Beth and Adam). (3/12/84)

The pattern described above was typical of what occurred following group
time. Children would disperse, and the first to get to an activity or area would
have first rights to use it. The remaining children, if they asked, would be placed
on a waiting list and when a place became available, they would be notified and
could then choose whether or not they still wanted it. Initial claiming of a place,
therefore, occurred on a first-come-first-served basis.

Regardless of the presence of a waiting list, the children in the room used
a number of strategies to try to obtain a place in a "filled" activity. That is, even
if a child was not first on the waiting list, he or she might use one of several
approaches to attempt to gain a place. A description of these approaches follows.

The most direct way to attempt to get a place was to grab a seat should one
of the participants in a desired activity get up and leave. Should one's patience
not allow for that, then walking up to the group in question and asking each of
the current participants for a seat when he or she was done was the next best
thing. This approach was used many times by many of the children, with mixed
results. If the answer was no, the strategy seemed to be to ask each of the
participants until one obtained a positive response. If everyone said no, there were
a number of responses that were possible: the child might just walk away and
return at a later time; the child might complain to the teacher that he or she was
not being given a turn, at which point the teacher would add the child's name
to the waiting list or create one if none existed; finally, the child might cry, fight,
or argue, at which point one of the adults would most likely become involved.

If the answer was yes, it was still not clear when the exchange would take
place. The child granting the permission might get up and leave immediately or
might stay in his or her place indefinitely. The following example contains several
instances of a child's approach:

(4)   [Tammy, Nicholas, Kenny and Thomas are sitting at a table playing with
Play-Doh.] As with popular activities, waiting lists develop and students
begin to ask if they can take someone's place. David approaches the table and
first asks Tammy "Can I be after you?" Tammy: "I'm going to take a long
time." Then David asks Kenny the same thing and he says quite emphatically
"Yes!" David goes to stand behind Kenny and keeps asking him "Now is my
turn? Are you going to take a long time?" Eventually, he pushes Kenny over
on the seat and tells him he will wait there, but at the same time picks up a
small piece of the Play-Doh and starts rolling it on the table. He leaves when

[adult] reminds him that only four are allowed to sit there at any given time. [Approximately five minutes later] Nicholas gets up from table 5 and David walks over and sits down. Nicholas comes back and says it is still his turn. David gets up and Nicholas sits back down. David asks him if he can be after him and Nicholas says no. He then asks Tammy and she says yes. David goes to stand behind her and starts playing with her hair. He then tells her that he is going to sit behind her until she is done and forces himself between her and the chair. Tammy calls to teacher who asks David to ask Tammy if it's OK with her. He asks, but Tammy just gets up and leaves the table, leaving her place open for David. (4/19/84)

Faced initially with a negative response from Tammy, David persevered and asked Kenny. Had Kenny said no, chances were he would continue to ask each of the participants individually. This was the case on numerous other occasions when not only David, but other children as well, were attempting to get a place. Note also the use of the phrase "I'm going to take a long time" as a rebuff against a request for participation and the fact that David never questioned Tammy's right to turn him down. Over time, the statement that referred to how long a student was going to be involved in a given activity became a powerful mechanism for maintaining a claim and will be discussed in detail in the next section.

Once he received an affirmative answer, David would initiate a series of actions that the other children found irritating. With both Kenny and Tammy, David physically occupied part of their chair. In so doing, he was appropriating a piece of the territory he eventually wanted to occupy since the chair was literally a place at the table and symbolically a "place" in the activity and group.

Other children, faced with an affirmative answer, tended to be more patient and to wait until the child whose place they would take had finished before taking their place at the activity. There were also instances when, even having gotten a positive response, a child would leave after getting tired of waiting for the other child to relinquish his or her place. In light of this, it is possible to understand why David, having been told he could have a place, undertook the harassment tactics that guaranteed that the other child would leave.

A variation on the above strategy consisted of the same type of tactics described above, except that the initial request was missing. The following example demonstrates this:

(5)   Today, the art activity, and the thing everyone wanted to do, was to cut catalogues with scissors. Joel went over to table 5 to do it, but couldn't because all of the places were taken by Francie, Tammy and Nicholas. He sat next to Nicholas and began to pressure him to finish so that he could take his place. Nicholas eventually moved to table 4 to get away from Joel and Joel followed him there telling him he could still reach him. Then he told Nicholas that he wanted to write his (Nicholas's) name on his catalogue with a marker he had just picked up. Nicholas handed Joel the catalogue and Joel wrote on it, asking Nicholas what his name started with. After writing on it for a bit, Joel then went over to table 5 to get some scissors and he started to cut [the] catalogue. Teacher noticed what was going on and told Joel to give [the]

catalogue back to Nicholas, who by this time was complaining that he didn't have it. After several attempts, teacher was successful and Joel gave materials back to Nicholas. Joel yelled in Nicholas's face, but then sat down to wait for his turn. (3/21/84)

Analogous to David's attempts to take over Tammy's and Kenny's chair, Joel attempted to take Nicholas's place by taking the catalogue away from him. The catalogue was essential for participating in the activity since there were only three of them, whereas there were many more pairs of scissors. By getting the catalogue, Joel managed to obtain one of the ingredients necessary for his successful takeover. Through his harassment he had managed to get Nicholas to leave his seat at the table where the activity was occurring. All he had to do once he obtained the catalogue was to return to table 5, get another pair of scissors, and sit down in what had been Nicholas's place. The plan failed when the teacher, having heard Nicholas's complaints, intervened and returned Nicholas to his rightful place. Note again that Joel never questioned Nicholas's right to the place. He merely chose to attempt to get the place away from Nicholas by any means possible.

The strategies described above involved obtaining one of the necessary ingredients for participation in the activity. In the examples presented, both Joel and David managed to secure a "beachhead" through devious means.[2] It is clear from these examples, and many other instances that occurred in the classroom, that obtaining a place in a desired activity was a task that was taken quite seriously by the children. It also seems to be the case that adult notions such as "waiting list" and "patience" were not always valued highly by the children.

Given that there were such zealous attempts at wresting away a place, the children also developed ways of protecting their turf, thus ensuring their continued participation in an activity. It is to that issue that we now turn.

Marking Time

In example (4), David began by approaching the table and asking Tammy if he could have her place when she was done. Her answer, taken literally, might seem to be indirect and irrelevant: "I'm going to take a long time." David, however, accepted her statement as a negative response and then moved over to ask Kenny about his place. Several things are curious about this answer: (1) when asked a yes-no question, Tammy responded with neither; (2) even though she was asked a question about her place, that is, about a physical space, Tammy responded by alluding to time; and (3) David accepted Tammy's response without argument. That is, he never questioned her right to turn him down.

Tammy's time-reference statement could be viewed as a typical example of a three-year-old child's egocentrism. However, we prefer to interpret it as constituting a response to an implicit contract among all of the children that place claims are to be honored, to the extent that they are reasonable. That is, the child who has been participating in an activity can claim the place as his or hers. The lack of a challenge on the part of the child making the initial request for a place seems to support the existence of this tacit contract.

Tammy was not the only child who did this: many of the children in the room responded to the question "Can I have your place when you are done?" with answers that referred explicitly to time. Instances of the use of time reference in this way are found throughout the field notes during the months of March, April, and May. Through its repeated use in this context, it took on the quality of a verbal routine with which all of the children were familiar.

Another example of the use of the routine follows. This incident occurred the same day as example (5):

(6)   This occurred immediately after he [Joel] had been playing with Beth at the water table and David had come over and wanted to play. Only two are allowed there so David asked Beth if he could do it after she was gone. Joel told him no, because they weren't ever going to be done. [Researcher] told David that [he] would save his place there and that he would be next. Joel then took his smock off and gave it to David and told him he could do it. (3/21/84)

Notice that Joel, in responding to David's question to Beth, also answered using a time reference ("ever"). In this case, because of the interference of the researcher, we don't know David's response. However, in example (4), David responded to a time reference as though it was a negative response. In fact, following the incidents reported in example (4), David himself used the time routine in this manner:

(7)   [Nicholas, Thomas, Kenny and David are playing with Play-Doh at table 5.] Nicholas gets up to wash his hands and Adam comes over and takes his place. Nicholas says he's not done and that he is coming back, but teacher, who has been observing this, tells him he can't because he got up and is washing his hands. That means he has now lost his turn. (He has also been at table 5 since they came down from gym.) Joel comes over to table 5 and asks David if he can go after him and David says yes. Kenny looks across at Adam and says "You going to take a long time, right?" Adam says yes. Then David says he will take a long time, too [thus reversing his previous affirmative answer]. Then Joel goes to Thomas who also says he's going to take a long time, too. Joel goes away to house area crying. All four at table 5 laugh at him loudly and say they will take a long time. (This is one of the few times I have seen anyone ridiculed for crying, or really for anything else.) Joel gets angry at them and he goes back to table 5. They again say they will be a long time. Teacher, who is standing near by, reprimands those at table for laughing at Joel and then says that Joel will still get a turn, even if it does take a long time. David says he will take a long time "forever, until my mommy comes." (4/19/84)

In example (7), David, having initially given a positive response to Joel, changed his mind after he heard Adam answer positively Kenny's question about taking a long time. In fact, David demonstrated his complete understanding of the time-reference statement by saying categorically that he was going to be there forever, at least until "my mommy comes."

Following the lead of the others, Thomas responded to Joel's request in the same way, and all four of them then told Joel that they would take a long time. In this case, they seem to have been doing more than saving their individual places; it appears as though they were also using the time-reference routine as a way of marking solidarity with each other and excluding Joel from their group. Joel's response, going away and crying, seems to indicate that he felt hurt and rejected by the four boys who were participating in the activity. His crying led to taunts and teasing, which only served to mark even more definitively the boundary between those who were doing the activity and those who were not. The time-reference routine, then, serves to mark not only physical boundaries, but social ones as well. It separates those who are part of the group (i.e., those who are taking part in the activity) from those who are not.

It also appears that chronological time had little to do with the time-reference routine, as evidenced by Joel's behavior in example (6). Shortly after telling David that he and Beth were not ever going to leave, he took off his smock and handed it to David. The smock was a prerequisite for participating in the water-play activity. By handing it to David, Joel was essentially turning over his place to him. He reinforced this nonverbal action by telling David at the same time that he could do it. The point, however, is that very little time passed between the point at which Joel said that he was not ever going to leave and the moment when he handed David his smock.

In fact, there appears to be little relationship between the use of the time-reference routine and the actual amount of time that elapsed. After saying they would be there for a long time, children would sometimes stay for a few seconds, sometimes for a few minutes, and other times for much longer. Viewed in this light, the routine can be seen as having little to do with actual time, and the argument of its use as a metaphorical marker of physical and social boundaries is enhanced.

A question this analysis raises in our minds is where did the children acquire the notion that time reference could be used in such a fashion? If our analysis up to this point is accurate, then it seems as though the children in this study have a fairly complex notion of time, one that goes beyond a measurement of an abstract concept related to duration. We believe there may be a clue to be found in conceptions of time as they have been described and analyzed by social scientists. These notions of time might provide the beginning of an answer to the above question.

Conceptions of Time[3]

Concepts of "time" and "matter" are not given in substantially the same form by experience to all men but depend upon the nature of the language or languages through the use of which they have developed. (Whorf 1964: 158)

For Benjamin Whorf, as stated in the above quote, conceptions of time are based on linguistic and consequently cultural assumptions. For speakers of English, part of the group Whorf identifies as "Standard Average European," time is

> objectified, or imaginary, because it is patterned on the outer world . . . Concepts of time lose contact with the subjective experience of "becoming later" and are objectified as quantities, especially as lengths, made up of units as a length can be visibly marked off into inches. A "length of time" is envisioned as a row of similar units, like a row of bottles. (1964: 139–140)

For speakers of English, then, time is something that can be measured, chopped up, and counted. It is an "object," not a personal or subjective experience. Hall (1973) describes American conceptions of time in much the same way: "Time with us is handled much like a material: we earn it, spend it, save it, waste it" (7). Implicit in these descriptions seems to be a belief that time is a valued commodity: the more we have of it, the better off we are. Even though it is a countable item, it is also finite, so that it must be distributed and budgeted efficiently and competently. The aphorism "Time is money" sums it all up.

Zerubavel (1981), however, conceives of time as more than just a quantity:

> Despite the growing prevalence of the quantitative description of temporality in the Modern West . . . people clearly do not relate to time only as a physico-mathematical entity. They also view it from a qualitative perspective, as an entity imbued with meaning. (101)

If time is "an entity imbued with meaning," then it should be able to be used as an effective medium of communication. In fact, Zerubavel argues that

> time functions as one of the major dimensions of social organization along which involvement, commitment, and accessibility are defined and regulated in modern society. (141)

In building his argument, Zerubavel urges that time be viewed from a new and different perspective: that of territoriality (142). By this he means that we need to understand how time is used to define what he calls a "niche of inaccessibility" (142). On the basis of this, he discusses what he calls "temporal boundaries of social accessibility" (144) or the ways in which persons use time to regulate their accessibility to others. He does this by differentiating between what he calls "private time" and "public time." Time is used to draw boundaries and create distinctions. It then becomes much more than merely a neutral physical concept. Through its use, it becomes a powerful semiotic vehicle.

In combining these various views of time, we realize that time can now be seen as both something to be valued and cherished and as a mechanism for drawing distinctions and defining boundaries. Much more than merely the ticks of a clock, time has been described as one of the most valued commodities in our culture, to which these children, and perhaps many others, are continually exposed in their everyday lives, from sources such as parents, teachers and television. How many times are children presented with unassailable comments such as "Not now. Later. I don't have the time."?

Remarking Time

We said earlier that David interpreted as negative Tammy's response to his question about whether or not he could have her place. In light of the above discussion, we can reconstruct his understanding of Tammy's utterance "I'm going to take a long time" to read something like: "I'm doing this and you can't do it nor can you be part of the group." We see their use of time reference as a way of defining social and physical space, adapting this conception of time for their own use. It seems clear to us that the use of the phrase "I'm going to take a long time" can be construed as creating what Zerubavel would call a "temporal boundary of social accessibility," or in this case, inaccessibility. Time is being used by these children to communicate access or lack thereof to the activity in question.

Simultaneously, this metaphorical use of time to define boundaries does not imply another of the connotations of time reference: that is, as a measure of chronological duration.[4] As we said earlier, after a child uttered this statement, he or she might get up and leave immediately or might keep doing the activity for several seconds, several minutes, or even longer. The uttering of this statement seems to have little to do with how much actual time will elapse before the child stops doing the coveted activity.

Finally, the use of time reference to deny access to a desirable activity implies an understanding on the part of these children of the value of time not merely as duration but as a commodity, such as it has been described by Whorf and Hall, among others. That is, the value placed on participation in the activity is heightened by the reference to how long the child plans to retain his or her place. Combining this with the way in which they use time to create social boundaries and to limit access to others, referred to above, produces a picture of a group of children who seem to have a fairly complex notion of the social uses of time.

CONCLUSION

In writing about education in Taleland, Meyer Fortes discusses the uses of imitation in learning and play:

> But the Tale child's play mimesis is never simple and mechanical reproduction; it is always imaginative construction based on the themes of adult life

and of the life of slightly older children. He or she adapts natural objects and other materials, often with great ingenuity, which never occur in the adult activities copied, and rearranges adult functions to fit the specific logical and affective configuration of play. (1970: 59)

If we might include "concepts" along with "natural objects and other materials," we can join with Fortes in celebrating the ingenuity, imagination, and creativity with which children construct worlds of their own. They are not merely passive receptors of knowledge, nor do they simply accept what adults propose and teach. Neither are they incompetent or incomplete social beings. They do not just take: they absorb, transform, and create.

What this implies is that children play an active role in their own growth and development and create worlds of meaning. Only by understanding their ways of making sense can we truly expect to capture the essence of what it means to be a child.

NOTES

We are grateful to the director and teachers of the day care center in which this study was conducted. Our deepest debt and gratitude are owed to the twelve children, aspects of whose lives we hope we have portrayed accurately. Any misrepresentations or inconsistencies are ours and ours alone. A version of this paper was presented at the Annual Meeting of the American Anthropological Association, Denver, Colorado, November 17, 1984.

1. In the sections that follow, portions of the text that are indented are copied verbatim from field notes. They are numbered to allow for easier reference. Following the excerpt, the date on which the notes were taken is added. Only three kinds of changes have been made to field notes found in the text. First, names have been changed to protect the identity of the participants. Second, when needed, clarifying comments have been added. These are enclosed in brackets. Portions of text that are enclosed in parentheses appeared that way in the field notes. And third, complete words have been substituted for the abbreviations used in the field notes.

2. In both cases, adults intervened to restore order and to return the place to the child who initially had it. It is not apparent what would have happened, that is, how the children would have resolved the situation, had the intervention not occurred.

3. We are aware that the conceptions of time described here do not account for regional, ethnic, or social class variations in what is generally referred to as "Western" or "European" time. What we are arguing, however, is that these children seem to have a complex and well-formed notion of time that is a variant of those described in this section, rather than one that is "incomplete," "immature," or "deficient."

4. George Spindler (personal communication) suggested that the children's notion of time may be more analogous to the Hopi conception of time described by Whorf as "a relation between two events in lateness" than it is to the European-American conception

of a "length of time" (Whorf 1964: 140). That is, the phrase "I'm going to take a long time" might be better paraphrased "You cannot have my place after me" rather than "I'm going to spend a great deal of time doing this." We don't mean to imply that these children have acquired Hopi notions of time. Instead, the Hopi conception as described by Whorf may provide a more accurate way of describing the way in which these children think of time.

CHAPTER 3

English Communicative Competence of Language Minority Children: Assessment and Treatment of Language "Impaired" Preschoolers

Li-Rong Lilly Cheng

Communication and communicative competence go beyond having a command of the forms of language. Yet, many traditional assessment instruments focus only on this aspect of language. This issue exacerbates difficulties in the assessment of non–English-proficient children, because communication is culturally bound and must be assessed with respect to the social and cultural contexts in which it occurs.

Educators and clinicians need to consider methods that go beyond traditional assessment techniques. In particular, ethnographic and naturalistic approaches to assessment of language minority (LM) students are considered in this chapter. Such methods allow practitioners to consider individual social and cultural differences when they interpret children's communication. For the purposes of this study, language minority students are those who reside in the United States, whose home culture is different from the majority culture, and whose home language is not English.

This chapter addresses three fundamental issues regarding the philosophy that underlies language and communication assessments of language minority students. First, what are the implications for our understanding of children's communicative competencies when our testing practices involve the administration of isolated tests? To what degree can these separate scores be put back together to provide a picture of the whole child's ability to acquire knowledge?

Second, what about social, cultural, and cognitive competencies required for effective communication? The forms of language do not exist in a vacuum. Third, the function(s) of particular language forms may vary across different individuals and within the same individual depending on their intentions and on the contexts of interaction. Several case studies are presented to illustrate the variations of language skills in culturally and linguistically different children, viewed in specific sociolinguistic contexts.

COMMUNICATIVE COMPETENCE

To be a competent communicator is to be competent at meeting the social, cognitive, cultural, and linguistic demands of language interactions (Hymes 1974; Hatch 1980; Gumperz 1981). This notion of communicative competence was discussed by Cook-Gumperz and Gumperz (1979):

> The notion of communicative competence was originally proposed by socio-linguists to account for the fact that, to be effective in everyday social settings, speakers and listeners depend on knowledge that goes beyond phonology, lexicon and abstract grammatical structure. Language usage . . . is governed by culturally, subculturally, and context specific norms, which constrain both choice of communicative options and interpretation of what is said. . . . By applying the term competence to communication rather than to language as such, ethnographers of communication advance the claim that there exist measurable regularities at the level of social structure, and social interaction, which are as much a matter of subconsciously internalized ability as are grammatical rules proper. Control of these regularities . . . is a precondition of effective communication. (12–13)

Thus, communicative competence is more than the application of grammatical or phonological rules in a speech act. It is the interactive realization of communication within specific contexts that are themselves coded as part of that communication. Becoming communicatively competent is a means of extending our knowledge of the interactive uses of language.

In all languages there are rules or conventions for verbal and nonverbal communication that apply to the form, content, and use of language in particular situations (Bloom and Lahey 1978). Such conventions are both linguistic and social in nature and are learned through communication experiences within the context of particular cultures and linguistic systems. In other words, communicative competence is demonstrated when the right thing (content) is said to the right person in the right social context (use) in the right way (form).

Defining the right content, form, and use involves making use of social, cognitive, cultural, linguistic, and paralinguistic knowledge that has been acquired through interpersonal interactions in the particular language and culture. Judgments of communicative competence are based on the degree to which one follows the linguistic and social conventions of the particular language and culture in which the communication occurs. Thus, judgments of incompetence may occur if one lacks the opportunity to become familiar with the rules of the particular language and culture. Mastery of the conventions that govern form, content, and use is required for effective judgment of communicative competence.

APPROACHES TO LANGUAGE ASSESSMENT

The emergence of a more holistic and complex view of communicative competence suggests the need to reexamine the assumptions and practices that characterize language assessment. Historically, researchers and practitioners have tended to focus on observable aspects of language. The specific aspect observed varied according to the needs of a particular discipline or the training of the assessor, or both. Practitioners, for example, have tended to focus on the phonological and grammatical aspects of language. An implicit assumption of such efforts would be that one can meaningfully isolate and assess different aspects of language. This has led to the development of separate tests or subtests to measure isolated aspects of language behavior. Typically, the aspects measured relate to language form and are limited to test items for which the correct answer is unambiguous. For example, a child may be asked to repeat the sentence "Billy had made a beautiful boat out of wood with his sharp knife (Mecham, Jex, and Jones 1977) or to repeat the five digits 3-1-8-5-9 (Zimmerman, Steiner, and Pond 1979). Measurement is derived by comparing the accurate with the inaccurate responses to a small number of given test items delivered by the examiner or teacher.

Test items such as these ignore the communicative repertoire of the individual child. Partially as a reaction to this assessment tradition and partially in response to our growing understanding of the complexity of communication, a number of researchers, clinicians, and practitioners have been placing greater emphasis on function and context in language assessment. These may be conceptualized as five aspects of language: phonology, syntax, morphology, semantics, and pragmatics (Gallagher and Prutting 1983). These five aspects cover the form, content, and use of language. While these five domains represent an improvement over the traditional form of assessment, they still neglect the social and cultural knowledge—the paralinguistic codes in operation in each of the numerous cultures within the multicultural American society that are required for effective communication.

To assess paralinguistic as well as linguistic codes, a number of practitioners have turned to ethnographic methods that can be adapted for the assessment of communicative competence in "rich" environments (Bryen 1975; Bartel and Bryen 1978; Lund and Duchan 1983; Leonard, Perrozzi, Prutting, and Berkeley 1978). Children may be observed in low-structured activities conducive to naturalistic communicative interactions. For example, children may be observed playing with siblings, friends, classmates, and caretakers in different settings—at home, in the classroom, or at the playground (Lund and Duchan 1983; Cheng 1983).

The more naturalistic approach to assessment has led to the realization that children who fail as communicators generally do not use the variety of strategies that successful communicators do and tend to create breakdowns in communication (Lund and Duchan 1983). (The difficulties of assessment are even more dramatic when the child is not an English speaker.) All of the aforementioned assessment issues are intensified in the case of language minority (LM) students for the following reasons:

1. We do not have tests written in the primary language of the LM students, nor do we have developmental norms for most of the languages spoken by these students. It is highly unlikely that such tests will become available in the near future.
2. Even if some such tests were available, we do not have professionals with appropriate language training to administer them properly. Of the 55,000 ASHA members (American Speech-Language-Hearing Association), no one speaks Vietnamese, Cambodian, Lao, Hmong, or any of the Filipino languages. Only 1 percent of the total ASHA membership are proficient enough in a foreign language to provide clinical services to the estimated 3.5 million LM speakers who have a speech, language, or hearing disorder.
3. Translated versions of standardized tests do not take into consideration the pragmatic and cultural factors involved in testing children from the many different cultures and languages that are reflected among LM students.
4. Speech-language clinicians traditionally have not received preservice training in bilingualism and multiculturalism and, in general, are unprepared to work with the LM population.

THE LANGUAGE MINORITY STUDENT AND THE ASSESSMENT PROCESS

The salience of paralinguistic codes and the social and cultural context of assessment is particularly evident where LM students are concerned. One critical issue is the degree to which the assessment situation is an appropriate and successful communication interaction and one in which the child is receiving comprehensible input (Cummins 1983). If the test instructions themselves are not comprehensible, inability to perform a particular task is not interpretable.

The diversity of home and culture that exists among LM students also presents a serious problem in the assessment process. The dilemmas educators face in the assessment of LM students are complex and difficult to solve due to the very nature of the complicated process of language acquisition and our lack of understanding of what is considered different and what is considered disordered. Children learn to be proficient in language by continued exposure and input. They gradually become communicatively competent through experience and use. They learn the meaning and form of their primary language by using it in its social and cultural context. A Cambodian child was asked the question, "Which room do you sleep in?" by his teacher, who was hoping to get the answer "The bedroom." The child looked puzzled and asked for clarification: "What do you mean?" The teacher was also puzzled and asked again "Where do you sleep?" The child still looked puzzled and answered "Everywhere." Another example is presented here to illustrate the social and cultural relatedness of the meaning of words. A clinician asked a Chinese-speaking child to point to the thing that she would use to eat with and the child was very puzzled and finally pointed to some pencils, since the pencils looked like a pair of chopsticks. If the children cannot make sense of the task or item given because of their sociocultural-linguistic differences, their abilities can not be properly assessed. As a result, educators have the enormous and ultimate responsibility of providing an assessment procedure that is linguistically relevant, culturally sensitive and, socially meaningful to LM children.

When a monolingual speech-language clinician attempts to assess the language ability of a LM child, English is used. Tests are often translated with the help of a family member or a friend. Such a procedure has proved to be ineffective since many items cannot be translated directly. Furthermore, items that can be translated may not carry the same degree of linguistic complexity of the original item. For example, the English word "elated" can be translated into Chinese as "很高興," which can be transliterated as "very happy" and carries different linguistic weight.

Another problem that arises in the assessment process concerns the relationship between the linguistic code and the conceptual code. The command of a diversified and flexible vocabulary is an important feature of communicative competence (Simon 1979). The ability to demonstrate such flexibility, however, may depend not on the vocabulary per se but on the way meaning is expressed in the first language. For example, in Chinese one word, "shang" 上, is equivalent to five English expressions: on, up, over, above, and on top. Conversely, Spanish has two expressions for "leg:" "pierna" for a human leg and "pata" for an animal's leg. In English, we may use leg to refer to an animal even though there are a number of species-specific terms. In Spanish this usage of "pierna" would not be acceptable. Thus, conclusions about the presence or absence of flexible vocabulary may in fact reflect linguistic difference rather than deficiency and linguistic interference in the semantic domain rather than disorder.

Less specific problems may also be related to cultural differences. The culturally acceptable conventions of communication differ from culture to culture (Wong-Fillmore 1984; Heath 1984a, 1984b, 1984c). In the school setting, eye contact is generally considered an appropriate behavior in interpersonal communication; however, the parents of many LM children may tell them not to "stare" or return eye contact to authority figures. Asking questions is also considered appropriate in the school setting, but many LM children are raised with the notion that such behavior is impolite. By examining the above issues, one may question whether LM children might behave differently in turn-taking, topic maintenance and other pragmatic considerations as a result of their cultural background. Hispanic LM children generally have not been exposed to the experience of recounting a past experience and are not asked to label objects at home (Heath 1984a). Chinese LM children in general are not encouraged to volunteer information or offer commentaries at home (Wong-Fillmore 1984). We need to look for possible identifiable sociocultural-linguistic features that may contribute to their different styles of learning and communication. The use of ethnographic methods in the observation and description of LM children's communication reveals how children use language (Heath 1984b, 1983).

Ethnographic analyses have raised questions about the validity of traditional test results and the interpretations based upon them. Should LM children be labeled language impaired if they seem unresponsive to questions asked? The misdiagnosis of LM children may lead to mislabeling children as language handicapped when in actuality they may be acquiring a second language normally. Such misdiagnosis often leads to children's perception of themselves as failures —"severely disordered," "culturally deprived," or "mentally retarded."

A functional-ecological approach needs to be adopted when we examine the communicative competence of LM children. We need to have some understanding about their home culture, language, and community. There is a set of community norms, operations, principles, strategies, and interpretations (comprehension) of language (Smith 1982). LM children may bring to us very different world views when they lack interpersonal involvement with the majority culture and language. We need to examine LM children and their families' exposure to the English language and their familiarity with mainstream culture.

To systematically pursue a broader and less traditional assessment procedure for use with language minority children, I adopted a microethnographic methodology that included the use of video and audio tapes and participant observation (Erickson 1978; Trueba and Wright 1980–81). By using audio and video material, the interactions can be studied and examined frame by frame and second by second (Mehan 1978; Greenfield and Smith 1976). Three case studies are presented on the following pages.

CASE STUDY 1

Languages Spoken at Home: Capampamgan, Tagalog, and English

Background Information

The two-year, seven-month-old boy was referred for speech and language evaluation by Dr. H., who reported that the boy had "language impairment and no intelligible speech." Pregnancy and birth history seemed uneventful. After birth, the baby boy had jaundice and was hospitalized for five days. He achieved gross milestones within normal limits. The medical history revealed a history of mild ear infections in the first year. According to the parent, the client used his first words at age two and a half but used mainly gestures to communicate. The client had been cared for by an elderly woman (live-in) who spoke Capampamgan (a dialect of the Philippines).

At the time of the evaluation, the client lived with his parents, a sister (age one year and two months) and the sixty-four-year-old live-in baby sitter. According to the parents, the client did not have any playmates. They lived in an apartment complex and the children did not play outside. They also did not have many friends or relatives. The client basically did not have the opportunity to interact with people other than his baby sitter and family members. The mother reported that the baby sitter did not speak very much to the child and took care only of his basic needs for food and toilet.

The father, a police officer, worked in the afternoon and went to school in the morning. The mother had a full-time job. The parents spoke to each other in Tagalog and spoke to the boy in English. The boy's daily activities included watching T.V., playing with cars and trucks, and playing or fighting with his younger sister. The father remarked that the client had no playmates besides his sister.

Evaluation Results

The client refused to separate from his parents, and he demanded to sit on his mother's lap by pulling at her leg and crying. An interview with the parents revealed that the child did have single words that were intelligible (e.g., mommy, daddy, baby, apple, car, etc.) and that he could put two words together, although he seldom did. After much coaxing, the client interacted with the clinician in a play situation. However, he never spoke and refused to speak when asked. An observation of parent-child interaction revealed that the boy could use one to two words to respond to a question but rarely spoke voluntarily. The majority of the parent's utterances to the child were questions and were unrelated to the client's actions. This could have had some effect on his spontaneous expressive language.

On the Preschool Language Scale, the client received an Auditory Comprehension age equivalent of 2:3 years. Although the score was slightly low in relation to the client's chronological age, his true score could have been a little higher since he became distracted and irritable towards the end of this section. It was not possible to complete the Verbal Ability section because the client refused to talk to the clinician or to his parents, either in English or in Tagalog.

The client showed good gross motor skills and coordination. He was able to stack six 1-inch blocks in a tower. His father reported that the client had climbed a six-foot fence to the next yard recently. The client was able to problem solve and to request help when needed, although he preferred to play independently.

Clinical Impressions

The client appeared to have receptive-language abilities within normal limits. His expressive language was difficult to assess. It appeared to be developing normally although at a slightly slow rate. Articulation and voice characteristics were also within normal limits. The client's refusal to speak and his uncooperative behavior made formal assessment very difficult. The clinician did not feel comfortable in describing the child as delayed or impaired and wanted to evaluate the child further, using a naturalistic ethnographic approach.

The results were discussed with the parents. Methods of language stimulation at home were modeled and explained to them. The possibility of enrolling the client in a preschool in order for him to have interaction with his peers was also discussed. It was recommended that the parents use Tagalog at home to stimulate language development for a duration of two months and to then bring the child back for a reevaluation.

Progress Notes

The client was brought back by his father for a reevaluation two months after his first appointment. His mother could not leave work to come. According to his father, they could not enroll the client in a preschool because he was not toilet trained. The father reported that his work and study situation had not changed. The client was still being cared for by the elderly woman, who spoke very little to him. According to the father, he and his wife tried to read some books to the child and occasionally asked him to name a few objects. He also reported that the neighbor made a remark about the boy, that "He is like a parrot because he repeats everything." The father concurred that the client did exhibit such parrot-like echoic behavior in repeating the last word or syllable after his parents had said something to him in Tagalog or someone had said something to him in English.

The clinician attempted to elicit some verbal responses from the child in the following excerpt, which demonstrates the parrot-like speech pattern.

Looking at a picture book
s = Speech clinician
c = Child

c: Bone (telephone).
s: Good. (turned the page) What's that?
c: S dat (s that?).
s: Ya, what's that?
c: S dat (s that?).
s: Window.

 c: Wibo (window).
 s: Great. Do you have a window in your house?
 c: House.
 s: Yes, do you have a window in your house? (pointing to the window in the room)
 c: You house.
 s: Window. This is a window. Do you have a window in your house?
 c: House.

The excerpt demonstrates the client's echoic speech pattern and also provides information about the client's lack of understanding of the questions being asked and the topic of the question (window).

  Later on, the picture of a church was presented. (According to the father, the family goes to church every Sunday.)

 c: Church.
 s: Right, a church. Do you go to church?
 c: Church.
 s: Do you go in there? (pointing to the entrance of the church)
 c: In de (in there).
 s: Yes, do you, your mommy, your daddy and your sister go to church?
 c: Church.

The client consistently did not answer any yes-no questions. He did give labels to a few objects such as car, gun, and vacuum. Speech therapy was recommended, the primary reason being the child's lack of opportunity to interact with others.

  Attempts at assessing the client by using a formal articulation test such as the Goldman-Fristoe Test of Articulation and the Expressive One-Word Vocabulary Test were not successful. The clinician asked the parents to bring the client in for weekly therapy sessions.

  The clinician spent the first few sessions playing with the child, observing the interactions between the client and his father or his baby sitter. His mother was not able to leave work. At first, the father just sat in the room and watched the child play. He occasionally would ask the child to label by asking, "What is that?"—but not any other kind of question. When the child failed to label, the father would respond by saying, "You know what that is, say it." If the child still did not respond, then the father would provide the answer! "That is a cup."

  The baby sitter appeared passive, rarely asked any questions and frequently did not even respond to the child's questions—"s da?"—and sometimes seemed impatient when the child repeatedly asked her "s da?" (what's that?). It was also noted that the baby sitter spoke very little English, and whatever she spoke was telegraphic and choppy, and sometimes unintelligible. The client did repeat or mimic the few words uttered by the baby sitter.

  By playing with the child, the clinician noticed that the child would not only mimic the sounds, such as the engine sound or the bird chirping, and the words, such as bird or boat, but also the actions that describe verbs, such as sleeping and flying. The clinician decided to use dolls, animals, a toy house, a toy kitchen, cars, a toy school, a tool set, a picnic set, and other toys with detachable parts. The client began to ask more questions about the labels, and the clinician began to introduce action words by manipulating the toy people and describing the acts, such as "The boy is going to bed," "The mother is cooking a dinner." The child began to imitate parts of the sentences and also to copy the act. He smiled a lot and was able to concentrate on the activities and did not seem to be tired of them. He imitated what the clinician did all the time and appeared to truly enjoy the tasks. The following excerpt demonstrates the point:

C: S da? (what's that?) (pointing to the bathtub)
S: Bathtub.
C: Baster.
S: Do you have a bathtub at home?
C: Home.
S: You take a bath in a bathtub.
C: Take bath. (turned the page) S da? (what's that?)
S: Feather, remember?
C: Member.
S: Feather on a bird.
C: Feather.
S: Let's see this one (turning the page).
C: See this one. See this.
S: Yes, a flag.
C: *Baj* (flag).
S: OK.
C: OK.

The client did not know how to label many of the common everyday words used in his environment and was learning very quickly to ask the important questions, such as "s da?" (what is that?), "s di?" (what's this?), and "doing?" (what's he doing?). The child seemed forever inquisitive and curious about the world. The clinician, by observing the child playing with toys, realized that the child had not played with most of the toys and seemed intrigued by them—the car that could go in circles and the pair of shoes that could walk after winding, and so forth. Furthermore, the child needed to ask the clinician to wind the toys and become more talkative to make his demands known. The father was asked to bring the toys the client was playing with at home, and the clinician found out that the client had only a few trucks and cars and a number of torn books. Noting the limited variety of toys at home, the clinician provided some old and new toys for each session and talked about them in a variety of contexts. The parents were encouraged to play and talk with the client whenever they could, for example describing things along the road while driving, talking about the dinner while eating, asking different kinds of questions, and so forth, so that a rich language environment for home language could be nurtured.

The child was placed in a child-language group and was also seen with a child his age. During the group activities, the client was observed through a two-way mirror: he did not appear to be shy and began to imitate the other children. He gradually learned the rules of participation and became an integral member of the group. Initially when he was seen with another child his age, he was aggressive, consistently wanting to grab the toys. Gradually, he became more collaborative and started to verbally interact with his playmates.

Three months later, the clinician took another sample of the child's interaction:

Play with a comb and brush set
C: Oh, comb.
S: Is this a comb?
C: This comb.
S: Brush.
C: I have brush.
S: Yeah.
C: Brush my hair.
S: I brush my hair.
C: Brush my hair.
S: Right, your mom brushes your hair.
C: Brush my hair.
S: Look, the boy is brushing his teeth.
C: Brush teeth. Brush teeth in room.

The clinician was pleased with his progress and the initial clinical decision to not label the child "language-impaired" without further ethnographic assessment. The ethnographic-naturalistic-experiential approach was useful in providing the clinician with information that could not have been found using formal testing procedures. Furthermore, the observation made by the clinician of the interaction between the client, his baby sitter, and his father supported the appropriateness of providing opportunities for intensive language bombardment and environmental stimulation as the remediation strategy. This allowed the child to grow and experience the use, form, and content of language in a variety of contexts so that he learned how to learn, how to negotiate, how to interact, and how to enjoy the socialization process.

At the time of this report, the client still did not initiate topics, talked mainly about the here and now, and occasionally made a four-word utterance. However, based on the background history and his progress, the clinician suggested that he be enrolled in a preschool as soon as possible for more exposure to social and linguistic interaction and more opportunities for cognitive development.

CASE STUDY 2

Home Language: Vietnamese

Background Information

This three-year, five-month-old Vietnamese boy was referred by Dr. V. due to apparent lack of speech. His mother was working in a factory and could not come to the evaluation session. His father, who worked the afternoon shift, brought him in. His father, who spoke very little English, tried to explain to the clinician that his wife had been very sick and depressed during pregnancy. The child was born in the United States a few months after his parents arrived. His mother started working three months after his birth. His father took care of him for the most part. His father described his daily activities as playing with blocks and watching T.V. Vietnamese was the only language used at home. His father further indicated that he talked very little to his son since he was busy learning a trade by studying during the day. The child was reportedly communicating by pulling and pushing people to get whatever he wanted. The child did not seem to understand Vietnamese, according to the father. Developmental history as well as medical history seemed uneventful.

Evaluation Results

Even though the clinician could not speak Vietnamese and there was no test instrument available in Vietnamese, the clinician wanted to find a way to assess the child. The Preschool Language Scale (Zimmerman, Steiner, and Pond 1979) was presented. The child was asked to point to the pictures named by the clinician and translated by the father. The child did not seem to understand the instruction made by the father in Vietnamese. The father even showed the child how to take the test by pointing to the right picture. The child did not appear to understand the task required even after the father showed him several times what he was supposed to do. The clinician produced the Photo Articulation Test and presented the photographs to the child with the intention of eliciting some verbal responses from the child. The child did not name any pictures. The clinician then tried to administer the Denver Developmental Screening Test. Again the child failed to understand what he was supposed to do. All attempts to test the child formally by using standardized tests failed. It was not possible for the clinician to report the results of any test since the child did not respond to any test and did not seem to understand the tasks involved. Informal testing based on observation was used by the clinician.

The father was asked to play with the child and the clinician observed the interaction. The child played mostly by himself throughout the session. The father said words in Vietnamese to him, such as "Sit here," "Come here," "Don't do that." Verbalization by the child was present but was not clear. He was not attentive to his father or to the clinician. Some interaction was noted while he was playing blocks with the clinician. After several repetitions of the word "block," the child repeated what appeared to be the word. It was felt that an ethnographic method was the only alternative for assessing the child. It was recommended that he be seen for speech therapy and that the parents provide home-language stimulation in Vietnamese and peer association with children in their own community. It was further suggested that the parents take him to a preschool program. The clinician attempted to analyze the child's interactions by viewing videotapes and by talking to the father. The father was also asked to keep a diary of observations and of the child's utterances at home.

Progress Notes

The father reported that he disliked the YMCA program and felt that he could not afford it anyway. During the first few sessions, the child babbled a lot, but no meaningful speech was noticed. He appeared only to understand a few commands, such as "pick up the toys." However, these commands were generally given with a gesture. He exhibited some symbolic play behavior, such as eating pretend food.

After a month of therapy, he began to say "cookie" and "popcorn." The clinician asked the father to play with the client, and the child began to say some Vietnamese words to his parents. He also said "hello" on the telephone. While the child was playing with the blocks, the clinician noticed that he spelled "CBS and ABC Sunday and Saturday night movies." And when the clinician spelled the program "You Asked for It," the child read it out loud.

At the persuasion of the clinician, the father took the child to a preschool, but later withdrew him from the school because, according to the father, the child was playing by himself and no one talked or played with him. The teacher, as reported by the father, was reluctant to interact with the child because she said she didn't know the Vietnamese language and that the child did not speak English. It appeared that the child was "neglected" because he did not have the skills to communicative effectively, and that he did not learn because of the lack of opportunity for social interaction with his peers and his teacher. The father reported that he was frustrated and could not play with the child.

The clinician arranged one special session where the whole family came— father, mother, the child, and his cousin. By observing the interaction, the clinician noted that the mother and the cousin did everything for the child. He cried hysterically when his mother left the room (he was not bothered when his dad left). The mother gave him what he wanted and spoke for him. He did not seem to understand the Vietnamese spoken by his mother.

The clinician continued to observe the child in play and used blocks and spelling games during the sessions. The child continued to spell many words and seemed interested in reading the words out loud. He spent many hours spelling words and looking at them. Attempts to get him to play with other toys were not very successful. The clinician built the sessions by introducing different concepts and objects through the use of spelling blocks. Very little progress was made in eliciting verbal responses from the child. At the same time, the child continued to exhibit a lack of understanding of his home language and second language— English. He rarely responded to a command or a question. He concentrated on spelling and responded occasionally to environmental stimuli. It was after repeated observation that the clinician decided to make a referral for a psychological evaluation. The results of the psychological evaluation revealed that the child had an above-average performance IQ, which might be the explanation for his strong interest in spelling and reading. His interest in written symbols led the clinician to look for ways of working with him. It was through the written symbols that he tried to communicate to the world what he learned by watching television. His autistic-like behavior could have easily misled the teacher, clinician, and family into thinking that he was mentally retarded. Yet, repeated attempts to elicit verbal responses from him failed. It was not because his family spoke Vietnamese and that he was not exposed to languages that the child did not respond. A more complex neurological picture was contributing to the confusion. The fact that clinicians and teachers are generally confounded by children whose home language is not English may blur and obscure their vision when the problem of the individual may be neurogenic in nature. We need to keep in mind that children all over the world learn language in a naturalistic way, and when one child does not respond to the stimulation, it is safe to assume that one may be looking at a neurological problem and not a social, cultural, or linguistic problem.

CASE STUDY 3

Home Languages: Spanish and English

Background Information

This client was seen initially for a speech and language evaluation when he was a two-year, six-month-old child. He was referred to this department by Dr. S, who indicated that he was slow in acquiring language. He is one of two children. His seven-year-old brother, according to the mother, occasionally stuttered. His mother also indicated that her older son talked very late. This client did not start talking until he was two years, three months. At the time of the evaluation, he was saying some single words intelligibly, and occasionally he would string a number of words together. The client had been taken care of by a Spanish-speaking baby sitter. The client's mother is from Venezuela and works as a bilingual teacher. She uses Spanish with her children at home. His father is a monolingual English speaker, and his older brother also speaks to him in English.

According to the mother, the child did not interact very much with his father. At the same time, the father felt very frustrated that the child could not be understood. The mother further described the father as being "impatient and cold." The mother described the child as "loving, curious, active, and cute."

Birth history and pregnancy appeared normal. Developmental history seemed unremarkable. The boy's medical history and developmental history seemed uneventful. According to his mother, he is a good eater and plays well with other children. In his immediate environment, he has his brother to play with. In his baby sitter's home he plays with a four-year-old girl who speaks only Spanish. The mother further indicated that the client is mixing some Spanish words with English. For example "más" for "more," "agua" for "water." At the time of the evaluation, the mother was concerned about the client's development in speech and language.

Evaluation Results

Due to the young age of the client, the clinician chose to start the assessment session by presenting some objects. The client seemed to have difficulty labeling the names of some of the objects and animals, such as elephant, turtle, zebra, and giraffe. He did, however, imitate every word that the clinician uttered. His attempts to imitate polysyllabic words were unsuccessful. His repetitions of single words were generally successful. However, he did name a few objects that he seemed to be familiar with, such as shoe, chair, and paper. To assess auditory comprehension, the clinician asked the client to follow one or two level commands. The client was able to follow those commands without much difficulty. When the client wanted something, he mainly used gestures. His spontaneous utterances were very limited. The following phrases were uttered by him spontaneously: "What this?", "All gone," "You see," "I get it," "Okay."

A brief oral-speech-mechanism examination revealed structures to be within normal limits. The client seemed alert and appeared to be cooperative. His attention span was short. He would not stay with a task for more than a few minutes.

Formal testing was not appropriate for this client. After looking at the informal testing results, it was the clinician's opinion that the client exhibited a problem in communication. The family was going to Venezuela for the summer and Spanish would be the only language used there; the mother hoped that the client would develop more Spanish during the summer. The clinician provided the mother with suggestions for stimulating his home language.

Progress Notes

The client was seen after the summer, after he had spent four months in Venezuela. When he was asked some questions, he responded in Spanish. When he wanted something, he used Spanish also; however, his Spanish output was limited to one-or two-word utterances. At the same time, he was also producing some one-and two-word utterances in English. He obviously was mixing the two languages at times. His mother indicated that he seldom talked to his father but spent a lot of time playing with his brother, who spoke English to him. Although his overall intelligibility was poor, he produced many utterances. In other words, he talked a lot even though he was not always understood. He combined English and Spanish frequently in his communication. Informal observation of his cognitive development revealed normal cognitive knowledge for his age. Furthermore, he was constantly imitating what the clinician was saying. In one month, he began to use many three-word sentences, such as "Let me see," "You want more," "I want more," "I go shopping," and so forth. He also demonstrated his ability to conceptualize such concepts as hot and cold, big and little, more or less. Even though his words and sentences were very unclear, his cognitive abilities seemed to be developing steadily. The clinician asked the mother to speak Spanish to him at home to try to elicit clearer articulation from the client. The clinician also introduced polysyllabic words from his interest areas, words such as helicopter, ambulance, fire engine, fire station, and so forth. More games were introduced and more questions were asked about the present, the here and now, and the past. The client began to make sentences such as "My brother is at home," "That is camera," "That is TV," "Let me show mommy," "Let me show you," "Let me do it." He also became more curious and began to ask more questions, like "What you doing?", Why?", "Where are you going?", and to make more statements, like "I want this one," "I don't want that one," "I like this," "I don't like that," and so forth.

Since therapy sessions were conducted in English, the clinician was able to report improvement of the child's English over a period of nine months, from basically not saying single words clearly to the point at which he was speaking in sentences. He continued to be cared for at the Spanish-speaking baby sitter's home, where he played with the Spanish-speaking girl. According to the mother, the child spoke Spanish to his baby sitter, the little girl, and his mother. She reported that he was improving in Spanish and in English. In the past, because of his inability to speak intelligibly, he and his father seldom conversed. His father began to take the initiative by bringing him for therapy. By observing the child's interaction with the father, it was clear that the child's ability to speak English helped to strengthen the father-son relationship and to provide effective communication between them. The mother reported that the father is now willing to take the child out to play, while in the past the father had always refused to take the child anywhere. So the ability to communicate effectively seemed to be the crucial factor in strengthening the father-son relationship. This closer bond helped the client feel better about his father. He began to talk about his father during therapy sessions, which he had never done in the past. In the past he had always referred to his mother. From this progress note it was clear that the client's lack of intelligible output at one point was not enough evidence for labeling him language disordered.

The father reported that he was able to communicate with his son and was extremely pleased about that. The clinician felt that the child was able to interact appropriately with different interaction participants and to communicate effectively, while less than nine months ago he had been considered unintelligible. It is the clinician's opinion that this child will continue to develop language and that at this point he does not exhibit a language-delay problem.

During the nine months of therapy, formal speech-language tests were not administered due to the child's lack of interest and investment. As a result, no formal test results could be obtained. However, an abundance of data was collected by watching the child interact with his brother, other children, his mother, and later his father. Initially, he was quite agitated and moved from one task to another, from one object to another; usually after spending a few minutes in the room, he wanted to leave and "go home." His "lack of cooperation" was indeed disturbing to the clinician. However, after observing the child playing with his brother for a while, it was clear that he had a strong interest in family members. Things in pairs and sometimes three or more of the same objects were introduced. Coins (one cent, five cents, ten cents, one dollar, etc.) were used during the session. The child was very interested in playing the role of a shopper and the role of a storekeeper. He did not seem to get tired of the activities of shopping, buying, and selling, and as a result the therapist built many activities around that. Later he told his mother that he loved to go to the clinic and asked his mother if he could go every day. The motivation and the environment were clearly favorable, and the rapid growth of language development in the child certainly made us clinicians think about the value of using the functional-ecological approach to understand the children's home environment, and of using observation and in-depth ethnographic analyses of interactions.

RECOMMENDATIONS

The following recommendations were found to be useful in working with LM children:

1. Observe children. Find out what they like and dislike. Learn what they know and do not know. Find out what is motivating to them. Watch them play, work, and negotiate. Watch them interact with peers, teachers, siblings, parents, or even strangers. Watch them over a period of time, keep records of the observations, and analyze the interactions. Observation methods must focus on verbal, nonverbal, vocal, intelligible, unintelligible responses or the lack thereof.

2. Work with the family. Learn about the home culture and the community

of the children. Find out about their social and cultural activities and attempt to understand their world and world view. Use their experience to construct meaningful activities for them. LM children and their families need to feel that being bilingual is an asset. Parents of LM children need to be encouraged to maintain their home language and culture and to provide opportunities for their children to optimize their communicative experiences by using the home language, which is the most natural and comfortable way of communicating for them. Encourage parents and children to become more familiar with the majority culture and language. By working with the family members, educators are able to indirectly influence the learning outcome. By encouraging and involving parents in the educational process, educators are able to gain insight into how best to teach the children. Clark (1983) reported that, in view of the fact that children spend only 18 percent of their time in school, what they learn outside the school, in the community and at home, contributes significantly to the development of how they negotiate meaning, understand concepts, structure and classify them, analyze and synthesize them, store and retrieve them, and generate their own concepts in oral or written forms. These forms have to be meaningful; learning them is based on the children's experiences.

3. Primary language plays an important part in preparing children to interpret the meanings of the messages and cues they perceive. Each child constructs his or her own reality based on a complex network of linguistic-sociocultural knowledge. Educators need to be sensitive to the children's need to create their own meaning based on what they perceive, on their own frames of reference, and on their experience in order to understand what is being said and interpret what is not being said. Children need direct encouragement. They function better when teachers are able to provide contexts that are familiar to them and that have high communicative demands. Children can try many strategies, including elaborations and clarifications, to facilitate smooth communication.

4. Attempts at assessment and intervention should target engaging the children in genuine communication in naturalistic environments with low anxiety and high motivation. Tasks need to be cognitively challenging, linguistically meaningful, and culturally appropriate. The key to successful communication is mutually congruent and comprehensible input. Without that, communication barriers and breakdowns are created. The educator or tester or facilitator needs to encourage children to talk, express, read, write, explore, share their experiences, and feel confident about themselves. Interesting toys such as leg blocks, toys with detachable parts, books, photographs, clay, and crayons should be made available for children to play, create pictures and objects, and make stories.

5. Clinicians need to develop their cross-cultural communicative competence, which includes the following:

a. Sociolinguistic knowledge
b. Cross-cultural sensitivity
c. Flexible communicative styles

d. Nonauthoritarian attitudes
e. Knowledge about differences and disorders, normalcy and deviance

6. Language proficiency (which includes literacy) must be learned through practice. It is imperative that we provide ample opportunities for LM children to practice and use the language. Nursery rhymes are excellent for practicing the language, and words that rhyme are also ideal for raising children's curiosity and interest. Some children lack the opportunity to become familiar with games, group activities and stories, resulting in their lack of participation. It may be helpful to expose children to different situations, arrange for them to have different partners, and physically act out the activity and practice it with the children. The following is a list of some suggested activities and games:

a. Play the barrier game in which the child follows other people's instructions to manipulate objects hidden from him with a board.
b. Show an object that has a missing part, is broken, or does not make sense (e.g., an unplugged lamp whose light is on).
c. Work with the children on a small project, such as making some Christmas decorations, birthday card, Mother's Day card and so forth. Ask the child to tell you the things required to complete the project and the sequence of events that took place from the beginning to the end.
d. Read stories to the children, introduce new vocabulary in context, act out those verbs, use them in multiple contexts, have children role-play and use their imagination to make inferences, comparisons, and analogies; capitalize on what they bring to school from their home experience and culture, such as photographs of fiestas.
e. Show them a picture and ask them to tell a story about the picture.
f. Ask them to choose a game and ask them how the game is played, or create with them new games, like the fishing game, and ask one child to teach another child or a group of children a game or how to make something.

In conclusion, further study and research is indicated in the area of understanding the process of language acquisition. We need to examine current assessment procedures and construct heuristically useful instruments that are linguistically meaningful and culturally appropriate. Furthermore, we need to question vigorously the relationship between language and culture, and between sociocultural knowledge and linguistic knowledge. Observational methods need to include verbal, nonverbal, and vocal productions; to record productions in various contexts with multiple partners; to examine units of discourse to see how children sequence events, organize ideas, react to pressure, express abstract thinking, make inferences, store and retrieve networks of information, and negotiate meaning. Furthermore, research on literacy has strongly suggested the relationship between oral language competence and literacy. In other words, the language competence that a child brings to school becomes the basis for future language learning (reading and writing). LM children bring to school a different language and culture, which often results in feelings of tremendous dislocation and incongruence and a lack of linguistic competence. Practitioners need to respect such linguistic and cultural differences, to be cautioned against "pigeon-holing" children for their English linguistic incompetence, to learn more about the language and culture of LM children in order to conduct ethnographic studies, to nurture the growth of the children's home language and English, and to improve observation methods and intervention strategies when working with these children.

CHAPTER 4

Contrasting Acculturation Patterns of Two Non-English-Speaking Preschoolers

Jerri Willett

INTRODUCTION

Despite a growing interest in the social context of second language learning, research investigating and documenting the child's sociocultural environment in the process of acquisition is in a nascent state (see Saville-Troike 1982a, 1984; Willett forthcoming; Wong-Fillmore 1976, 1982a, and 1982b; Wong-Fillmore, Ammon, and McLaughlin 1985; and Cazden 1986).

Ethnographies of communication and schooling have made clear that communication is embedded in cultural systems (see collections of Green and Wallat 1981; Heath, 1983; Saville-Troike 1982b; Spindler 1982; and Trueba, Guthrie, and Au 1981). Cultural values and assumptions directly affect the nature of communication and its emergent qualities, which in turn affect cognition and transmission.

Observations from this ethnographic literature suggest that to capture the dynamics of second language acquisition, research must consider the learner's and his or her interlocutor's present and past sociocultural environment. Research in second language, however, has been narrowly focused and has not looked at these global aspects of acquisition. This report attempts to consider these neglected areas of second language research by examining the sociocultural environment and language development of two non-English-speaking children immersed in an American nursery school.

THE STUDY

Procedures

Having a daughter enrolled in the school, I was able to gain entry into the classroom as a parent participant. I spent five months observing the children every day for thirty minutes. In addition, I also participated in the classroom activities, for approximately four hours each week for four months. As a parent participant, I read stories, played with the children, went on field trips, and helped prepare and serve snacks.

I kept a running narrative of events and conversations in a notebook, which was filled out immediately after each session. After first obtaining folk terms for activities and events that occurred in the classroom, I focused on the interaction patterns of the teachers and English-speaking children. Using the children's and teachers' categories for activities and events, I classified who played with whom, when, and how. I then focused on the two non-English-speaking girls, noting differences and similarities between their patterns of interaction and those of the English-speaking children. Finally, I concentrated on activities and events in which the two girls displayed different patterns of interaction from each other.

In addition, I interviewed the mothers of both non-English-speaking children and the two classroom teachers. Each interview was approximately five hours long over several meetings. During the interviews, I elicited opinions, attitudes and, value statements about child-rearing, language learning and education, as well as reactions to specific events that I observed in the classroom and reported to the parents and teachers.

The Setting and Participants

The Kid's Center is a cooperative day-care center for the preschool children of affiliates of a private university in California. Parents participate in the governing, maintenance, and daily activities of the school. The community from which the school draws its children is marked by both its academic orientation and its international character.

The seven boys and twelve girls in the four-year-old room represented a variety of nationalities and life experiences. Many of the children would eventually return to their native countries after their parents finished graduate studies in the United States. All except three of the children were fluent-English speakers, including the two girls who are the focus of this study. The children could be considered privileged, if not economically, at least by virtue of having well-educated parents of high status.

Two teachers, both in their mid-twenties, supervised the activities in the four-year-old room. Interaction between the teachers and the children seemed natural, playful, and easy. One teacher described the interaction thus: "We really get down at the level of the children. After class, it is sometimes difficult to readjust to an adult level. I have to shower as soon as I get home to help me readjust." The two teachers had very different personalities and each appealed to different types of children. Both teachers seemed to thoroughly enjoy the children.

In addition to the teachers, a parent participant and a university student played with the children and assisted the teachers. Parent-participant roles were not well defined. Some parents entered the child's energetic world comfortably, while others were more reserved and tried to find activities that were more clearly defined, such as pushing swings, reading stories, or helping the teachers to tidy up. The children, however, saw the participant roles very clearly. They would often ask an unoccupied adult, "Are you participating today?" If there was an affirmative answer the child would plop him- or herself into the empty lap with a book. Participants were supposed to give "under-pushes" on the swings, chase and tickle the children, and assist with putting on jackets and shoes.

The two girls selected for the focus of this study were both non-English speakers upon their recent arrival to the United States. The girls lived in the same court in the married-housing complex for students of the university. At the time of the study, the fathers of the two girls were students, while the mothers stayed at home. Alisia, the child from Brazil, had one younger sister. Jeni, the girl from Korea, had one brother a year older than she.

The Activities: A Typical Day

The atmosphere in the room was a continual flow of energy, loosely contained at one level by the activities that structured the four hours, and at another level by the interests of the children. The following is a description of a typical day:

The afternoon session begins with an hour of free time. A variety of activities is placed on each table (playdoh, crayons and paper, puzzles) and children choose whatever they wish to do. Children tend to start out with solitary activities, gradually making contact with those sitting next to them, until they are ready to join into the energy flow.

After an hour or so, the teachers announce clean-up time. The teachers start picking up as they cajole the children into helping. Although a few "hide in the oven" (a toy under the loft), most of the children follow along with the cleanup. Without a break in the flow, one of the teachers starts passing out mats for nap time. Each child finds a space, usually extending the definition of a "permitted area" as far as possible. Children are found draped over blocks, behind bookshelves, or between legs of chairs. The teacher puts on a Judy Collins's album, *Both Sides Now*. The flow ebbs momentarily but never stops. Although the children lie quietly on their mats, not a limb is still. During one side of the album, the defined length of the rest period, the teachers set up the project for the day. There are monthly or weekly themes, such as dinosaurs, space, or any conceivable holiday, upon which the project will be based. Today's theme is space.

At the end of the record, the children jump up and put away their mats. Without instructions most children find their way to the tables where one of the teachers has already started creating a space ship. She begins to narrate her actions: "I'm going to Mars so I'll need a space ship. I'll use this box for the body." The children join in to build their ship, using paper, glitter, egg boxes, and paint. They talk about what they will find on Mars. The other teacher is handing out paint brushes full of paint to splatter on a roll of black construction paper, which will end up as the Milky Way. Gold stars are randomly stuck on the mural. They talk about the Milky Way and how far away the stars are. Another group of children is coloring planets, which have been cut out by the teachers during nap time. Some of the children become engrossed in their work, some ask questions about space, and some run off to play on their own. The children and teachers talk throughout the project work.

As interest wanes, one teacher sits on the piano bench with a book while the other teacher starts cleaning up. Soon the children start gathering around. She waits until everyone is seated on the floor before she begins to read *The Empire Strikes Back.* There is dialogue throughout the story between the children and the teacher, but the focus is fully on the book, which she holds up as she reads so that the children can see.

Snack, which was prepared by the second teacher, is announced. Each child sits down at a table. The child whose parent provided the snack selects two other children to be "waitress" for the day. They pass out oranges, crackers, and cheese. The teachers place small jugs of milk on each table so that the children can pour out their own milk. The children chatter throughout the snack. At one point during the snack, Tommy shouts out, "Please pass the wig!", which he does nearly every snack time, and the children break out in laughter.

After snack, the children disappear outside. Initially, they run to the swings and climbing frame, but soon the children begin to form spontaneous fantasy play groups. One child announces the roles: "You be the mommy and I'll be the baby." "I wanna be the sister," says another. "O.K. and this can be the bed." "Let's pretend this stick is the bottle." The children narrate every action. Some talk is interactive and some merely fills in the details of the environment as it evolves. Once the groups are formed, intruders are quickly rebuffed.

After forty-five minutes, the teachers start herding the children inside. A variety of new activities are found on the tables. Some of the children continue their fantasy play indoors, while others explore the new activities until parents begin arriving.

The afternoon described here was typical, although field trips, singing, show-and-tell, plays, films, swimming in the sprinklers, or watching soccer on the playing fields were also common. The activities that filled the children's afternoons seemed to evolve smoothly and gradually into one another in a rhythmic focus-release-focus-release pattern. Of course, occasional flare-ups, lost tempers, and deviations from the flow of activity occurred, but generally there were few breaks or sudden jerks. Focus was rarely on the teacher but on some common activity that she introduced and the children developed. In fact, the focus was so diffuse that an obvious focus was not always discernable. Generally, the teacher started an activity, and gradually the children became interested and changed their focus.

The View of Foreigners by the Class

Living in University Village, the children interacted with people of different races and cultures on a daily basis. They heard a wide variety of foreign languages and accents and saw divergent customs, food, and dress. A high proportion of the children in the class had lived outside of the United States or had parents who were born in another country. A few of the children (in addition to the subjects of this study) had acquired English as a second language. Every year the school enrolls non-English-speaking children, so that both the teachers and the children had frequent experience with children struggling to learn English. Anglo parents frequently commented that they appreciated their children's living in a multiethnic environment.

The school exploited its multiethnic environment in several ways. Many of the project themes, snacks, stories, and festivals stressed international understanding. Parents were encouraged to give presentations about their native countries and to provide ethnic snacks. However, no specific policy concerning the treatment of non-English-speaking children existed. Generally, the children were "immersed" into the classroom without special treatment.

Both teachers felt that the fluent-English-speaking children did not really appreciate or empathize with those having to learn a new language and cultural rules, even though they might have gone through the process themselves earlier. Typically, the English-speaking children ignored the non-English speaker, until the new child could competently operate in the "new culture" (language was not necessarily needed to operate competently in many aspects of this culture).

The teachers seemed to accept the children as part of the group whenever the foreign child decided for him or herself to join in. Attention was mostly on a physical level and did not necessarily require language. Hugs, kisses, and rough-and-tumble play were plentiful and available for whomever happened to be around. The teachers' behavior was not inconsistent with their expressed views of childhood development. They felt that when children were ready and able, they would participate on their own terms, without pressure from the teachers. This appeared to be the operating principle of the classroom, whether or not a child was a non-English speaker.

Jeni—the Korean child.   The teachers could not remember a time when Jeni cried or acted upset, but they recalled that she followed them around "like a shadow" during the first two months. By the time my field work began, however, Jeni had stopped her shadowing and had developed distinctive interaction patterns that did not change much during the five-month study. In contrast to the other children, Jeni did not interact with her peers. Normally, Jeni could be found sitting at one of the small tables working on a concrete task, such as a puzzle, playdoh, or drawing. Jeni avoided moving around the room except at the transition points in the day's structure. The other children, however, moved around frequently, even when working on a project at a table. Outside, Jeni spent most of her time swinging on a swing. She seldom participated in spontaneous group activities, unless structured by the teacher, and it was common to see Jeni sitting alone. When children were playing around Jeni, she seldom entered into their conversations, even when she was linguistically capable of doing so.

Jeni did not seem interested in or even aware of what the other children were doing. One particular example illustrates this point well. Virtually every day for weeks, girls would bring leotards from home, which they traded around, and would pretend to be ballerinas. The girls became so engrossed in the play that some parents complained. Jeni never entered into this play, and more interestingly, she never mentioned the dancing at home (this particular event was critical in the other foreign child's case). This type of behavior seemed to prompt the "shy" label from most adults and other children.

In striking contrast, Jeni was quite talkative with adults. Not only was she talkative, but she often initiated contact with adults and worked hard to maintain the contact. Frequently, Jeni's conversation with an adult would attract the attention of the other children, who would join the conversation. The adult would then include the other children, although Jeni never picked up on their conversations. A sample conversation between Jeni and me illustrates Jeni's fixation on adult conversation, while ignoring children around her:

> [Jeni and Alisia are sitting at the table, coloring.]
> JERRI: What are you making, Jeni?
> JENI: I making rainbow. [She reaches for a crayon.] Yellow. [Heather comes over to the table carrying a doll.]
> JENI: [directed to Jerri] This Heather baby.
> JERRI: Did you bring this for share day, Heather?
> JENI: Here for you [gives Jerri her drawing].
> JERRI: Thank you Jeni—that's lovely. [Stephanie sits in Jerri's lap, while Heather begins coloring.]
> JENI: This fire.
> STEPH: What are you making? [directed to Jeni, but Jeni does not respond] I want this!
> JENI: You can't. You can't [pulling away the scissors. The squabble ends almost as quickly as it started.]
> JENI: I write fire name. [John joins the table and shows me his drawing.]

JERRI: That's great, John. I like the colors, especially.

JENI: This my mommy cookie.

JERRI: Cooking?

JENI: No, cookie. This triangle cookie. [She starts drawing a triangle.]

During the entire proceedings, Heather, John, and Stephanie were in constant conversation, discussing such things as the proper word for hole puncher, their favorite colors, and narrations of their drawings. Jeni does not enter into these conversations, except for the one altercation with Stephanie.

With the exception of the opening statement, where I asked what Jeni was making, she initiated and developed each topic change throughout my conversation, but she ignored the conversation of the other children. Discussions with other parents and observation of Jeni with other adults, revealed that Jeni frequently sought out interaction with adults, inside and outside school. Typically, Jeni was able to elicit talk from adults and actively manipulate their speech in spite of her limited English.

The family interaction patterns reported by Jeni's mother were very different from those of the nursery school. When discussing her views about how children learn, Jeni's mother agreed that Confucian values had a strong impact on the socialization of her children. She felt that children learn by watching and imitating: "If parents set a good example, the child will learn how to behave correctly. A wife shows respect to her mother and husband so the child will learn to respect her family and teachers. If a child has respect for her teachers, she will pay attention and work hard to learn what must be learned."

I was unable to observe Jeni's mother in a "teaching" interaction with Jeni, but I was able to watch Jeni's father interact with her at school. Jeni was seated at a table playing with playdoh. There was a box of kitchen utensils in the middle of the table. Jeni had made a playdoh figure, using her hands. Her father told her she should use the utensils, and then he demonstrated how to do it. Jeni picked up each utensil and copied his actions. Observing another adult, from a Western background, I noticed a very different strategy of interaction. The adult attempted to capture the attention of the child with an enthusiastic tone, saying, "Hey, look at this!" The adult then asked the child what he thought could be done with the utensils. When the child did not respond, the adult feigned discovery: "I know, I bet you could make some squiggly worms!"

I asked Jeni's mother about any adjustment problems Jeni may have experienced. She thought that Jeni felt a little ashamed because her brother, Paul, could speak English, while she could not. However, Jeni rarely expressed her frustrations and she rarely cried. She pointed out that they had to be stricter with Jeni because her grandmother had been too "soft" with her. In addition, Jeni was a little too tomboyish and aggressive, since she played with her brother so much. She explained that in Korean families the father is the authority figure to whom everyone was obedient. Her husband often used spanking to correct misbehavior of the children, but generally they were well behaved.

I asked her if Jeni talked about school or the children at home, to which she replied that Jeni mentioned a few names, but normally she did not talk about the other children very much, "The children are not patient and do not want to play with her because her English is not good, and so Jeni ignores them."

Jeni's mother felt that many differences existed between the way American and Korean mothers socialized their children. She said that American mothers seemed to fuss over unimportant matters, like insisting that the children say thank you for everything, but that when it came to important matters, like learning, the children were left to their own devises with no guidelines. She liked the greater warmth and affection that American mothers showed their children, but sometimes the children seemed "uncontrollable."

In response to a question about her views on nursery schools, she said that Korea did not have many nursery schools and Jeni had not attended one. Usually, the mother or grandmother looked after the children at home. Once a child started school, it was very competitive and children had to study many hours, but before entering primary school the children had plenty of time to play at home. She said her children did similar things at home to what was done in nursery school and she would take the children to play outside every day. In response to a question about the age children were allowed to play outside alone, she said, "usually about six or seven."

Jeni's mother believed that the Kid's Center was quite nice and provided a lot of things for the children to do. Her only criticism was that she had hoped the teachers would spend a few minutes every day teaching English to Jeni, but that the teachers seemed reluctant to do so. Consequently, she spent time at home giving Jeni English lessons, using a book she brought with her from Korea.

Alisia—the Brazilian girl.   Alisia's approach to language acquisition was very different from Jeni's. Alisia had a difficult and stressful initial adjustment. She hated going to school and begged her parents not to send her. She was frequently tearful, and the teachers described her as "a little hysterical." They learned a few words in Portuguese to help reassure her. Alisia's mother felt that because Alisia was very verbal and sociable in Brazil, she was devastated by not being able to communicate.

By the time I began my field observations in January, Alisia had calmed down, but she was not yet saying much in English. "Don't" and "Stop" seemed to be the extent of her verbalization. Although she would smile, and she seemed to respond physically, she would not respond verbally when I attempted to elicit English from her.

Alisia did not remain stationary, as did Jeni. She frequently moved around the classroom space, watching the other children and eventually returning to Jeni's work space. While Jeni was usually seated, Alisia normally worked standing up.

Alisia soon made attempts to join the "flow." She first attempted to gain entry by breaking the flow. I frequently observed her trying to run off with toys the other children were using. One day during the nap two girls were quietly engaging in a tug-of-war over a book that each girl wanted. The girls were momentarily distracted by the teacher, so Alisia grabbed the book and hid under the loft. "Hey! Who took my book?" said one of the girls. When she was informed that Alisia had the book, the girls lost interest. I noted that on many occasions, the children would "give in" to the non-English speakers. Whether they were aware that it was an unfair battle or whether they thought they would "get into trouble" could not be ascertained. An episode the very next day led me to realize that Alisia was not interested in the toys she was grabbing but in the contact she hoped would follow. The next day when nap time was announced, Alisia led me to her "cubby" and pointed to her satchel. Puzzled, I handed it to her. She took out a book written in Portuguese and went over to the same girls, who had struggled over the book the previous day. With exaggerated movements, she sat down next to them and opened her book so that the girls could see. The girls soon took notice and gingerly reached for the book, which smiling Alisia allowed them to do.

Alisia soon learned how to join the flow of peer activities. When the other children raised their hands (e.g., volunteering for roles in *Star Wars*), she would also raise hers, even when she did not know why she was doing so. During songs, she would sing and mime when she did not understand the words. She managed to participate in fantasy play groups by making contact with one child, who could then help her join the group. One day I observed Alisia first make eye contact with one child. She then dropped down behind a bookshelf and popped back up again, while giggling. Her "contact" soon followed suit, dropping down and popping up. Soon they were in the midst of a hide-and-seek game that attracted several other children. Although the original game soon dissipated, her "contact" stuck with her when the next peer group evolved.

The turning point in Alisia's adjustment concerned the ballet fad mentioned earlier. Wearing a leotard seemed to be a prerequisite for joining in the ballet fantasy play. One by one, each girl in the class managed to convince her mother to allow her to wear a leotard to school. Unlike Jeni, Alisia asked her mother if she could bring one. It turned out to be her ticket into the group fantasy play. From this point on, Alisia loved school. With the leotard, she was fully accepted by the girls, even without language. Shortly after her "acceptance," she began speaking. The teachers recalled the first time they heard her speak. During snack time, Alisia said in the same intonation pattern used by the other children, "Please pass the bananas."

After she started speaking, Alisia would use her limited English in the same appropriate way that she played. A casual outsider might not have realized Alisia was a limited-English speaker. The following scene illustrates how Alisia used her English to participate in group fantasy play, but it cannot capture Alisia's native-like intonation patterns:

Kara and Alisia were stacking cardboard bricks, in order to make a wall for their house. Jonathan grabbed one of the bricks under loud protests from both of the girls. Kara went into the house (under the loft), while Alisia continued building. "Jonathan!" cried Alisia in a menacing voice, which deterred Jonathan for the moment. Alisia questioned Kara: "Kara, three blocks here?" "Yes . . . ah, no, three reds," Kara responded, as Alisia finished off the wall. The girls started setting up the inside of the house. Alisia, taking a handbag from the costume box, said, "I want this, O.K.?" She took out a red purse and handing it to Kara said, "Here." Kara responded in a mock-grown-up intonation, "Thank you, Alisia." Using the same intonation, Alisia said, "Goodbye, I have to go now." The girls pretended to walk to their new house. Alisia put down her handbag and picked up the play teakettle, saying, "More?" "Yes, please," replied Kara. Alisia ran to the bathroom to fill up her kettle with water. Upon Alisia's return, Kara said, "Put it here." "No. Here," Alisia countered. I was called away by the teacher, but the girls continued playing for another ten minutes.

In contrast to Jeni, Alisia focused on her peers for discovering "ritual constraints." By imitating and participating in the energy of the class, she was able to pick up the details as she went along. Once she discovered various appropriate rules, she avoided behavior that labeled her as an outsider.

Alisia's interaction patterns at home were also quite different from Jeni's. Alisia spent much of her time in the play area with other children, and her mother rarely went to the play area with her children. Alisia's mother commented, "Only mothers with toddlers and Asian mothers supervise their children's play in this area. Sometimes Latin American mothers go to the central area, but only to socialize—not really to supervise their children."

Alisia's mother described the difficult time Alisia had adjusting to the "court life." Alisia was shocked to discover that she was not competent socially, as she had been in Brazil. The mother noted that the children formed exclusive cliques. When they would not let Alisia play, she would come home crying, because she didn't understand the "rules of the game." In spite of her difficulty, she finally learned how to be competent with the other children and eventually adjusted. "Perhaps I could have helped her more, but I had problems myself. We had to work out our own adjustments. I don't feel any guilt, because ultimately it worked out for the best."

I asked whether or not she and her husband helped Alisia with English at home. She said they considered using English in the home, but they decided against it. Some of her Brazilian friends had children who had forgotten their Portuguese. She felt that ultimately the children would have learned the language anyway. She said she would never directly teach her children English.

I asked her about the differences between her culture and the American culture that made their adjustment difficult. She felt that there were not many differences in the basic values or lifestyles between Americans and upper-middle-class Brazilians:

It's just a matter of learning "terminology" or getting used to a new color of the same style. Brazil was much closer to the American way of life than other

Latin American countries. Brazilians are like Americans. They are informal, friendly and sociable. Other Latin American countries are more similar to the formal European style.

She did not find much difference in the rearing of children, although she believed that Brazilian mothers were a little more careful about the appearance of their children and less concerned about "politeness." She also thought that some American mothers felt that the behavior of their children reflected directly upon the mothers' ability to raise their children, whereas she did not believe this was true. One reason posited for these differences was the fact that "most upper middle class Brazilian families have servants, so that there is time to attend to the children's appearance. You can also blame children's unacceptable traits on the servant's influence."

In Brazil, Alisia had a very busy and independent social life, partly because of the servants. Alisia, at the age of three, could call up a friend and make arrangements to meet. The servant would take her and stay with her, until Alisia was ready to come home. I asked how closely the servants supervised the children's play, to which she replied, "Hardly at all. The servants socialize among themselves, and children do as they please."

I asked about her views on discipline. She said she had no consistent policy for guiding her demands on the children; it really depended on the situation, the parent's mood and the child's mood. She did not expect children to obey blindly. She negotiated with Alisia, who was quite rational, but Anna, her younger daughter, she normally distracted.

I asked her which values she hoped her children would possess and how they learned these values. She said that she hoped they would be independent, sociable, and critical (not blindly accepting of others' views). She would be disappointed if they were aggressive or selfish. Although these traits seemed contradictory, she said one should attempt to achieve a balance between them. She felt that children were partly born with specific personalities and were partly influenced by their environment. She praised the children when she observed independent or sociable behavior, but basically she felt that they learned from other children.

Alisia's mother saw the role of the parent as providing the child with opportunities and options. The children decided for themselves how to use the options. For example, providing music and dance lessons or a college education would equip the child with skills to handle whatever situation he or she might choose to compete in. However, it was up to the child to use the skills as he or she wished. Pressure to acquire skills was not usually needed if parents provided an environment in which there were peers who were interested in acquiring skills. In Brazil her "class" ensured that Alisia would be motivated to acquire skills and social graces, so the parents did not pressure their child.

Although a parent must protect children from physical and psychological harm, they must also "release" the child from the parent's guard as soon as possible, so that the child is free to develop his or her own individuality. The quandary for the parent is deciding when to give protection and how much to give.

Alisia's mother saw the role of the school as similar to her own. Children needed opportunities to play with other children, and preschool ensured that for so many hours each day the children would have these opportunities, without the mother having to make special arrangements each day. Although social and intellectual skills were important, she could not imagine her children having difficulty in school. If there should be learning problems, she would provide them with extra help. Both her "class" and her family take for granted the acquisition of these skills.

INTERPRETATION

In this study, the Brazilian and American views (represented by Alisia's mother and the teachers) have been almost identical, contrasting on every point with the Korean view (represented by Jeni's mother).[1]

Alisia's mother and the teachers had the same views about peer socialization, adult roles, values, and discipline. They both saw their roles with respect to the children as providers of stimulating environments rather than as teachers or supervisors in the Confucian sense. They both left the responsibility for interacting with the children themselves. A similar informal, friendly, and noncoercive relationship occurred between them and the children. Jeni, on the other hand, had been socialized to expect focused interaction with her parents, and, by extension, teachers; and so she sought out adult relationships in the school. Within those relationships she was talkative. The content of the talk was task-related and centered around what Jeni was trying to do. There was pressure from her family to learn English and Jeni put great effort into this task.

Alisia's difficult adjustment, despite congruity between the cultures, was predictable. Since her identity derived from her peers, she had to reconstruct a new identity, without help from teachers or parents. Unlike Jeni, who had been trained to be self-controlled, Alisia had been allowed to express her emotions as loudly as she wished. Jeni, on the other hand, did not appear to have a strong inclusion need, since her identity did not derive from peer acceptance. Jeni and the other children had "no relationship"; she was inclined to ignore them and avoid interaction with them on an ad hoc basis. Furthermore, the other children did not act the way Jeni had been taught to behave. The other children were comfortable with unsupervised space, had short attention spans, and moved around following peer activity. Jeni selected the structured activities and stayed in one place.

The values being transmitted, the activities, and the relationships in the classroom were in conflict with Jeni's cultural values and relationships. Adult guidance and supervision directly transmitting Confucian values is lacking in an American nursery school. In a Korean context, play is shaped by continual adult feedback. In the Kid's Place the teachers structured the environment, offered stimulation to spark new interests, defined the parameters in which play must take place, and provided warmth and affection for those children who temporarily needed refuge. However, ideas and relationships were predominately shaped by peer feedback. By contrast, Alisia was not required to act differently from the way she had been socialized in order to discover the "new rules." She knew where and how to look for the rules. She had been raised to need integration with her peers, and so the motivation was strong. Because she did not expect help from an adult, she was not at a loss, as was Jeni when she did not receive focused supervision.

LANGUAGE ACQUISITION

Alisia and Jeni were both successful language learners. When the two children entered kindergarten the next year, Jeni was not required by the school to attend special English as a Second Language (ESL) classes, and Alisia was dropped from the class after a few months. The girls' approaches to learning, however, were very different. Since classroom conversations were not recorded, to gain information it was necessary to depend on quick notes and on-the-spot analyses of the children's English development and reports from the parents and teachers.

Although the girls developed quickly, it was possible to compare and contrast a few of the more general trends of their development. The following patterns in the children's limited speech samples were observed:

Jeni began using English almost immediately. While she used a few formulaic expressions (as described by Wong-Fillmore 1976), she preferred to nominate topics by using single words, which were then expanded by her adult interlocutor. By her third month, Jeni had an extensive vocabulary and was beginning to syntactically process her language rather than to rely on learned patterns. Turn-allocators were among the earlier patterns used by Jeni. She did not appear embarrassed by her numerous errors. Her English pronunciation and intonation patterns were very poor. Teachers reported that they and the children had a difficult time understanding Jeni.

Alisia did not start using English until after she had been accepted by her peers. She first used memorized chunks of language appropriately and correctly to help her integrate into the peer group. She spent several "silent" months observing and noting how the chunks were used by her peers; however, she waited until she was fairly confident that she was correct before she started using her learned patterns. Her intonation patterns and pronunciation were native-like, and she was able to use her "routines" in a variety of situations, by merely changing the intonation pattern.

Literature on first- and second-language acquisition helps to relate these descriptions of language output from the two girls to the interaction patterns described earlier. This literature gives credence to the possibility that Jeni's predominant interactions with adults and Alisia's predominant interactions with peers may have affected the language acquisition process.

Peters (1977, 1983) distinguishes "analytic" and "gestalt" styles of first language development. In the analytic style a child uses words to label and refer, and therefore follows a "one word at a time development." The adult expands these referential words from which the child develops a syntactic system. A "gestalt" style user attempts to use whole utterances in a socially appropriate situation. Having committed routines and patterns to memory, the child is ready to have the language-processing mechanism extract the syntactic rules operating in the memorized patterns. Krashen and Scarcella (1979) have posited that "input type" may determine which style a child prefers. The "analytic" child may receive clear caretaker speech, while the "gestalt" child may receive more rapid, conversational input.

Therefore, it is possible that Jeni's rapid syntactic development and one-word-at-a-time development may have been the result of her adult interactions. Alisia's use of phrases and her rapid phonological development may have been the result of her peer input.

Literature exploring differences between child-child interaction and child-adult interaction further supports the hypothesis that Jeni's interaction patterns affected the type of input she received, thus defined the type of learning style she needed to use, and finally, affected her language output. In comparing child-child and child-adult discourse, Peck (1978) found the latter to contain a greater number of questions and requests for clarification and referential speech. Topic nomination was easier for the learner. In adult-child interaction, the adult spoke slowly and clearly. All contributions made by the child were considered potentially relevant, but the adult showed the child, through expansions, how to make the contribution relevant. Relevancy, however, was narrowly defined. Peck suggested that adult-child interaction aids the child in semantic and syntactic development. Scollon (1974) found that child-adult discourse had a vertical construction in which the child nominated the topic, often by a single word, and then the adult expanded the child-nominated topic into a full sentence. Hatch (1978) suggested that such vertical constructions enable a child to discover the syntactic rules of language. Again, Jeni's interactions followed this pattern very closely, and this could account for her rapid syntactic and semantic development.

In child-child discourse, on the other hand, Peck (1978) found that there was a large amount of repetition, a greater range of functions expressed, and more varied input. The second language learner had more difficulty nominating topics, but repetition and sound play were considered relevant responses. A word or sound might be used as a take-off for free association or sound play. In other words, the second language learner had to be "socially appropriate" to be accepted by the native-speaking peer; there was a greater range of behavior that was considered socially appropriate. Sound play in child-child discourse was frequent, but sounding different was more of a stigma than not making literal sense. The exchanges in child-child interaction were rapid and did not take into account the fact that the second language learner did not understand. Therefore, the child had to memorize "chunks" of sound in order to participate. Peck hypothesized that child-child interaction increases phonological development. Alisia's almost exclusively peer relationships would have necessitated that she use the gestalt approach and would account for her phonological development and acquisition of appropriate chunks.

In addition to the syntactic and phonological differences between the girls, there were also differences in the early use of turn-allocators (wh-questions, yes-no questions, verbs of notice, and imperatives), which might explain the differences in the approaches of the girls.

Keller-Cohen (1980) found that children who learned turn-allocations early were able to get their interlocutors to "create a linguistic context," and as such, to provide the child with information about the new code he or she is trying to learn. However, turn-allocators are used more frequently (as effective turn-allocators) in child-adult discourse than in child-child discourse. Keller-Cohen noted that a child who does not learn turn-allocators early "must rely on the willingness of others to talk to him, and must depend on less direct means of gaining information about his new linguistic code." However, as Peck (1978) points out, children do not always pay attention to the formal turn-allocators and seem more interested in whatever is more relevant to their play at the moment. Therefore, it might be that the child who can figure out how to be relevant (quite often physically or through sound play) has a greater chance of maintaining contact with peers. Again, we see that Alisia's hours of observation of her peers was necessary for her to learn what was relevant in order to maintain peer contact. Alisia demonstrated her awareness of her peers and their "rules," time and time again. Turn-allocators were not relevant in her situation. Jeni, who developed turn-allocators early, used her ability to initiate interaction with adults, from which she could control the input she received.

CONCLUSIONS

This report suggests that the culturally shaped interaction patterns of the participants in this study influenced the type of language input received by the two girls who were the focus of the study, and may explain, in part, their learning styles and developmental language output. Jeni's Asian background may have led her to seek out situations that were adult and task centered. Jeni's frequent adult contact and infrequent peer contact may have influenced her "analytic" approach to language learning. Clear, slow, and simplified input from adults increased the likelihood that Jeni would be able to discover linguistic constraints fairly quickly. The adults' emphasis on semantic and syntactic clarity and on referential function made it likely that Jeni would develop these aspects of language first. Phonological development, functional variety, and rules of appropriateness, emphasized in peer interaction, would be learned later.

Alisia's culture, on the other hand, highly values independence and social competence in peer situations, as does the American culture into which she was placed. Identity with peers was both a necessity and a possibility for Alisia, thus decreasing the time she needed to discover how to behave like the other children. Alisia's peer interactions may have necessitated a gestalt approach to language acquisition. Sensitivity to her peers exposed Alisia to rapid, varied, and appropriate models. However, the only way she could work out linguistic rules was to memorize chunks (which, if memorized correctly and exactly, were accepted by her peers), and later to process the chunks syntactically. Children's interest in sounds and sound play helped Alisia process phonological rules early in her development.

I am not suggesting that there is a fixed relationship between cultural values, social strategies, and learning approaches. All of the participants displayed adaptive strategies in dealing with the tasks of learning, teaching, and communicating. Nevertheless, an understanding of how cultural assumptions influence interaction and learning patterns can help educators interact with children more effectively.

NOTES

1. A few studies support the cultural interpretations presented in this paper. Park, Cambra and Klopf (1979) found that in oral communication Koreans were talkative, dominant, task oriented, and had low inclusion needs, whereas Americans put a greater emphasis on personal-emotional aspects of communication. Smart (1977) and Underwood (1977) point out that in Korean communication, relationships are the basis for interaction and that Koreans avoid interaction in which they do not feel competent or where no relationship has been established. There are no comparable studies of middle-class Brazilians. However, Schumann (1976) has noted that Latin American professionals are solidly acculturative in their integration patterns. Kahl (1968) found that values of high SES families in Brazil stressed low integration with relatives, individualism, high integration with friends, activism, and that education was taken for granted.

CHAPTER 5

Learning Failure: Tests as Gatekeepers and the Culturally Different Child[1]

Donna Deyhle

Anthropological studies of American educational institutions have increasingly focused on single events, activities, or processes that dominant and minority children encounter in school. These ethnographic studies have focused on such topics as reading (McDermott and Gospodinoff 1981; VanNess 1981), teaching and questioning styles (Erickson and Mohatt 1982; Heath 1982), and classroom participation (Ludwig 1981; Philips 1983). A recurring problem revealed by these studies is the cultural discontinuities that often exist between the home and school environments. In particular, this research points to significant educational problems or mismatches that minority-group children experience due to the lack of cultural congruence between their home culture and that of the schools they attend (Au and Jordan 1981; Heath 1982; John 1972; Boggs 1972; Philips 1972, 1983; Mohatt and Erickson 1981; Shultz, Florio, and Erickson 1982). Participant structures, questioning styles, social organization, the absence of contextually relevant materials, and physical structures in the classrooms all seem to be factors contributing to some children's disorientation in the school environment. However, the testing event, as the major device for determining success or failure in school, has not been examined as a possible culturally incongruent activity for some children.

This chapter presents the results of an ethnographic study of tests and test-taking among Navajo students in a Bureau of Indian Affairs (BIA) day school and Anglo students in a large Western city. Its purpose was to examine how testing was structured and presented in classrooms and how students developed an understanding of the concept of test-taking or the role it played in their schooling experience. Results of this study lead to the conclusion that (1) not all children approach the event of testing with the same understanding of its importance in the context of the schooling process, (2) this difference can be viewed in terms of differences in socioculturally determined styles of displaying competence, (3) failure is an educational concept that is learned and reinforced by test-taking for Navajo children, and (4) teachers' test presentations served to misrepresent the role of testing among Navajo children and reinforced its importance for Anglo children.

TESTS, CULTURE, AND SCHOOLING

Although not without criticism (McDermott 1982; Padilla 1979; Hilliard 1979; Tyler 1979), the role of the test is firmly entrenched as a repeated event associated with schooling. In anthropological terms, testing can be seen as a "rite of passage," which a student must successfully complete in order to move on to the next stage, grade, or position within the institution of schooling. In this sense, the role of a test is synonymous with that of a gatekeeper—to allow the passage of some and ensure the failure of others. When examining those students who often have difficulty in successfully passing through this gatekeeper, studies show that minority students consistently score lower on tests than do students from the dominant sociocultural group in American society (Coleman et al. 1966; LeVine 1976; Rohwer 1971).

Many educators and students see testing as a device that is helpful in promoting learning: a test is the judgment of what has or has not been learned in the classroom. Another view of the role of testing is that it serves as a device for sorting children and youth, pushing out those who are judged least promising and encouraging a few to go on in school (LeVine 1976; Tyler 1979). According to LeVine, the achievement test contained important social values: it emphasized ordering individual differences, and it served the social functions of rationalizing the allocation of scarce resources and settling social conflict by providing a natural, "scientific" form of evidence. These factors shaped test forms and ensured the acceptance of tests as they became very much a part of dominant culture as a measure of educational accomplishment and personal self-worth.

Literature and research that oppose tests exist; their concerns focus on the cultural biases inherent in testing (Gay and Abrahams, 1973; Anastasi 1949; Gerry 1973). This research points out that tests are designed for and validated against the values and lifestyles of the middle class, which in turn discriminates against other socioeconomic groups and nondominant cultural groups. The bias-criticism arguments are divided into two areas of concern—the bias of test content and the bias in the environment of the test itself.

The method most frequently used to examine the depressed achievement of minority students has been a psychometric statistical analysis of tests and test scores (Coleman et al. 1966). Mercer (1972a) indicated, "What the IQ test measures, to a significant extent, is the child's exposure to Anglo culture. The more 'Anglicized' a non-Anglo child is, the better he does on the IQ test" (95). Mercer (1972b) goes one step further in a psychometric study that attempts to rectify the disparity of test scores by developing a sociocultural index. This index creates pluralistic norms, which are then interpreted along with standardized norms of the test as published in the test manuals. The other method used in examining test bias has been to analyze the cultural differences of the students, relying on sociological or anthropological data to support differences of learning styles, attitudes, language, and values (Cohen 1969; Gay and Abrahams 1973; Harris 1976; Hernandez 1973; Maehr 1974; Piersel 1977). Within this method, attempts have been made to develop cultural-free tests, to adapt present tests for cross-cultural applications, and to develop distinct tests for particular sociocultural groups. This has not resolved the problem that tests are cultural products. As Cole (1975) points out, the notion of a test being culture-free or culture-fair is very difficult to accept, as this implies that a test can be "independent of experiences" (52).

Both of these approaches have been valuable, but ultimately, they do not address the basic processes involved in the actual event of testing. How does the idea, concept, and importance of a test as a personal-assessment device develop among students? Research that starts with the test scores themselves obscures or neglects the processes the students are involved in up until they actually put pencil to paper to take a test. How has the classroom teacher presented the test to the students? What knowledge of the event of test-taking do the students have before they sit down to take a test? Research that looks at students' cultural or socioeconomic backgrounds for explanations of success or failure on tests addresses some of the possible differences with which students might enter the testing situation. Such research analyzes the content of the test itself as being either appropriate or inappropriate according to the students' backgrounds. Again, however, the processes involved in learning about and developing an understanding of tests and their importance in the context of the classroom experience are neglected.

This study attempted to fill this void by examining and describing the processes occuring during test-taking with regard to two groups of children—Navajo and Anglo. Are there certain lessons, skills, or attitudes—beyond the factual content of a test—which need to be learned in order to perform well on tests? Is it possible that failure to perform adequately on a test might be connected to some students' failure to interpret the importance of tests in schooling rather than simply to their lack of knowledge of the content of the test itself? Do some children enter the classroom with more of a formal understanding of tests and their importance, and does this in turn put them "ahead" of other students in terms of success in schooling? In short, how do these two groups of students perceive the "What?", "How?", and "Why?" of the testing event?

RESEARCH METHOD

Sites and Population

Research for this study extended over a three-year period and occurred at two different sites located in the inter-mountain West. The site of the first two years of the study (1979–1981) was an all-Navajo Bureau of Indian Affairs (BIA) day school of approximately 210 students, grades kindergarten through eight, located on the Navajo reservation. Throughout this article this site will be referred to with a fictitious name, Red Canyon.

The academic performance of the students at Red Canyon mirrored that of many other minority group children: they performed poorly on tests and often did not succeed in school. In order to examine the opposite experience—that of students who successfully maneuvered through school in general and through test-taking in particular—a second site, White Hill (also a fictitious name) was studied during the 1982–1983 school year. White Hill represented almost exclusively a nonminority Anglo population of approximately 600 students, grades one through six, and was located in a large metropolitan area.

The community of Red Canyon was composed of approximately two thousand people. The average family income in the community was very low, with wages derived primarily from work in the local mining industry, the community school, and arts and crafts work at home. Some individuals commuted to a nearby metropolitan area for jobs. The school was the largest employer in the community.

The Red Canyon school, first established in the 1930s as a boarding school, was converted in the 1960s to a community day school. Due to the small size of the school, each grade level consisted of only one class, with class sizes ranging from twenty to thirty students.

Although not as isolated or traditional as in some parts of the Navajo reservation, the community members of Red Canyon proudly asserted their identity as Navajo people. Squaw dances, powwows, and healing ceremonies, although not frequent, still occurred in the community. Most of the children came to school from homes where both Navajo and English were spoken. However, many grandparents were reported to be monolingual Navajo speakers.

At the time of the study most of the teachers at Red Canyon were Anglos. Exceptions to this were two lower-elementary teachers, one Hispanic and one black, and one upper-elementary teacher who was a Pueblo Indian. Each classroom in all of the grades at Red Canyon had a bilingual Navajo teacher aide, typically Navajo men and women from the local community. In most cases the aides had worked at the school for at least five years. All of the school's support staff—secretaries, cafeteria workers, and bus drivers—were Navajo.

The academic level of the Navajo students at Red Canyon in all grades was considerably depressed when compared with national norms. An analysis of the 1979 Comprehensive Test of Basic Skills (CTBS) pretest results revealed that a total of 95.8 percent of the students, grades two through eight, scored below the national average on the total test battery. One-half of these students scored below the 30th percentile on the CTBS. By the time the students reached the eighth grade, they might have been as many as three or four grade levels behind, according to nationally established norms on the CTBS.

In many ways White Hill lies at the opposite end of the descriptive spectrum from Red Canyon. It was one of twenty-seven elementary schools in a district that prided itself on having dedicated, well-trained teachers, and students who consistently scored above national norms on standardized tests. White Hill was considered a well-run, model school, which boasted traditional as well as open classrooms and which had a large gifted program. The school was nestled among middle- and upper-middle class homes in an area of the city that was considered affluent or professional. Teachers described strong parental involvement in the school's activities and considerable parental pressure on the children to perform successfully academically. Class sizes throughout the school ranged from twenty to thirty students.

Academically, White Hill was in the top 25 percent when compared with other elementary schools in the district. Analysis of the total reading and mathematics subsection scores on the CTBS reveals that according to school averages, the students all scored above their respective grade levels. By the time students had reached the sixth grade, as a class average they were scoring at the eighth-grade level in mathematics and reading.

It must be emphasized that this study examined the testing situation of only one group of Navajo and Anglo children. Variations exist within, as well as between, cultural groups. Therefore, it is suggested that generalizations to all Navajo, American Indian, and Anglo children be made with caution.

Research Rationale and Procedures

Tests are imposed on students from "above," and this testing situation has traditionally been interpreted in an etic manner. The etic approach is concerned with the assessment of an outside observer, who may or may not have the same categories as the students being observed. That is, tests are given and analyzed by teachers, administrators, and researchers with little input from, or regard for, the students' perceptions of the event. Etic statements may bear little relation to the students' notion of what is significant, real, meaningful, or appropriate. An emic approach, on the other hand, is an attempt to view the situation or event from the perspective of the group or culture being observed. An emic approach to purposes, goals, motivations, and attitudes is premised on the assumption that, between actors and observers, it is the actors who are better able to know their own inner states. An emic approach also assumes that information concerning the actors' inner states is essential for an understanding of their behavior and for a proper description of the culture or situation in which they participate. For purposes of this research, the emic approach was used to discover what the students themselves were feeling and thinking about tests and testing. According to Edward Sapir, "[Emic study] helps one to appreciate not only the culture of language as an ordered whole, but it helps one to understand the individual actors in such a life-drama—their attitudes, motives, interests, responses, conflicts, and personality development" (in Harris 1968: 571).

Descriptive data were gathered over a three-year period in a range of classrooms from first through eighth grades. These data included teachers' explanations of the need and purpose of testing, students' perceptions and feelings concerning testing, and extensive classroom observations. In addition to community and classroom observations and informal discussions, in-depth formal interviews were conducted with a sample of 103 students and 10 teachers from Red Canyon and 41 students and 3 teachers from White Hill. The interview questions focused on three areas of concern, as expressed by the students during field observations and informal conversations. These were (1) definitions of tests, (2) purpose of testing (why), and (3) feelings surrounding tests. Interviews ranged from ten to fifteen minutes and were tape-recorded with the students' and teachers' permission. Verbatim transcriptions were obtained from the tapes.

Data gathering centered on the lower-elementary grade levels in order to explore students' understanding of tests developmentally. At Red Canyon, due to the absence of standardized testing and the lack of formal classroom testing at the first-grade level, primary data-gathering efforts were centered on the second-, third-, and fourth-grade classrooms. In replicating research efforts at White Hill, I started observing and interviewing at the second-grade level. When it became clear that these students were responding at a level similar to the fourth grade Navajo students, I made two decisions: (1) to move down to observe and interview at the first-grade level to see if Anglo children were entering school with an understanding of the importance of testing or were learning this information in school, and (2) to move over to the third and fourth grades to determine how this level matched with the Navajo fourth graders. A more extensive description of the field methods used are outlined elsewhere (Deyhle 1985; Deyhle, in press).

CULTURAL DISCONTINUITY: LEARNING WITH AND WITHOUT FAILURE

Ethnographic literature on Navajo children stresses that observation rather than verbal instruction is a predominate mode of learning among Navajo children. According to this literature, Navajo children repeatedly observe an activity, review the performance in their minds until they are certain that they can do the task well, and only then undertake its performance (Longstreet 1978; John 1972; Leighton and Kluckhohn 1948). In the home environment the Navajo child has learned to learn privately through self-initiated self-testing. Children certainly make mistakes during their learning process; however, mistakes in general are not publically acknowledged. This contrasts sharply with the school's general mode of teaching through public questioning techniques (informal testing) and in particular with assessing learning through failure as measured on individual tests. In analyzing "learning without public failure" for the Navajo child, as compared with the situation he or she faces in the classroom, Longstreet (1978) wrote,

> Compare this with the prevailing tendency of school teachers to help children
> by correcting them and encouraging them to try even if a few mistakes are

made. There is obviously the possibility of considerable tension arising between Navajo children's ethnic heritage and scholastic ethnicity. (2)

Werner and Begishe (1968) also reported that the Navajo approach stressed competence as a prerequisite for performance:

> Navajos seem to be unprepared or ill at ease if pushed into early performance without sufficient thought or the acquisition of mental competence preceding the actual physical activity. . . . This philosophy of learning can be summed up . . . "If at first you don't think and think again, don't bother trying." The Anglo approach stresses performance as a prerequisite for the acquisition of competence. . . . This philosophy of learning can be summed up . . . "If at first you don't succeed, try, try again." (1–2)

Appleton (1983) also found this pattern of reluctance to display competence prematurely among Yaqui students. The Yaqui student tends to avoid educational situations in which trial and error or an inquiry method of reasoning is demanded. According to Appleton, this is due to the child's respectful attitude toward any task and the importance of doing that task well:

> A task done well is a task done according to recommended or correct form. For Yaquis, the activity itself is as important as the purpose or goal of the activity. If it cannot be done well, there is little reason to engage in the activity at all. Teachers must carefully prepare children for such activities and avoid asking them to perform or recite before they have mastered the task. (173)

In relating these examples to classroom testing, one can see that the structure of a test requires students to perform inexpertly as a prerequisite, in order to develop competence.

Viewing failure to learn as an individual or private act (to be ignored in public) is not unique to the Navajo sociocultural learning system. Philips (1972) reported that the mode of instruction of the Warm Springs Indians also ignored failure and required long periods of observation preceding performance:

> First of all, children are present at many adult interactions as silent but attentive observers. . . . A second way in which this type of instruction among the Warm Springs Indians differs from that of non-Indians is the absence of "testing" of the child's skill by the instructing kinsman before the child exercises the skill unsupervised. . . . It appears that in many areas of skill, the child takes it upon himself to test the skill unsupervised and alone, without other people around. In this way if he is unsuccessful his failure is not seen by others. (385–386)

Testing in this form, to learn a particular skill, is done without the acknowledgment of failure; however, in contemporary classrooms, skills and materials are taught through children's (often public) failure as an example of what they still need to learn.

In existing educational systems the use of tests as the main vehicles for assessing learning determines who is not learning. A child is expected to demonstrate his or her knowledge during testing. In preparation, teachers require students individually to answer questions in the classroom in the presence of fellow students. Philips (1972) contrasted this Anglo style of learning with the process followed by Warm Springs Indian children in acquiring competence:

> In the classroom, the processes of acquisition of knowledge and demonstration of knowledge are collapsed into the single act of answering questions or reciting when called upon to do so by the teacher, particularly in the lower grades. . . . The assumption is that one will learn, and learn more effectively, through making mistakes in front of others. (387–388)

Mohatt and Erickson (1981) also discussed the problem for Indian children of the discontinuity between the Indian style of teaching and learning and the Anglo "teacher searchlight" phenomenon. The issue is not the positive or negative reinforcement of the "searchlight" interaction but the required public response of individual children in front of other children:

> In such a participation structure, the Indian students showed much more inappropriate behavior (silence, failure to answer questions, nervous giggling) than did White students in the classroom. The teacher's way of organizing interaction in the classroom seemed culturally congruent with the White students' expectation for how things should happen, but culturally incongruent with the expectations of Indian students. (108)

As the ethnographic literature indicates, Navajo children enter the classroom having learned primarily by observation, listening, and supervised participation; their previous failures have been ignored or not publicly acknowledged. Indian children's avoidance of public verbal displays in the classroom has also been documented. However, how Indian children's preschool experiences affect their concept of test-taking and how these children respond to the testing situation in the classroom have not been studied before.

THE CONTEXT OF TESTING: THE TEACHERS AND THE CLASSROOMS

The Test

When first observing a weekly spelling test in the second grade at Red Canyon, I expected students to be serious and quiet while preparing for and taking the test. This event was designed to judge their personal knowledge and I therefore assumed that the students would approach the test with some anxiety as they attempted an accurate performance. These second graders, however, presented a different understanding of the testing event (Deyhle, 1983). When the teacher reminded the class that there was to be a test that day the class exclaimed, "Ahhh," and the students were observed to turn around to each other and exclaim, "Test! Test!" Two female students, who were standing next to the pencil sharpener, turned to each other and hugged, with wide eyes and smiles, as they said, "It's a test!" In her excitement preceding the weekly spelling test, one student even spelled the word "test" aloud: "T . . . E . . . S . . . T." In general, the atmosphere surrounding this test was one of excitement. The students, who were eager to start taking the test, had to be quieted by the teacher and the teacher aide.

The teacher then wrote each of the ten spelling words on the board for student review. The class recited each word as the teacher erased it. The teacher distributed precut half sheets of paper as he asked students to take out their pencils, put their names on their papers, and number their papers from one to ten. While the students were eagerly complying with the teacher's directions he continued,

> This is a test. This means you are not to look on someone else's paper. If [aide] sees anyone looking at another paper we will take your paper and tear it up and throw it away in the wastepaper basket, and you will not be allowed to go to recess but instead will have to stay in the room and take the test. Does anyone want to stay in during recess and take the test? [students exclaim "No!] (Deyhle, 1980)

While they were actually taking the spelling test, the students excitement was visible in their body movements: some students bounced in their seats and others mouthed the spelling of the various words. When a student had attempted to spell a word, he or she would look up and around, with continued body movements, at the rest of the class. The teacher and aide continually walked around the classroom during the test reminding the students to keep their words covered. The students appeared very protective of their papers at times, although they frequently strained to examine each other's papers and at the same time exposed their own papers. At the conclusion of the test, one student at each of the tables picked up the spelling test papers and gave them to the teacher aide.

This level of excitement carried over to the events following the test. For example, after the teacher had given all of the spelling words, they were repeated for the students to check their lists. The entire class said "Yes!" after the teacher repeated each word. This exclamation was spoken very loudly, and by the time all ten words had been repeated, the children were shouting "Yes!" After the children exchanged and graded the tests, the teacher asked the children to pass the papers back to their "owners." He then asked those who got 100 percent to raise their hands, those who missed one to raise their hands, and so forth, until all the children had raised their hands. All of the children were observed to be excited and exclaimed, "Ahhh," as they raised their hands. Even the children who had missed more than five or six out of the ten spelling words raised their hands high and smiled as they looked around the room at the other children.

Testing situations in the second and third grades, consisting primarily of spelling and math tests observed over the two-year study at Red Canyon, revealed similar patterns. The younger students approached testing eagerly, without apparent anxiety or concern. This excitement was observed among the "good" as well as the "marginal" students and was connected to these students' understanding of what tests were all about in general and in particular to a system of rewards or prizes in the form of different colored stars the teachers applied to the class spelling and math charts. In explaining why they liked taking tests, two students quickly said, " 'cause I get a lot of red stars" and "Yes (I like tests), I told you 'cause of green and red." The consequence of doing poorly on a test—not getting 100 percent or a star—carried no repercussions for the students. In fact, tests were an opportunity, not a burden: the more frequently tests were given, the more chances a student had to obtain stars. If one lost such a "game" one could simply wait to try on the next one. The implicit purpose of testing from the perspective of the teacher and the school—to learn what one did and did not know—was not part of the younger Navajo student's concept or understanding of a test.

As these Navajo children moved through school and began to develop an understanding of the true purpose of tests in the context of their classrooms— as devices for judgment of personal failure—the testing scene changed. The observations of test-taking in the fourth grade revealed a much more serious approach to test-taking than in either the second or third grades. Students were observed to be actively studying with each other before taking tests. Some students sat alone at their desks quietly reviewing. Others worked in pairs at the blackboard. Students at this grade level had redefined tests, from game-like or nonserious events to be enjoyed and looked forward to, to events that must not only be tolerated or attempted, but passed successfully. Failure on tests meant failure to move with their friends to the next grade. This understanding of the connection between a test, failure, and lack of promotion increased the level of anxiety and apprehension in the minds of the students as they approached the event of a test.

The rhythm and flow of student movement during test-taking at White Hill was very different from that observed in the lower grades of Red Canyon. Here, students at all grades levels were observed to quickly and quietly follow their teacher's pretest directions—taking out their pencils and labeling and numbering their half sheets of paper. Students who were away from their desks quickly ran to their desks as they fumbled to locate the "right" pencil with a sharp point. Others quickly sharpened their pencils and moved back to their desks. Not unlike the testing scene at Red Canyon, teachers would recite the words with the students for a review before proceeding with the test and would also remind the students about what they were *not* to do during the test:

Is there anyone who is not ready to go? Put your names on your paper. Pencils down, turn up your hearing aid. So, what do we do when we're through with the test? [no time for student response] Be considerate. I told you last time if you're noisy and disturbing I'm going to take ten points off your score. So, if I were you I'd be quiet. And keep your eyes on your own paper. (Deyhle, in press)

Students were observed to perch precariously forward on their seats as they twisted hair and quickly counted with their fingers or silently mouthed the spelling words. The end of the test brought both relief and concern to these students' faces: relief that the test was over and concern for their individual performance. Test papers were hesitantly passed forward to the teachers as the students moved directly into the next assignment. When test papers were returned to the students a hush would fall over the class. Students who received 100 percent or missed only one or two words or problems turned with smiles to show off their papers to their neighbors; others, who were not so successful, quickly shoved their papers into their desks and started other classroom work.

Teachers: Test Givers

Although teachers in this study frequently complained about the pressure it puts on students and in turn on themselves for accountability, the role of testing was viewed as firmly established in the schooling process. As one teacher at Red Canyon said, "For one thing everybody knows we have to have it [tests] so we pretty well just accept it. We have to be taught, we have to learn, and we have to live with it" (Deyhle 1983: 359). This feeling was echoed at White Hill:

I think testing is just part of the school system. . . . I think the test is to confirm what you already know. I use them mainly because I think parents are more satisfied if you can show them why the child got the grade. In a way it's a very selfish thing but those tests protect me. It's the system. When you're in an area like this where the parents are so concerned and all of them think every kid ought to have an *A*. . . . I just think it's a shame we have them. I don't like to put a label on a kid and that's what you're doing with a grade. I think they're terrible. (Deyhle, in press)

At both schools teachers, to some extent, viewed the acceptance of tests in the system as a "necessary evil". The teachers, however, responded in two distinct ways in "protecting" their students from the impact of testing. The teachers at White Hill, who felt strong pressure from parents to ensure the students' academic success, tried to gently encourage a serious approach to test-taking. As the second grade teacher said,

> I know if you're going to get the most from them you have to give them some
> concerns about it. You have to put a little pressure on them or else they just
> simply don't do their best on the test. I'm sure they get a little up-tight. I hope
> not too much. I try to do it just right. Put some pressure on but not too much.
> . . . A lot of pressure from home. You wouldn't believe the pressure on some
> kids. If they don't bring *A*s home they're in trouble. (Deyhle 1980)

The teachers at Red Canyon, feeling very little pressure or encouragement
from the Navajo parents to work for student academic success, tried to minimize
the importance of test-taking. In the lower grades, in an attempt to minimize test
anxiety, tests were often presented as gamelike events with a reward system to
make it easier for them (Deyhle 1983). One teacher, describing his presentation
of tests to the fourth graders said,

> I hate to say this, but I am probably as guilty as anyone else. They're from
> a minority group background and I don't place a lot of emphasis on tests and
> I think the kids pick this up from me, and they probably don't do as well on
> tests as they should because they know that I really don't place that much
> emphasis as far as a grade is concerned. . . . When they don't do too well I
> try not to get down on them. I tell them that they made the mistakes, I go
> over the mistakes, but I'm not going to jump all over their cases. (Deyhle
> 1980)

The teachers at Red Canyon chose to view the academic failure of their
students as being "caused" by the Navajo culture. They thus avoided analysis of
their own classroom presentations. In discussing testing and Navajo students, the
teachers spoke with pride of the gamelike testing environment they had created.
At the same time, they repeatedly expressed disappointment at their students'
lack of concern about *F* grades and their general lack of academic achievement.
From the teachers' perspective, their students' poor achievement was not in any
way related to the students' confusion about what grades were or to their misunderstanding or rejection of what testing was all about.

Teachers felt that parents, having had little formal education, saw little need
for schooling and, therefore, passed this attitude on to their children. As one
teacher explained, "I blame an awful lot of it on parents and maybe too much,
I think, but there is no support for an education in most of the kids." Homes with
educated parents, a minority at Red Canyon, were perceived as supporting
schooling. Parents who had limited formal education were viewed as caring little
about their children's involvement with the community's school. The fourth-
grade teacher felt that the students at the top of his class did get encouragement
from their parents, were more attuned to Anglo culture, and often thought about
going to college to get a good job. In describing the rest of the students in his class,
he explained, "Ninety percent of the kids hear their parents say, 'Well, I only
went to the third grade, and it hasn't hurt me. I eat every day and I have a couple

of sheep and I have some cattle, I have a home, so what's the big deal about school?' "

The second-grade teacher expressed what many of the other teachers viewed as the major problem surrounding student achievement in school:

> I don't think they see the value in going to school. Many times they look at their own parents or someone in their own family who has never been to school and they are getting along okay. They are living, and so I don't think they think that it is important for them to learn. They know they have to be in school—this is something for them to do and some place for them to go, just to hang out. They get to visit with their friends, they get a free meal, and it's better than staying home and doing nothing. (Deyhle, in press)

In formulating the opinion that the students' lack of motivation in school was tied to the parents' lack of support for schooling in general, the teachers continually cited the students' physical treatment of their school papers: test papers were quickly thrown away, homework papers were lost, and report cards were returned to the teachers without parent comments. Physical abuse of the objects of schooling was seen by the teachers as evidence of a lack of valuing or appreciating education. In describing this behavior, an upper-grade level teacher said, "Some of them take their paper and immediately, as soon as they get it, they crumple it up and they are ready to throw it away. It can be any grade, it doesn't make any difference to them." Another teacher talked about the behavior of throwing away papers as an indication that the students did not care about grades or school: "The reason I said that is because I'll return papers with grades on it, and if I pass it out during the first of class, I spend the next ten minutes getting them all to sit back down 'cause they've all walked to the trash can to throw papers away, whether it is an *A* or an *F*. They do not take papers home."

Teachers at Red Canyon assumed that, because school papers were so quickly discarded and destroyed, students and parents did not value or appreciate schooling and disregarded the importance of tests. This was based on the assumption, however, that the students actually understood the various papers as products or evidence of an important event. Observations and interviews indicated that the Navajo students did not share an understanding of the importance of testing as representative of personal progress in school.

As shown in the previous section, Red Canyon and White Hill teachers differed somewhat with regard to the emphasis they placed on the importance of test-taking. However, there was a surprising similarity in the physical structuring and presentation of the testing event at both sites. Teachers were observed to be consistent in the information they provided the students before test-taking. This information included the proper labeling of the test paper and rules surrounding cheating or copying and talking. Absent from most of the testing situations observed was any information that might give students an understanding of the significance of the test they were about to take—the "why" of test-taking. At all levels teachers assumed that the students understood *why* they were taking tests and therefore needed only technical information about *how* to take tests. As will be shown in the following section, about students, the Navajo students did not express this understanding, whereas the Anglo students entered their testing situation equipped with the "why" of test-taking.

STUDENTS: THE TEST TAKERS

Children entering the classroom for the first time are presented with concepts and words that are foreign to them but that they must learn in order to function in their new environment. Children are confronted with the word *test* very early in their schooling, and over the years they develop a definition or a concept of a test and its role in their schooling experience. This concept may or may not conform to the teacher's or school's definition of the purpose and significance of testing and assessment. Differences may also exist between cultural groups. What is presented in the following section is the "image" of testing in the minds of the Navajo and Anglo students studied here.

What Is a Test?

In general the second-grade Navajo students' definitions of tests centered on vague descriptions of the placement of desks during tests, rules of cheating and copying, the location of test materials on the various classroom blackboards, and on the teacher as the individual whom one had to listen to during a test. This was clearly illustrated by one student's response: "It is when the paper is in half [spelling tests are taken on one-half of a sheet of paper] and you put the words from the board and listen to the teacher." Some students defined tests according to the content of tests they had experienced: "It's spelling"; "Like when you take a test on stuff . . . like when you take a test on words"; and "A thing that you write . . . words." All of these younger Navajo students' responses emphasized the procedures or technical rules required when they were taking a test. What is missing from these students' responses is any mention of the significance or importance of tests for assistance in or judgment of learning.

The second-grade Anglo students, like the Navajos, often mentioned the rules of test-taking when they defined a test, but unlike the Navajo students, half of the Anglos indicated that a test was an activity that helped them to learn. The rules the students mentioned were similar to those the Navajo students cited, and they centered on the location of test materials, the placement of desks, and rules about not talking or copying other students' papers: "It's something like when there's this piece of paper and there's this thing up on the board that you've done for a long time. You have to capitalize it and put punctuation at the end. You do that. Then you don't have to do it anymore. That's a test"; "It's something like you have to not look on people's paper"; and "A test is when you have to be quiet." Whereas grades were never mentioned by the Navajo students, the Anglo students connected grades to tests: "It's something . . . you kind of do something and you're trying to get a hundred and stuff"; and "It's something that you really have to work hard on. Sometimes you have to practice on it so you can get a good grade."

The greatest difference between these two groups of second graders' definitions of a test was in reference to learning. Almost half of the Anglo students connected a test and learning: "A test is when you learn. You learn everything and then you see if you know how to do it"; "Make you get smarter"; and "You have to do these things that the teacher tells you. It helps you out on your work. It tests you how you're doing." Anglo students had a clearer understanding of tests as events arranged to see if they had learned their school work. None of the Navajo students mentioned learning when they talked about tests. The Navajo students saw tests as events that were distinct from other classroom activities only due to the unique behavioral or procedural rules.

In defining a test, over half of the Navajo fourth graders responded that a test was connected to promotion and that tests were taken in order to pass on to the next grade. Unlike the second grade Navajo students, who used the procedures or rules occurring during testing to define a test, most of these fourth graders understood that tests were special events and that they had to be taken and passed successfully in order to move to the next grade. Frequent responses included, "It's a thing you take and if you miss a lot you stay in the same grade"; "If you get all the answers right you can go to another grade"; and "Its something that you take before you can go to the next grade."

All but one of the fourth-grade Anglo students indicated that a test was an activity that followed in-class work and was important for assistance in learning and promotion: "A test is just when you go over something like a chapter or unit. After it you just sort of take a test to see what you've learned. Sometimes a test determines what you get on your grades if you pass what grade you're in." At the fourth-grade level, then, the outcome of a test, rather than the teacher-directed processes one went through in taking a test, was used by both Navajo and Anglo students to define testing.

What Makes a Test a Test?

Students are confronted with a variety of activities during the school day. They must learn the reasons for each of these activities and the behaviors they require in order to function well in the classroom. At all grade levels the children saw tests as originating with actions from the classroom teacher. The teacher verbalized commands indicating that a test was about to be given. The students responded to these instructions with the awareness that an event called a "test" was about to take place. The event of testing was, therefore, set apart or defined according to the behavior that was learned as appropriate to the test-taking situation. Students learned that appropriate behavior in one situation was not necessarily appropriate in another. They thus learned to segment or divide classroom activities according to the rules that they had learned surrounded that particular event or activity.

When Navajo and Anglo students talked about teachers' presentations of tests and what happened before they took a test, they all spoke of the technical or explicit rules they had learned to associate with test-taking. In both situations students carefully explained that their teachers required certain test-taking behaviors that must be adhered to. The behaviors the teachers demanded included rules for proper set-up on the test paper, with name, date, and number, and rules against cheating, copying other students' papers, talking, and excessive body movements. Navajo student responses included, "He tells us to be quiet, and look at your own papers, and don't copy"; "Don't look on others, put your desks right on, move it. Don't look at others' paper"; and "You be quiet, put your books in the desk and he gives you a piece of paper you write on." Like the Navajo students, the Anglo students spoke of the importance of having the correct "test set-up," which is followed by silence—and no wandering eyes:

> She tells us to get out our pencils. She passes out the test. Before she tells us
> to sharpen our pencils. Sometimes she tells us to be quiet so other people can
> write. The big hand goes around and it goes up to twelve and she says go and
> we start going . . . I hurry up and get my pencil out. If it needs sharpening
> I have to run really fast to the sharpener and sharpen it and hurry back and
> start. (Deyhle 1980)

Both groups emphasized no cheating or looking at others' papers as the most important rule to be followed, but when they were asked why, their reasons were different. The Navajo students told me that the rule was important because if you violated it your paper was torn up and "You get no stars or rewards." The Anglo students, however, carefully explained that you could not look at other students' papers because this violated the purpose of testing—to display your acquired knowledge to the teacher: "Don't cheat on other people's paper because she wants to see if we really do know that or if we're just looking on other people's paper"; "Because if they get it wrong then you'll get it wrong. It doesn't make you learn."

What is interesting from both the Navajo and the Anglo students' responses was the general *absence,* in the teachers' presentation of a test, of any information that would encourage the students to do a good job or that would explain that the test was important to help them master necessary subject matter. Rather, according to the student responses, tests were presented and framed by behaviors that were *not* permissible. There was no exception to this among the Navajo students and only two of the Anglo students said that their teacher gave them encouragement: "Do good"; and, "She says don't look . . . so that you would get smart."

Observations supported students' re-creations of what occurred during test-taking. The teachers of both Navajo and Anglo students provided the same pretest information. However, a very different picture of the "why," or importance, of taking a test emerged when students continued to describe their understanding of the event of test-taking.

Are Tests Important?

Both teachers and school administrators see tests as important assessment instruments. Teachers use tests as an "objective" measurement of the students' progress in the classroom, and the school uses tests for an overall measurement of the students' progress in the school. However, as the following section illustrates, not all students share the same understanding of the importance of tests.

When asked the questions, "Why do you take tests?" and "Are tests important?" most of the Navajo second graders were unable to respond and merely shrugged their shoulders and said, "I don't know." These students were confused when they tried to explain why one activity they did in class, a test, was more important than other activities. They sensed that the event was different from other activities, but it was too early in their school experience for them to explain how testing would affect them in their schooling. *Learning* was a key word in only two students' responses: one indicated that tests were taken "to spell, and so you can learn it"; another said that tests were taken because "we don't learn." A different picture emerged when the second grade Anglo students were asked about the reasons for and the importance of tests. All of the Anglo students clearly articulated that tests were important and that they took them to "learn" or "get smart." As one second grader said,

> So we can learn and we won't have any problems in third and fourth and fifth and all that with tests. Because if you don't do a test then you'll get a bad grade and get expelled sometimes. Sometimes you have to stay after school and do something like bounce the ball or something like that . . . So we can have a good education. We can get a good job when we grow up . . . So you won't have any trouble or anything through your whole life. . . . You learn tests to learn. (Deyhle 1985: 123)

After four years of exposure to testing as a regular event in their schooling experience, the fourth-grade Navajo students' responses consistently matched the Anglo students' understanding of why they took tests—to demonstrate learning in order to pass to the next grade: "Because I have to take . . . because I have to pass the fourth grade . . . pass the test. Because you have to pass a grade" (Deyhle 1985: 124). It is important to remember that very few of the second-grade

Navajo students had this understanding of why they took tests, whereas all of the Anglo second graders clearly understood this purpose behind testing. As would be expected, the Anglo students at the fourth-grade level continued to clearly articulate the significance and importance of test-taking:

> That's what school is for. Tests to make sure you know it so you don't have to go over it. So the teacher knows where you are and what you're doing so she can help you with stuff you're behind on. (Deyhe, in press)

Navajo and Anglo students seemed to begin their schooling experience at different "starting points" in their understanding of what testing is all about. The second-grade Anglo students all understood testing as a regular event in their schooling experience that was used to determine success or failure in the learning process. In contrast, the second-grade Navajo students saw tests as distinct events separated from other classroom events due to special rules, but not necessarily as being more important for learning. At the fourth-grade level, however, these two groups of students converged with regard to their understanding of what testing is all about. They clearly connected the consequence of test-taking to learning and promotion or failure and grade retention.

Attitudes Towards Test-taking

It is clear that there is a difference between Navajo and Anglo students in their understanding of the significance and purpose of test-taking. Germane to this difference might also be a dissimilarity in motivation or attitude toward test-taking. As these children approached the event of testing, their distinct and different understandings created an equally dichotomous set of attitude responses.

The feelings expressed when they took tests differed dramatically between the two groups of second graders. The Navajo students indicated that they felt "good" and "happy" when they took tests. They did not see tests as particularly important events for judging personal success or failure. On the other hand, second grade Anglo students spoke about feeling trepidation when they recalled how they felt during test-taking: "I feel sort of nervous, shaking all over"; "Sort of scared. I hate it when I do it"; and "Sort of worried, because you think you won't do it as best as you can. It's just hard."

As the Navajo students' understanding of why they were taking tests developed to more closely match that of the Anglo students, in the fourth grade, attitudes and feelings of nervousness became characteristic of both groups. Both groups of fourth graders indicated that they felt nervous and scared when they were taking a test. These feelings were vividly expressed by one Navajo boy: "My body feels like I'm scared. I want to run away from school. And I . . . when I take a test, and I feel like I'm gonna tear the book." A parallel comment was expressed by one Anglo boy: "Oh, no!—butterflies in my stomach. Sort of, oh no, not again! Because I hate taking tests." Both groups of students said that they were nervous after taking a test because of concern about their grades. One girl clearly summed up the feelings of the Navajo students: "Sad. Because you get an *F.*"

Test Knowledge: From Home to School

If all of the second-grade Anglo students, unlike the Navajo students, clearly understood the importance of tests in their schooling experience, the question arises, how did they acquire this understanding? Observations in both the Anglo and the Navajo situations revealed that teachers did not provide any information that would lead to this kind of understanding. Also, if at the second-grade level, Anglo students clearly saw tests as important events that evoked nervousness and concern, which was not the case with the second grade Navajo students, did the Anglo students have these feelings when they began their schooling experience? It seemed that Anglo students were either entering school with this knowledge or picking it up outside their classrooms. I therefore moved down to observe and talk with Anglo first graders.

As was the case with the Anglo and Navajo second graders, the first grade Anglo students defined tests primarily according to the rules presented by their teacher: "It's a thing you have to write on, we can't look on other people's paper." Their explanations of what happened before they took tests matched those of both Navajo and Anglo second graders and centered on test-taking rules, with the general exclusion of any teacher directions that included the significance or importance of test-taking: "I think she tells us that you should do them. You shouldn't just wander off and go to the back of the room and get a drink or just play"; and "She says don't look on other people's papers and that. Keep your answers covered. Don't talk." However, like the Anglo second graders, these children clearly understood the "why" of test-taking in their schooling experience. All of the students told me that they took tests in order to learn: "It makes you learn things. Once you do it you get smarter and smarter"; and "Because you can go to college. To learn."

Over two-thirds of these Anglo first graders expressed nervous feelings with regard to test-taking: "Nervous sometimes. Because I might get a wrong answer and I don't like getting wrong answers. Then you don't feel very good . . . starts to shake a little . . . nervous"; and "Scared, because maybe I won't have a hundred." Along with entering school with an understanding that tests were important "learning" events in their schooling experience, these first graders generally expressed nervous feelings about approaching a test. Their success or failure somehow depended on their performance during this event.

In summary, in articulating the importance of test-taking the Anglo students in this study showed that they began their schooling experience with a clear understanding of what they needed to do in order to succeed. Tests were one of many activities they faced in the classroom, and they knew it was the most important event. The Navajo students, on the other hand, began their schooling experience with the perception that test-taking was one of many new experiences and that it differed from other activities only according to required behavioral rules. They did not understand the importance of a test as a sorting device or gatekeeper for success and promotion until they had experienced test-taking for three or four years.

LEARNING THE CONCEPT OF FAILURE: BETWEEN HOME AND SCHOOL

Learning through mistakes or failure, informally in classroom discourse and formally on classroom tests, is clearly not a method that works for all children —though some children do learn quite well through individual performance in the classroom. The Anglo students in this study entered their classrooms with a set of learning experiences that included the knowledge that displaying individual competence during an event called a test was an important part of their schooling experience and that this event would help them "learn." Members of their families, who themselves had been indoctrinated through a formal educational system, incorporated this lesson in preschool socialization and also conveyed the idea of the importance and inevitability of school in general. This information was transmitted either explicitly through verbal instructions from parents or possibly from older brothers and sisters, or implicitly through experiences of testlike situations in their home environment in preschool years. These testlike situations might have been in the form of praise or rewards for verbal or physical tasks accomplished individually. Observations of Anglo verbal interactions often consisted of the adult "testing" the preschool child by asking questions as they observed an event: "Look! What is that? Yes, it's an elephant, good!" An image comes to my mind of a refrigerator gaily decorated with little Johnny's first attempts at writing. Even though the words are misspelled, the child is praised for his attempt and rewarded with the public display of his work. Heath (1983) also reported that the interactions between adults and children in the Anglo communities in her study consisted of adults viewing children as both information-givers and information-receivers, which was reinforced by a series of questioning or testlike interactions. "Adults ask for the names of items; if the child gives an unsuitable name, the adult proposes another and then follows with a series of questions to test the child's reception of this term" (128). Thus, children who have experienced this type of "instruction" or "testing" come to school with the advantage of having already learned the valuable lesson of performing as an individual information-giver.

In families whose economic or cultural settings exclude them from participation in a formal educational institution or are different from the dominant culture of the school, this kind of "testing" experience might not be a part of the child's preschool socialization. For the child who does not have this understanding, learning the importance of tests as a measure of personal failure in schooling is a crucial and often difficult task. That was the situation with the Navajo children in this study.

When the Navajo children in this study began school, they faced tests as one of many new activities. They learned that testing was set apart from other events by distinct behavioral rules. Without previously understanding the test concept as a device for judging personal success or failure, and with misinformation from their teachers, the children regarded the test as a nonserious or gamelike activity that resulted in rewards if all the rules were followed correctly. Verbal and physical test anxiety was minimal among students as they approached test-taking eagerly in the hopes of acquiring additional stars or tokens (Deyhle 1983). In general, the classroom test was not seen as personally important, nor was it feared.

As these Navajo children moved up in grades, they began to see tests as events that judged personal academic performance in their classrooms. Observations and interviews revealed an increase in anxiety as the children tried to perform successfully. With older children, test anxiety caused them to became almost dysfunctional as they realized that the content, not the form, was the important reason for the test. The students' test anxiety turned to frustration, and ultimately to apathy, as they realized the seriousness of tests and their lack of achievement on them.

When Navajo children enter school, they come with a culturally determined understanding of the appropriate means of displaying competence. This is different from the processes required in school—demonstrating individual knowledge through public display (classroom questioning) or through testing. However, as they advance in grade level, they learn that their classroom performance is being judged and that by the school's standards they are deficient. It is at this point that they reject the importance of display on classroom tests. Research on adolescent American Indian children indicates a marked decrease in academic achievement by the fifth or sixth year in school (Zintz 1963). So dramatic is this decrease that the causal factors cannot be limited to lack of knowledge. Collier (1973) described Eskimo students "giving up" in classrooms. Wax (1976) examined the high dropout rate among Sioux adolescents, who saw themselves as having been "kicked out" or "pushed out" of an educational system that was at odds with their own culture. The teachers at Red Canyon also reported that the older Navajo children just "don't care" and that they stopped trying to perform in school. In describing the change in the students, the second grade teacher said, "They [the older students] start going from the little preschool kids into adolescence and there's more pressure on them there. They know they are not doing as well in school, and I think that they get discouraged because they can see that they're not doing that well and that the interest does drop off. They understand a little bit more of what is going on and you can't fool them" (Deyhle 1985: 126).

Generally, the teachers at Red Canyon assumed that Navajo students could not function adequately in their classrooms because of their cultural background.

Teacher frustration focused on the students' apparent lack of respect, acceptance, or understanding of personal failure on tests. The teachers assumed that because the students did not approach testing seriously or respond with remorse when they received poor grades, they were not serious or motivated about learning in general. This was the teachers' way of placing the blame for their academic failure on the students.

If the teachers regarded Navajo culture as the reason for poor academic achievement, the causal factors were removed from the classroom and placed in the home. Implicit in this understanding was the assumption that school was the only place to *learn* (or learn correctly) and that what occurred in the students' homes was "nothing." This attitude ignored the cultural conflict that apparently exists between the Navajo community and the Anglo school. In the home, Navajo children learned without the use of public, individual displays of knowledge. These children, therefore, entered school without an understanding that the school was going to require them to learn via questions and tests—through a constant and public display of mistakes and failure.

IMPLICATIONS: BETWEEN SUCCESS AND FAILURE IN TESTING

In the past, our educational institutions were only partly concerned with helping each student learn and paid a great deal of attention to grading, classifying, and other sorting functions (Tyler 1979). Today, demands are being made on schools not to sort students but rather to educate all, or almost all, of them. However, classroom and standardized tests, embedded with cultural biases, remain as gatekeepers for assessing success or failure in the schooling process. In seeking equality of assessment, the content of some tests has been modified in the hopes of providing a more culture-free or culture-fair instrument. Even with these improvements, the concept of displaying one's competence during an event called a test, or the idea that a test is a device for judging personal learning, also needs to be viewed as a culturally incongruent or biased activity for some children.

All children face some level of disorientation when they move from their home environment into the school environment (Ogbu 1982). However, for some groups of children, whose cultural background is distinctly different from that of the majority culture, the disorientation is severe enough to continually affect academic performance. A question that can be raised here is whether or not the different responses of the Navajo and the Anglo children studied was due to one group's privileged economic situation, as compared with the other, or to the differences between cultural backgrounds. In the case of the Anglo students, the data from this study does not enable me to separate "economic class" from "culture." However, what is important is that the information these Anglo students have concerning the role or importance of tests, as gatekeepers, comes from outside the classroom, from their home environment, and that this is distinctly different from the socialization the Navajo children receive in their home environment. This, I would argue, puts the Navajo students at a distinct disadvantage regarding test-taking in the context of formalized schooling.

It appears that this situation of incongruence is not unique to the Navajo children in this study. A parallel can be found with regard to other minority or lower-socioeconomic level children's responses to testing. At a National Institute of Education conference on testing it was noted,

> Some children, particularly those from middle class homes, take formal test situations seriously and try to respond. Lower class children, on the other hand, usually come from backgrounds where tests are rare and they appear to be silly games. (Tyler 1979: 43)

How children approached testing and became "test wise" was also seen by Rist (1978) as important in contributing to further understanding of the testing process. He recorded the following teacher's statement:

> The only way I got them even to sit still was to bribe them with candy bars. Every time they finished a test, they got some more candy. But what some of them did was just to race through marking the first answer in every row. You know, they sure were not test-serious like the white kids. Why, those white kids were just waiting for me to spring another test on them. The black kids couldn't care less. (221)

Student perceptions and understanding of tests is an important area that needs consideration when one is assessing failure in some children and success in others. This is not to neglect other factors, such as language for the non-English speaker—that certainly affects a student's performance on a particular test. Rather, in seeking to unravel the academic achievement disparity among culturally different children in the schooling process, it seems clear, from the results of this study, that we must examine factors other than lack of test-content knowledge.

As educational research has moved away from the deficiency model to the difference model in examining the school situation and the academic failure of many minority children, there still exists the danger of adopting a line of reasoning that asserts that these children lack knowledge of the dominant culture's values and should therefore be remediated. This reasoning ignores poignant questions about the social and intellectual competence of the children studied and tested and about the norms of educational practice and their lack of responsiveness to cultural differences and educational equality. To continue to judge children with criteria that will assure their continued failure is to ignore the underlying problem of rectifying an inappropriate system, not its participants.

NOTE

1. Modified portions of this chapter have appeared in previous journal articles and are appropriately referred to in the chapter text. The literature review and the field notes and observations are common to the journal articles and to this chapter. As often happens with ethnographic research, the chapter represents the fully developed ideas discussed in previous publications. The author, however, has made special efforts to prevent overlapping and to refer to earlier publications showing common data and theoretical frameworks.

CHAPTER 6

Learning Spanish and Classroom Dynamics: School Failure in a Guatemalan Maya Community

Julia Becker Richards

During the life of most highland-Guatemala Mayan Indians the most intense and sustained exposure to the national language of Spanish and to members of the non-Indian Ladino society occurs through years of attendance at a local primary school.[1] It is primarily through the teaching of Spanish in primary school that the Guatemalan government seeks to integrate Indian children into the national culture and economy. The assumption underlying this goal of linguistic integration through compulsory schooling is that a shared national language will generate a shared national identity and ultimately lead to effective sociocultural and economic incorporation of the indigenous population.

In Guatemala, as in the other Latin American nations in which indigenous groups speaking native-American languages form a sizeable proportion of the population (Mexico, Ecuador, Peru, Bolivia, Paraguay), the teaching and learning of the national language forms an integral part, if indeed not the focus, of school instruction.[2] However, as national statistics have repeatedly shown, school progress for linguistic minority children is limited, leaving them largely monolingual and functionally illiterate.

In this paper I use a case-study analysis in order to elucidate the problem of school failure among Indian children of Guatemala. The framework for this paper follows that established by Ogbu (1978, 1982), Heath (1982, 1983), Spindler (1974, 1982), Troike (1978), McDermott and Gospodinoff (1981), and others, which places the study of school phenomenon not only within the confines of the classroom but also within the wider social, cultural, and political context. I first discuss the sociolinguistic and cultural context of formal schooling in one indigenous community, and I then examine facets of classroom dynamics to demonstrate the role of schooling in the acquisition of two languages by Guatemalan Indians.

SOCIOCULTURAL CONTEXT OF SCHOOLING

Approximately one-half of the seven million people of the Central American nation of Guatemala are Mayan Indians, an economically and socially subordinated people within a castelike national sociopolitical structure.[3] They speak over twenty separate Mayan languages that are further fragmented into some seventy dialect groupings (Kaufman 1976). Partially as a result of the post-conquest colonial policies of "congregación" and "reducción," whereby Indians were forced to reside in nucleated, corporately isolated settlements, as many as three hundred distinct intra-Indian ethnic groups exist today in Guatemala. Geographically demarcated by corporate township boundaries, each "municipio" constitutes a group of people united by a common tradition differing from others in history, language, and cultural style. The inhabitants of each "municipio" are acutely conscious of their unity and stress the uniqueness of their differing patron saints, surnames, dress, economic specialties, and most important, their spoken language (see Tax 1937). Indeed, differences among dialects spoken by even proximal communities can be substantial, and even within the same defined language grouping, dialects can virtually reach the point of mutual unintelligibility.

Spanish is the only official language in Guatemala (Constitución de la República de 1965, Art. 4), and it is used exclusively in all government communication, in legal procedures, in the mass media, and for all practical purposes, in the public schools. Since the time of the conquest four and a half centuries ago, Spanish has been used by the powerful non-Indian Ladino elite to subjugate the indigenous majority. Some scholars (e.g., Heath 1972, and Hawkins 1984) have argued that the "reducción" colonial policy, referred to earlier, that geographically, culturally, and linguistically maintained Indians isolated in their corporate communities, was an important strategy for effectively controlling a client population. Shirley Heath, for example, quotes a popular seventeenth century maxim "(that it was better that the Indians not) learn the Spanish tongue and become ladinos, which is the first step toward their becoming impudent; . . . while they speak their own language, they are more humble" (Heath 1972:42).

A substantial rate of monolingualism exists among the indigenous groups of Guatemala today. One estimate (Stewart 1981) places the rate of monolingualism as high as 90 percent in certain regions of the country. The overall rate of bilingualism among the indigenous population is probably closer to 50 percent; for many, however, oral Spanish proficiency is limited to the production of terms needed for the sale and purchase of goods in the marketplace.

Despite limited oral proficiency, many of Guatemala's indigenous peoples do nevertheless maintain at least partial receptive or passive control of the language and can be considered incipient bilinguals (see Diebold 1964). As is often found in sociopolitical contexts of unequal power relations among different ethnic or racial groups, bilingualism in Guatemala is strictly a unidirectional phenomenon; rarely does a member of the dominant Ladino population speak or admit to knowing an indigenous language.

Panajtzib, the setting of this study, is an indigenous "municipio" of the central highlands. In terms of its participation in the regional economy and society, it is a marginal, backwater community with a present-day population of one thousand inhabitants. Until quite recently, access to this community was restricted to canoe and foot travel. Like several other of the nearby communities, Panajtzib continues to exhibit many characteristics of the archetypical localocentric closed corporate community (see Wolf 1957). Among other things, it still has a functioning civil-religious hierarchy, marriage patterns remain essentially endogamous, and land tenure is held in communal usufruct.

Even by highland Guatemalan standards Panajtzib is an unusually impoverished village. Land holdings are small, and because subsistence production is inadequate to meet household consumption needs, members of the community must rely on obtaining seasonal wage labor on coastal export crop plantations to offset the deficient return on their domestic agricultural system. Most villagers live in a state of perpetual debt, and any cash that is obtained through seasonal migration, wage labor, or the sale of fruit and cottage industry items is used to pay off yesterday's debts. The villagers are near the end of a long chain of inter- and intraethnic social and economic exploitation, and daily needs take precedence over long-range plans and decision-making strategies.

Because of geographic isolation, poverty, and a social history punctuated by cataclysmic events that have repeatedly ravaged the village, the inhabitants of Panajtzib, the Tzibeños, perceive themselves as being of high moral integrity, but nevertheless subject to a fate that places them at the bottom of the regional social ladder. They figuratively refer to their community as "ga siwan tinamit," which roughly translates as "our village clinging to the ravines." This expression denotes not only the physical characteristics of a town set on steep mountain slopes, but also metaphorically conveys the sense of a group of people fallen and entrapped by sociopolitical structures well beyond their control.

In this region of central highland Guatemala, Tzibeños collectively are some of the most poverty stricken and marginal peoples; to outsiders, including Indians from other towns, they frequently are stereotyped as well-meaning and hardworking, yet hopelessly backward. In a context characterized by both intra- and interethnic subordination, the bulk of the power and authority is held by, and major economic transactions are conducted by, individuals well beyond regular access to Tzibeños. As a result, the Tzibeño notion of who conducts the affairs of state and the economy and how they are conducted is obscured by a vast social distance. Until the relatively recent arrival of transistor radios and improved transport service, as well as increased political campaigning and intensified political violence, the social and geographical conception of the world remained at best confined to a radius of thirty kilometers.

Within the village of Panajtzib all language interactions among community members are carried out in the local dialect of Cakchiquel, a Mayan language spoken in the central highlands by approximately 270,000 people (Kaufman 1976). Language is the principal ethnic marker in Guatemala, and for the Tzibe-ños, the local dialect is indeed the primary symbol of their intraethnic identity. The Tzibeños hold great respect for the language they identify as "ga-tzojobal," "our language," and although the dialects of the geographically proximal com-munities are quite close linguistically, community members exaggerate their dif-ferences and readily point out their obvious deficiencies. It is apparent that the nonleveling of dialect differences among villages located even within walking distance from one another and whose speakers are in rather frequent communica-tion is due to the fact that the speakers consciously retain and manipulate the differences as identity markers[4] (see Giles 1977).

The Panajtzib inhabitants believe that their distinctive dialect was given to their ancestors by the patron saint of their community. This ancestral language and way of speaking "ojer tzij" ("ancient words") is believed to have been preserved through history in more or less its "pure" form in the formal speech genre known as "choloj." "Choloj" is oratorical, ritualized speech used in such contexts as lengthy sacred rituals, legal litigations, and interfamilial petitions. It is characterized by the interspersion of countless qualifiers and interjections as well as by the elaborate repetition of words, phrases, syntactic structures, and semantic forms. Community members say that it takes years to acquire it, and that only a few are fortunate enough to acquire it well.

In the sentences below we see examples of two common "choloj" discourse strategies employing the repetition of ideas and syntactic structures. In sentences 1a and 1b the idea is restated but in different terms and without adhering to the same syntax. (This is termed "nonparallel repetition" by Gossen [1974:76].) In 2a and 2b the idea is restated but the syntax is also repeated with substitution of only one or two synonymous or analogous words ("parallel repetition," Gossen 1974:77). This speech form, which is often dialogic in nature, is delivered in a slow, deliberate, redundant manner with the emphasis on conveying to the audi-ence a sense of completion in thought and deed as well as respect and humility.

1a. Yoj oj meba7i. Majun qa pwaq. We are poor. No money have we.
1b. Yawa7 rija7. K'o gan ruyabil. He is sick. His illness is great.
2a. Naq ruwach nu maj? Naq ruwach nu jan? What is my transgression? What is my sin?
2b. Xa jan nkibij. Xa itzel tzij nkiya7 Only evil do they say. Only bad words do they utter.

In contrast to "choloj," the informal speech genre "xa tzij" ("just words") denotes plain, ordinary, daily speech. Many speech events are included in this genre: casual conversation "(bi7in tzij," "passing words"), joking ("etz'anem tzij," "playful words"), gossiping ("molon tzij," "gathered words"), arguing "(kowilaj tzi j," "strong words"), and so forth. Unlike in "choloj," there are no restrictions on the form and content of this genre, except that the speech act be delivered in a careful, intelligible, grammatical, and appropriate way. Through the attention given to speech and the importance placed on words and their metaphorical usage, it is evident that the power of language and the importance of verbal competence is well recognized and highly valued by community members. Good communicative ability is prized, and only a few villagers are recognized as possessing true oratorical skills. In a community not marked by substantial differences in degrees of wealth, speech figures as an important marker of prestige and status.

Incorporated into the lexicon of Tzojobal, as in all the Mayan language dialects of Guatemala, is a considerable corpus of borrowings from Spanish. The density of loanwords, which are partially or fully adapted forms of Spanish origin that have been integrated into the native language lexicon, is an indication of the political, technological, economic, and cultural influence of the Spanish-speaking society on the indigenous cultures of Guatemala. The loanwords in Tzojobal are mostly direct transfers from Spanish and represent (1) lexical items with the same meaning in the two languages, now lost from the present day Tzibeño speech repertoire, (2) words expressing cultural concepts and material culture innovations introduced through various periods of contact with the Spanish-speaking culture and society, or (3) lexical variants currently competing with existing lexemes in the Tzibeño daily usage.

Although loanwords are found integrated into all word classes of Tzojobal, the majority of the borrowings are nouns. Early loanwords that were borrowed into the indigenous languages at the time of the Spanish conquest and the period of colonial rule consist mostly of words representing Christian themes, Spanish political offices and concepts, introduced foodstuffs, and certain material artifacts. These early introduced words are fully adapted to the native phonology. Indeed, Tzibeños regard these words not as borrowings at all, but as "puro Tzojobal," that is, words of Mayan language origin. In contrast, recently incorporated loanwords that demonstrate the variable adoption of all types of Spanish features into Tzibeño pronunciation (and to a lesser extent, less recently incorporated loans that show restricted adoption of Spanish features) are clearly identified as words derived from Spanish. Although Spanish word borrowings of material-culture items are tolerated in the speech community, borrowings used as progressive replacements for existing Tzojobal words are marked, and depending on the social context and the interlocutor, their use is checked with subtle means of social control.

In addition to the occurrence of word borrowing, a fair amount of code switching also occurs in the native language context. Code switching, a language-contact phenomenon under considerable cross-cultural scrutiny (see, for example, Amastae and Elías-Olivares 1982; Durán 1981; and Heath 1984a), involves the alternate use of two languages or language varieties in a given stretch of discourse. Generally, the switch into the alternate language occurs at major discourse junctures, but it may also occur at phrasal and word boundaries as well. In Panajtzib, code switching mostly occurs as a brief intrusion of a Spanish lexical and phrasal form into an otherwise consistent Tzojobal language frame.

Code switching in Panajtzib, which is referred to as "xolon tzi j," "mixing words," appears to have primarily a metaphorical function (see Blom and Gumperz 1972). Spanish is clearly the language of power in Guatemala, and the use of this elite code in the native language context evokes the status, power, prestige, and dominance inherent in the Spanish-speaking Ladino society. The switch to Spanish under appropriate psychosocial context thus lends force, magnitude, and credence to the Tzojobal utterance.

In the sentences below we see several examples of rather extensive code switching in which the symbolic function of Spanish as the code of power is quite apparent. In all of the examples below the switch to Spanish tacitly renders the Tzojobal utterance more authoritative and elevated. Sentence 1 is an example of a contextually determined (yet metaphorical in content) switch used by the speaker to quote what a Ladino had said to him in Spanish. The stereotypic familiar imperative command ("venidte pa acá, vos") is often used by Indians to typify the abusive nature of Ladinos in their interactions with Indians. Sentences 2 and 3 show the common switch that occurs for emphasizing monetary, calendrical, and time matters. Sentences 4, 5, and 6 are examples of the switch to Spanish specifically for the purpose of amplification, clarification, and evaluation. In sentences 4 and 5, Spanish is used in the narrative to convey the magnitude and seriousness of the illness condition. The switch to Spanish in sentence 6 is used to reinforce the semantic content of the utterance and to offer "proof" of the openness and modernity of the community (which is defined forthrightly by the availability of Ladino foodstuffs). As mentioned, switching occurs primarily at discourse junctures. In sentence 5, for example, we see the use of the Spanish evaluative expression "ay Dios" ("oh God") employed at a critical discourse transition point. Other common emblematic expressions include "ay hombre" ("oh man,") "ay jodido" ("oh so screwed up,") "ay pobre" ("oh you poor thing"). Less evaluative discourse markers include the use of Spanish "pero," "pues," "hasta," "entonces," "claro," and "tal vez," and are used the way "después" is used in sentence 2. In the examples below all words of Spanish origin (whether borrowings or switchings) are underlined.

1. Xubij ri mo7s, "venidte pa acá, vos." The Ladino said, "Come over here, you."
2. Las tres de la tarde xinqa pa muelle, y después xpe ri jab,' pero fuerte jab'. At three in the afternoon I went down to the dock, and then the rain came, but a lot of rain.
3. Caro rajil, ndata7, diez centavos jo jun pastilla. Expensive, my father, ten cents for just one pill.
4. Bien yawa7 rija7; ya mero xkam. He was very sick; he almost died.

5. Jun mej otro chorro k'ik'. Ay Dios, fuerte k'ik' nuban. A little later another spurt of blood. Oh God, there was a lot of blood.
6. Ja pa Panajtzib puro alegre. Ntej cualquier: rábanos, verduras, nojel taq cosa. It's very cheerful in Panajtzib. One can eat whatever: radishes, vegetables, all things.

Although metaphorical code switching is a discourse strategy used to a greater or lesser degree in the speech of all villagers, most consider the extensive "mixing" of languages to be a deplorable corruption and a violation of Tzojobal. Because Tzojobal is held as the code of ethnic solidarity, there are subtle sanctions against the inappropriate and over-extended use of Hispanicisms and code switching. "Heavy" users are commonly accused of being presumptuous and attempting to put on "Ladino airs," and hence may be subjected to ridicule and other subtle mechanisms of social control.

There are two strata in Tzibeño society wherein considerable hispanization occurs (although it must be remembered that in Panajtzib the overall rate of Hispanization is minimal compared to that found in biethnic communities where interethnic contact is high). One group consists of young single men, who, because of their age, economic, and marital status, have relatively few social commitments to the community. Instead of engaging fully in traditional economic pursuits, they rely primarily on income derived from day labor and seasonal labor migration to coastal plantations. In addition to supplementing their subsistence needs, the money they acquire is often used to purchase durable consumer items such as wrist watches, transistor radios, cassette players, sunglasses, and so forth, which they conspicuously display in the community. Because of their newly assumed posture in the community and their sometimes forthright disregard for traditional mores, older established community members look upon these "up starts" as self-serving and disrespectful. The fact that they use considerable nonintegrated, stereotypic, and often vulgar Spanish words and phrases in their speech confirms the elders' belief that "xujal ki na7oj," "their way of thinking has changed." Indeed, the familiar, authoritative, and abrupt Spanish employed in their language interactions with one another is reminiscent of the Spanish used by Ladinos toward Indians or among Ladino peers. Hispanicisms are used by the young cohort (particularly in the mildly obscene joking context) for purposes of in-group solidarity and to signal to other community members their preparedness and willingness to deal with the world outside Panajtzib.

The second stratum displaying above-average rates of Hispanization consists of older, more prominent community men. These men have had considerable exposure to Spanish through the years but, more important, they have acquired prestige and status through their association and advancement in the status-conferring civil and religious hierarchy. Because of their age and elevated social status, these community leaders are accorded the "right" to use Hispanicisms (although, again, limits are carefully monitored). In their public speech they rarely use the pejorative, somewhat obscene, and combative Spanish expressions characteristic of young men's Spanish and code switching mentioned above. Rather, their code switching is usually done in more formal contexts with the expressed purpose of lending authority and dignity to their Tzojobal utterances. It is interesting that these individuals, who have learned the art of skillfully integrating Spanish into their discourse, are generally regarded by community members to be the better village Tzojobal speakers.

Exposure to Spanish and actual Spanish proficiency do not necessarily correlate with high rates of Hispanization. There are men and women, children and adults, who have had both considerable exposure to Spanish and demonstrate significant Spanish proficiency and yet who tend not to "drop" Spanish in their speech because they do not possess the appropriate level of community stature. Women and children (whose resources in Spanish are often admittedly limited but also whose prestige in the public domain is marginal) have very low rates of Hispanization. Both are expected to adhere, and quite definitely do, to a solidarity code defined in terms of "pure" Tzojobal. In response to this expectation and reaction to social sanctions of presumptuousness, they thus monitor down and self-regulate their usage of Hispanicisms and code switching.

That the usage of Hispanicisms and code switching in public speech is more a reflection of male social status than of actual Spanish proficiency is made rather apparent when one observes drunken speech. More Spanish is used by both drunken men and women, old and young, and of either high or low social standing than among those same speakers when they are sober. Drunken speech is essentially unmonitored, but given certain social frameworks it becomes the medium through which a more generalized performance is enacted. In the right context, many inebriated Tzibeños temporarily assume an authoritative Ladino posture and allow a repressed, not uncharacteristically vulgar and abusive, Spanish language to come forth.

Aside from the ubiquitous blaring of Mexican rancheros and disc jockey chatter emanating from transistor radios, little elaborated Spanish is heard in the community. Few non-Indians come to the village, and consequently intracommunity Spanish language usage is limited to interactions with the handful of resident representatives of the national society—the five teachers, the municipal secretary and treasurer, and the postal agent. It is important to note that despite the fact that the town treasurer and one of the teachers are Indians from larger, more cosmopolitan-oriented communities, they are still addressed in Spanish by all who know even minimal amounts of Spanish, and they themselves use Spanish in their dealings with Tzibeños. These individuals are perceived as outsiders, holding positions of authority traditionally filled by Ladinos. The fact that they are addressed in Spanish and that they themselves use only Spanish within the community minimizes their ethnic identification with a local Indian group of people they regard as "menos desarrollada" and "menos despierta" ("less developed" and "less awakened"). This paternalistic and deprecatory attitude—one commonly held by Ladinos toward Indians in general but also held by more cosmopolitan Indians toward more traditional ones—is encoded in the use of

Spanish, the symbol of power, authority, and privilege. As we will see, these chauvinistic ethnic and language attitudes held within the framework of socio-political power relations have important consequences for the classroom, for they form the backdrop of endemic school failure.

In Panajtzib, communicative competence in Spanish is largely a reflection of one's sex and age. In Figure 6-1 below we see the distribution of Spanish proficiency among male and female community members based on self-report data. Although women tend to underplay their linguistic competence (and men nearly always underestimate the ability of women as well), this graph provides an indication of communicative competence, defined by Savignon (1983:303) as "the expression, interpretation, and negotiation of meaning involving interaction between two or more persons belonging to the same (or different) speech community (communities)." To demonstrate further the extent of bilingualism in the community, the graph differentiates among those villagers who command at least incipient, limited, and moderate, self-reported proficiency in Spanish.

For reasons that will become apparent in our discussion of classroom dynamics, children possess few Spanish language skills. They leave school at age fourteen with the foundations for bilingualism laid but with little more than very elementary proficiency in Spanish. Generally, they can use some stock or memorized expressions, but their ability to create language is minimal. They have

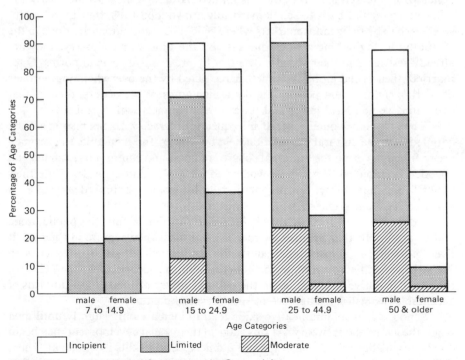

Figure 6-1. Communicative Competence by Sex and Age

almost no control of Spanish syntax, they speak largely by the juxtaposition of words, and their vocabulary is adequate only for functional interaction in restricted contexts. Because children are exposed to few appropriate Spanish-language contexts outside the confines of the school, their opportunity to develop the skills they may have learned in school is severely limited. Whether they ultimately acquire more bilingual skills in their life is determined largely by the structure of economic and cultural opportunities open to them as men and women in the regional society.

Girls receive almost as much schooling as do boys and, indeed, they leave school as proficient in Spanish as boys. Because of their domestically restricted role in Tzibeño society, however, women tend to acquire few additional communicative skills in Spanish. Many women claim that after having left school they quickly forgot much of what they had known. In the interim between leaving school and marriage, women are expected to begin displaying "k'ixibal" ("modesty"—"vergüenza" in Spanish) which means, among other things, that out of respect for oneself, one's family and the community, idle interactions with men, outsiders, and particularly Ladinos, are to be avoided.

As with the men, some women engage in seasonal migration to work in coastal coffee and cotton plantations. In these seasonal migratory episodes, however, they are accompanied by either adult relatives or peers from the village, and hence their interactions with others is limited. Although most women leave the village on a regular basis to sell domestically grown foodstuffs, they travel exclusively to nearby indigenous markets where economic transactions are done in the mutually intelligible indigenous dialects. By the time women marry, they are already restricted in their social movement by prescriptive societal norms. Once married, their social mobility is further restricted by the overwhelming burdens of rearing children and performing domestic chores. What occurs, then, is that over time women have fewer and fewer direct contacts with Spanish.

The fact that women overall infrequently interact with Spanish speakers, coupled with the cultural expectation held by women and men alike that women are to function within the "internal sphere" of home and community, defined and encoded in Tzojobal, leads most women to underplay and even denigrate their Spanish language ability. For pragmatic reasons, women at times deny and even mask their actual proficiency.

Adult males, in contrast, are expected to function within the public arena and to acquire further Spanish language skills. What they acquire in their adult lives, however, is not so much substantial additional linguistic proficiency in Spanish as further sociolinguistic proficiency in the second language. That is, they, as non-native speakers, learn the cultural contraints and cultural norms of acceptable Spanish language use in specific social contexts.

School-based communicative skills tend to increase only slightly until men reach the age of about twenty. At this stage in their social development men begin displaying highly prized and respected public speaking skills in Tzojobal. These skills of verbal competence tend to transfer to their production of Spanish. Within the structure of Tzibeño society, men have more economic and social opportunities to interact in Spanish-defined contexts and thus can increase their communicative competence. Their role in society lies in the public domain, and as such their participation in civil, religious and economic affairs more readily places them in contact with government and religious officials and Spanish-speaking entrepreneurs. They tend to buy and sell at regional markets, which both Ladinos and Indians frequent, and while working on the coastal plantations use Spanish with Ladinos and as a lingua franca with Indians from other parts of the highlands.

The overall Spanish language communicative competence of most Tzibeño men is relatively minimal, but in limited contexts it is usually sufficient to get basic messages communicated. Among the adult male population of Panajtzib, only 5 percent, at best, are substantially bilingual. These individuals are gainfully employed in nontraditional jobs that have arisen from the extension of Ladino institutions within Indian society, as well as in prestigious civil and religious offices. The individuals occupying these positions, in an effort to appear more progressive (i.e., more integrated with the national society) have made concerted efforts to make their Spanish less marked as Indian Spanish. In positions such as village mayor, Catholic Action president, cooperative officer, military commissioner, health promoter, and so forth, they require higher levels of communicative competence in Spanish, not only to make their messages more potent in the immediate community context, but also in an effort to be accepted and evaluated positively by their Spanish-speaking patrons. These men have secured their prestigious and relatively lucrative positions because they know the national language, but they also know the language as well as they do because of their acquired positions; the two components work together in synergistic fashion.

In summary, community members are keenly aware of the power of language and how language is used to exercise power. They are aware of others' bilingualism as well and the degree to which one language is used in relation to the other. Rarely, however, are the differences in second-language usage discussed without reference to one's progressiveness or conservativeness and social, economic, and moral standing, subtle as the distinctions are. Tzojobal is used by all community members as the language of ethnic identification and solidarity and as the means of acquiring and retaining resources within the community. Spanish is used within the community as the language of power, and it is implicitly valued for acquiring status and recognition and explicity for advancing oneself through employment if that opportunity were to arise. Tzibeños generally give two instrumental reasons children need to learn Spanish: (1) "para defenderse" ("to defend oneself") in order not to be deceived, ridiculed, abused, and exploited in a generally unfamiliar Ladino world, and (2) "para ser preparado" ("to be prepared") in order to know how to conduct oneself with outsiders and to seize an economic opportunity should one present itself. We turn now to an examination of classroom dynamics.

CLASSROOM DYNAMICS

The purpose of the national school system in Guatemala is to integrate individual citizens into the nation-state. The Basic Law of Education (Article 12), states, "[the reason for schooling is] to capacitate the pupils in order that they might live efficiently and beneficially within the national community." It is the role of teachers, then, as agents of the state, to initiate the children into Guatemalan citizenry, or as Moore (1973:132) puts it, "to direct the movements of large numbers of children over a six-year period, as the schools assemble them—away from their households, together with their peers—and ultimately aim at their incorporation into the nation."

Since the 1870s primary education in Guatemala has been both free and compulsory (see Gonzales-Orellana 1970). According to the public education law, all children aged seven through fourteen must attend school. The intent of primary education in the rural Indian highland regions is that children will enroll in Castellanización (a year of pre-school designed to help the indigenous child make the transition from home to school by teaching oral Spanish and introducing school culture) at the age of seven. By age fourteen, it is expected that the children will have completed the six grades of primary school.

In Panajtzib, as throughout most communities of the indigenous areas of Guatemala, the expectation of total enrollment and homogenous class age-grading is far from the reality. To begin with, less than 75 percent of the Panajtzib school-age population is officially enrolled in school. Boys, who are generally viewed as "street wise" at a younger age than girls, begin school at age seven and many remain in school through their fourteenth year. Girls, however, rarely begin before age eight and the majority leave by the end of their thirteenth year. There is considerable social pressure among parents to have one's pubescent daughter out of school (that is, off the village paths and away from male agemates and Ladino teachers) by age fourteen. Rarely do either boys or girls remain in school after the compulsory school age, because of peer pressure (school is perceived as falling within the domain of a children's activity, and fourteen-year olds are viewed as young adults) and because of the need expressed by parents and youth alike for young adults to begin "earning their tortillas."

Once enrolled in school, a child's attendance is quite sporadic. Class attendance is poor, partly because neither parents nor children understand the need for a continuity of learning gained through daily attendance, but mainly because child labor is needed for economic subsistence. Between the ages of seven and fourteen children begin to participate as members of the household economic unit, and consequently their attendance in school depends largely upon their response to the demands of the agricultural and domestic cycle. A major factor contributing to the general disarticulation of school and community is the periodic and cyclical nature of both domains. Peak agricultural demands coincide with the months of school attendance while the slack production months coincide with the months of vacation. Because child labor is needed for the many domestic and agricultural tasks, parents regularly pull their children out of school for days, weeks, months, and, not uncommonly, even years at a time.

Sporadic attendance on the part of the children is also a reflection of the relatively few days classes are actually held. Classes are supposed to begin in January and end in October. In Panajtzib they begin in February (January is used for school enrollment purposes) and end in September (October is used for evaluation). Of the possible 172 days that class could have been held from February through September 1980, in Catellanización, for example, only 116 days were devoted to instruction. Of the remaining 56 days, school was canceled for permission days, teacher in-services, and on a few occasions, low student attendance. Since students aggregately attended only approximately half the time in 1980, each student consequently received an average of 55 days of instruction. Because school is held only in the mornings, with one hour devoted to recess, the total hours of instruction are indeed few.

The effects of low attendance are reflected in high retention rates. In the history of schooling in Panajtzib, no one has progressed through schooling at the expected rate of one grade per year. In 1980, one-half of the children enrolled in Castellanización and the six grades of primary school were repeating for at least the second time the grade in which they were enrolled (see Table 6-1). The pattern of failure begins with the first year of schooling. To illustrate, in Castellanización in 1980, approximately 50 percent of the enrolled students were repeating the grade for the second, third, fourth, and even fifth time. At the end of the school year, only half of the repeaters successfully passed into first grade. Of those students who were enrolled in this grade for the first time, only 6 percent passed out of the grade that year (see Table 6-2).

TABLE 6-1.   SCHOOL ENROLLMENT IN OCTOBER 1980

Grade	Total	Number of students repeating grade	Percent of repeaters
Castellanización	62	30	48
First Grade	55	28	51
Second Grade	29	14	48
Third Grade	8	1	13
Fourth Grade	5	0	0
Fifth Grade	2	0	0
Sixth Grade	1	1	100
Total	165	74	45

TABLE 6-2.   CASTELLANIZACIÓN SCHOOL PROGRESS—1980

		Passed	Failed
Repeaters	30 (48%)	15 (50%)	15 (50%)
Non-repeaters	32 (52%)	2 (6%)	30 (94%)
Total	62	17 (27%)	45 (73%)

As can be seen in Table 6-3, which follows the Castellanización and First Grade cohorts from enrollment in 1979 to enrollment in 1981, this same holding pattern of failure is found in the First Grade as well. It is not difficult to see why nearly three-quarters of all the school children are enrolled in the first two years of school and why only approximately 10 percent of the student population ever advances beyond the Second Grade. Because pupils enter years behind schedule, because others repeatedly fail, and because others are persistently absent, there often is a tremendous spread of ages in the lower grades; it is not uncommon, for example, to find a thirteen-year old sitting beside a seven-year old in Castellanización.

By Second Grade the pattern of failure is clearly established and by mid-year teachers know who will fail and who will pass. Those whom they predict will fail are, simply enough, those who cannot read. Not surprisingly, though, those who cannot read are also those who have had a history of failing, who are currently repeating the grade, and those who are persistently absent. It is also these repeaters with persistent absenteeism (the ones who have been "dropping out" on a daily basis long before their failure is made official) who tend to drop out. As can be seen in Table 6-4, seven out of the nine second graders who dropped out by the time of the enrollment period in 1981 were repeaters in 1980. Two-thirds of the dropouts would have had to repeat the year again if they had remained in school.

There are many factors that contribute to low attendance, limited school progress, high drop-out rates and endemic school failure. A principal one, however, is that classes are taught in the nearly unintelligible language of Spanish by urban-oriented teachers whose training and pedagogical direction are ill-suited to the realities of rural indigenous Guatemala. With the exception of the Castellanización teacher (a "promotor bilingüe" [bilingual promoter], whose position derived from six years of formal schooling and an intensive one month short course), all of the teachers in Panajtzib have certificates in Urban Primary Education, which means that in addition to the six grades of primary, they received three years of secondary education and three years of teacher training. All the "maestros urbanos" (urban teachers) are Ladinos who were born and schooled in larger urban centers.

To the Tzibeños, the teachers represent the nation-state. Schooled in the virtues of nationalism, the teachers maintain a nationalistic orientation (with its attendant aspirations of geographical and social mobility), and they view their role as "uplifting" the Indian populace by disseminating the skills needed for their

TABLE 6-3.   PROGRESS RATE FOR 1979 COHORTS FOR THREE YEAR PERIOD

Grade	Dropped out	Demoted 1 grade	No promotion	Promoted 1 grade	Promoted 2 grades
Castellanización	4 (10%)		9 (22%)	24 (59%)	14 (34%)
First Grade	9 (20%)	1 (2%)	7 (16%)	17 (39%)	10 (23%)

TABLE 6-4. SECOND GRADE SCHOOL PROGRESS

| | Enrolled 1980 | Promoted | Failed | Enrolled 1981 | Dropped out | | |
					Total	Failed 1980	Passed 1980
Repeaters	14 (48%)	5 (36%)	9 (64%)	5 (36%)	9 (64%)	7	2
Non-Repeaters	15 (52%)	11 (73%)	4 (27%)	14 (93%)	1 (7%)	—	1
Total	29	16 (55%)	13 (45%)	19 (66%)	10 (33%)		

integration into national life. Although teachers often begin their tenure in Panajtzib with sincere idealistic fervor, they are not in any way prepared for the
harsh and lonely life they ultimately find in the village. After months of enduring
physical hardships and encountering, essentially, noncompliance in the community and silent defiance in the classroom, many become physically and mentally
ill and seek out any type of patronage possible to secure a post elsewhere. From
the teachers' perspective, teaching in Panajtzib is a hopeless and thankless en-
deavor.

The republic's official national study program delineates the teaching of the
Spanish language as the most important emphasis of schooling. Other curricular
areas (listed with decreasing emphasis) include mathematics, social studies, the
study of nature, aesthetic education, health and safety, agricultural education,
industrial arts and home economics. In Panajtzib, classroom instruction consists
of language arts and mathematics alone, since, in the words of one of the teachers,
"Tzibeños are so hopelessly behind we can't waste time on anything but language
arts and mathematics."

In Castellanización and First Grade, the focus of language arts is on oral
expression in the national language. Although the teachers' guide urges teachers
to be creative and imaginative, most language instruction consists of choral
recitation and drill. Students are asked to repeat long lists of Spanish words and
phrases that are painstakingly copied by the teacher from a text onto the blackboard. The Spanish the children hear in these lower-grade classrooms is essentially limited to the rote dissemination of a prepared lesson and the repetitive
reinforcement of classroom behavior rules. Due to the teachers' lack of training
in second-language pedagogy and their ignorance of and disregard for the language, society, and culture of the Tzibeño child, no effort is made to make the
language input interesting or relevant. Moreover, few opportunities are given the
children to interact meaningfully in a comfortable language environment so that
they might formulate, apply, and modify language learning strategies necessary
for the acquisition of the language in which they are being drilled (see Selinker
1972; Krashen, Long, and Scarcella 1982; Canale and Swain 1980; Krashen 1981,
1982a; Heath 1984b; Savignon 1972; and Paulston 1974).

An examination of one hour of class time in Castellanización illustrates the
type of language interactions that occur in the classroom. The arbitrarily chosen
hour opened with Spanish language instruction on a morning near the end of the
school year. The lesson was part of the unit "The Child and the School," the
second of four "centers of interest" outlined in the *Castellanización Bilingüe*
teachers' guide. The classroom vocabulary items targeted for instruction on this
day were "door" and "window." (In all of the excerpts below, the Spanish used
in the lessons is presented in English.)

The teacher began the lesson by showing a picture of a door. He then asked,
"What is this called?" and rhetorically answered, "Door." The students automat-
ically repeated "door," as they repeat any utterance cued by intonational emphasis. He then repeated the process for "window." The teacher then copied four

sentences from the teachers' guide onto the board. As he wrote each word on the board, he pronounced it and the students echoed his recitation until finally the teacher told the class not to repeat (but some continued to do so anyway). After the sentences were placed on the board, he engaged the class in several enthusiastic rounds of word-by-word choral repetition of the sentences in which he provided the model and joined the class in their response: "The-the school-school has-has windows-windows"; "The-the window-window serves-serves for-for light-light to-to enter-enter"; "The-the school-school has-has a-a door-door"; "The-the door-door serves-serves to-to shut-shut the-the classroom-classroom."

The teacher then called upon the class to answer in unison two product questions for which the echo response was a one-word answer (Teacher: "What is this called?" Teacher: "Door"; Class: "Door"; Teacher: "What is it made of?" Teacher: "Wood"; Class: "Wood"). The teacher then named two persons to answer individually the same product questions. The teacher signalled the end of the lesson in his customary way by tapping the floor with the yardstick and saying "good." He then instructed the class to copy the lesson in their notebooks. The rest of the hour focused on this task. As the students copied the lesson, the teacher busied himself by recording the lesson in his lesson plan book ("for the district supervisor's benefit") and walked about the room making certain that the students had copied the date in full, that the title of the lesson was underlined, that the students began copying at the top of a clean sheet of paper, and that each student's penmanship was acceptable.

During this hour of classroom instruction, the teacher elicited speech from the class on only ten occasions. On two occasions the teacher called upon the students to answer in unison a product question; on six occasions the teacher invited them to recite in word-for-word choral repetition; and twice the teacher named individual students to answer a product question. At no other time were the students invited to verbally participate in the lesson. On four separate occasions (occurring during the transition from the formal lesson to desk-work time and during desk-work time) students initiated a potential interaction by making individual requests for action on the part of the teacher, but two of the unsolicited initiations were ignored altogether and two were responded to nonverbally.

With the exception of the ten student-response elicitations, an informative statement, and three one-word evaluative utterances, all teacher talk in this classroom hour consisted of curt directives that were used to maintain control in the classroom. Twelve directives were imperative commands for procedural behavior ("Take out your notebooks and copy the lesson"); nine directives were imperative commands for prescriptive classroom behavior (i.e., for specifying necessary behaviors: "Pay attention right now") and restrictive classroom behavior (i.e., for specifying unacceptable behavior: "Rosaria, take your hand out of your mouth"), and three were interrogative directives ("Rocché, what is going on?") or indirect directives ("Navichoc, you're wasting time again").

It is important to note that all private interactions by the children among themselves both within and outside the confines of the classroom are conducted in the native language. Children quickly learn to tune out the teacher, particularly during the seemingly interminable desk-work time, and entertain themselves with whispered conversations in *Tzojobal*. Except for an occasional Spanish word from the lesson pronounced as the students laboriously copy them into their tattered notebooks, nonelicited Spanish is rarely heard in the classroom.

In all of the grade levels an inordinate amount of emphasis is placed on form and structure, with little attention given to comprehension and communication. In the excerpt below, taken from field observation notes, we can see the importance given to such matters as penmanship. Also apparent from this excerpt is the stressful and threatening ambience of the classroom.

The First Grade teacher begins the arithmetic lesson by asking Marcos to write the numbers on the board "big and separated." Marcos goes to the board and writes *A* instead of 1. The teacher shouts, "No, this is an *A*—NUMBERS." Marcos writes the numbers 1 2 but the teacher reprimands him: "No, use a dash." He begins again: 1-2 3 4 5. The teacher says, "No! A dash! Make them se-pa-ra-ted!" Marcos tries again: 1-2-3-4-5. Teacher: "No. No. The dash." Marcos makes it to number 7 and tries several times to execute an 8 but cannot. The teacher bangs his stick on the blackboard and shouts, "What is going on? When are you ever going to learn?" He makes a model for Marcos and Marcos copies it and proceeds to 10, but the zero is made too small. Teacher: "Big. Big. I want them BIG and the SAME size." The teacher calls on Eduardo. Marcos stays at the front of the room. (He was not told to do so but he knows from past experience that those who fail must remain at the front of the room.) Eduardo continues with 11 and 12, but the 12 is executed too small. Teacher: "Big. BIG. What a way ["costumbre"] you all have." The teacher calls on Marta Alicia; Eduardo remains at the front. Marta Alicia writes the numbers to 17 but the 7 does not meet the teacher's standards. Teacher: "This is no good. No good. I am not going to accept this." Mateo now continues. He successfully makes it to 21 but at 22 the numerals are of different sizes. Teacher: "Oh, man. I already explained—the same size. Not one big and one small, the same size."

By the time the students are sorted through the sieves of Castellanización and First Grade they have learned to copy well and have mastered the classroom behavior rules. But although they may have gained control of the sound system of Spanish, the students remain every bit as reluctant to utter Spanish in any form other than choral word-for-word repetition (and the enthusiasm for this activity has significantly waned). When students are put on the spot and are asked to respond individually to a question posed by the teacher, they either freeze, then lower their eyes and, by their avoidance, express total ignorance of the answer, or they answer the question (which usually has been simplified to elicit a one-word response) in a meek, muffled, reluctant, and embarrassed way.

In the excerpt below, taken from Second Grade—the only grade where the teacher made any effort to personalize the instruction—we have an example of the hesitancy on the part of students to respond to teacher's probes as well as the tendency among teachers to simplify process questions (where students must offer an opinion) to product questions (where students must offer an option) to choice questions (where students must chose an option, often only yes or no). (See Mehan 1979.)

The teacher is reading aloud the passage she has copied onto the blackboard. The poem is entitled "The Duck and the Duckling," and it is about a duck that goes out walking on her birthday wearing a silk dress, a straw hat, and woolen gloves. The vocabulary is difficult and the content is totally outside the students' cultural world (having been written, the teacher commented, "for children far more civilized and aware"), and so the teacher attempts to explain the vocabulary words to the students as she goes along:

TEACHER: Madame Duck. Duck. What are ducks?
    CLASS: [No response]
TEACHER: How many of you have ducks?
    CLASS: [No response]
TEACHER: Don't you have ducks?
    CLASS: [No response]
TEACHER: Filiberto, don't you have ducks?
FILIBERTO: No, only chickens.
TEACHER: Oh, you all don't have ducks but you have chickens?
    CLASS: [A few nod their heads in agreement.]
TEACHER: Oh, well, let's see. Birthday. Birthday is the day on which you were born. When is your birthday, Dominga?
DOMINGA: [No response]
TEACHER: Vicenta, on what day were you born?
VICENTA: [No response]
TEACHER: Do any of you know your birthday?

Mehan (1979, 1981) has argued that in order for students to be successful in classroom lessons, they must not only know the content of academic subjects, but they must also know the appropriate form in which to cast their academic knowledge. That is, while it is incumbent upon students to display what they know during lessons, they also must know how to display it. In Panajtzib, students generally refuse to display what they know and when they do so reluctantly, their knowledge is generally cast in a form the teachers consider unacceptable. Teachers become exasperated with the students' unwillingness to participate in the classroom lessons as they have been defined. This nonresponse by students, assuredly an adaptive coping strategy (see Ogbu 1978, and Trueba 1983), is interpreted by the teachers (and to a degree is internalized by the students) as stupidity and ignorance and a confirmation of their belief that the Indian child is both cognitively deficient and culturally deprived. Never do the teachers or the educational hierarchy question whether the structure of the classroom is conducive to understanding and communication. Indeed, no contexts other than ritualized choral elicitation and the anxiety-provoking formalized posing of questions about predetermined and segmented topics are ever provided for the students so that they may comfortably display their skills and abilities. The exasperation of the teachers, and yet their unwillness to restructure their lessons, is exemplified in the excerpt below:

The teacher of the Third/Fourth/Fifth Grade class is instructing the students to "prove" their subtraction problems. The teacher puts an example on the board and asks the students if they understand why proving the subtraction problem is a way of being certain the problem has been executed correctly.

TEACHER: All those who do not understand raise your hands.

STUDENTS: [One boy raises his hand.]

TEACHER: If you don't raise your hands and I find out you don't understand you will be punished. You will not be able to go out for recess. Now who doesn't understand?

STUDENTS: [Two more children raise their hands.]

TEACHER: Why won't you raise your hands? It is better for me if you raise your hands. If you raise your hands then I will explain it again. I will repeat it three, four, five—one hundred/three hundred times. Now, who doesn't understand? Raise your hands if you don't understand.

STUDENTS: [Three more students raise their hands.]

TEACHER: Why won't you admit you don't understand? I am not going to think you are stupid. You are not stupid. It is just that some of you don't have your minds developed yet. I am not going to think that Indian people are stupid. I am not going to think that because I know Indian people are the same as Ladinos. It is just that it will take a while. I know you are going to learn. Maybe not today but perhaps tomorrow . . .

CONCLUDING COMMENTS

The requisite for second language acquisition, as hypothesized by Krashen (1978, 1980), is language input that is (1) sufficient in quantity, (2) given in a non-threatening atmosphere, (3) both attended to and understood by the language learner, and (4) at an appropriate level (just a bit beyond the learner's present linguistic competence). Additionally, as Swain and Canale (1981) argue, in order for one to learn a second language successfully, "the second language learner must have the opportunity to take part in meaningful communicative interaction with competent speakers of the language, i.e., to respond to genuine communicative needs in realistic second language situations" (46). In Panajtzib, the delayed and meager acquisition of Spanish by schoolchildren reflects both the insufficient, incomprehensible, and inappropriate input of the second language, as well as the lack of opportunity to interact meaningfully in a comfortable and stimulating environment.

Upon completion of their years of attendance in the primary school, Tzibeño children, for the most part, have acquired only incipient bilingual ability. Those few children who remain in school beyond the second grade do show definite progress in Spanish language skill. We must remember, though, that few students ever progress beyond the second grade, having dropped out of school both literally and figuratively long before.

As the classroom interactions presented in this study show, early in their primary education experience Tzibeño children learn essentially all that they need to survive minimally in the classroom. They learn first and foremost to respond quickly to teachers' directives and to produce a small corpus of essential Spanish phrases. The end product of this type of classroom dynamic involving uncontextualized memorization and repetition is that, if not much more, the children acquire the basic sound system of Spanish and learn certain phrases and directives that will be heard over and over again in their interactions with non-Indians. Whether or not these children acquire greater bilingual ability in their lifetimes is determined largely by factors external to schooling that condition economic and cultural opportunities to interact in the national language context.

Adults in the society value the acquisition of Spanish for instrumental purposes. Spanish is the language of power in Guatemala, and, as we have seen, it is useful for gaining status and recognition within the community as well as for advancing oneself through employment, as limited as those opportunities are. Few who have acquired at least a fair amount of Spanish proficiency, however, credit the school for this ability—beyond recognition of the fact that the school did convey some basic language skills that lay dormant until they were needed at a later stage in life.

When asked about schooling, villagers allude to the mistrust, the noncooperation, and the apathy that has characterized school-community relations in the sixty years since primary education has come to Panajtzib. Only three children in the history of schooling in this community have ever completed the six grades of primary school, and no one has ever left the community to attend secondary school—that for which primary school has prepared them. Parents simply do not have the resources to send their children away for further schooling, and scholarships are next to impossible to secure.

Although primary schooling theoretically is designed as a type of gateway, leading to integration within the national society—a social system with a different language, different values, and different demands—Tzibeños, as a castelike minority group, are effectively excluded from this social system with or without schooling. Indeed, the sixth-grade graduate is not significantly better equipped than the first-grade dropout for any particular role within the community or the nation at large.

Because there are so few tangible rewards that accrue from the sacrifice of sending one's children to school, few Tzibeños value schooling beyond the minimal literacy and arithmetic skills it does impart. The limited economic and social benefits of schooling are the pivotal factors in the low school attendance, the limited school progress, the mental withdrawal, and the other coping behaviors and adaptive attitudes that are seemingly dysfunctional for achievement as defined by the school. The perceived futility of schooling is summarized by one parent as follows: "Before we had our corn fields, our hoes, and our cane houses. Now we have schooling, and we send our children there year after year, and we still have our corn fields, our hoes, and our cane houses. So what's the use?"

The causes of school failure in Panajtzib are many. I have argued in this paper that factors both within and outside the classroom inhibit the potential effectiveness of the school for promoting national language acquisition. Inappropriate teaching strategies, incorrectly articulated school policies, deficient resources, prejudicial attitudes, lack of communication, and cultural discontinuities contribute to the educational failure of the Guatemalan Indian child. Educational achievement in Guatemala, like educational achievement everywhere, is a reflection of the linguistic, social, and cultural context of schooling. It is only within this broader context of castelike subordination and structural disjuncture that educational failure can be fully comprehended.

NOTES

1. The research reported in this chapter is based on data gathered in Guatemala in 1974–75 and 1979–81. Work on language and education in Guatemala was supported through research fellowships from the Organization of American States, the American Association of University Women, and the University of Wisconsin/Madison Graduate School. An earlier version of this paper was presented at the meetings of the American Anthropological Association, Denver, Colorado, November 14–18, 1984.

2. The identification of schooling with the learning of a second language of wider communication is by no means unique to Latin America. Richard Benton, for example, describes formal education among the Maori of New Zealand as "almost synonymous" with learning English and indeed the "raison d'etre" of schooling (1978: 126,155).

3. The term *castelike,* used by John Ogbu (1978, 1981b, 1982, 1983a) is discussed earlier in this volume. For a discussion of the historical and contemporary subordination of the Guatemalan Indian, see Stavenhagen (1970), Martinez-Peláez (1979), and Warren (1978).

4. All of the dialects within this region of the central highlands are mutually intelligible even though they are dialects of three distinct languages, Quiche, Tzutujil, and Cakchiquel. See Hymes (1974) for a discussion of intelligibility and dialect differences.

CHAPTER 7

Parent Perceptions of School: Supportive Environments for Children

Concha Delgado-Gaitan

This chapter is concerned with the issue of Mexican immigrant families and their folk theory of success. That is, Mexican families have a perception of the way that the system operates and what it requires for them to succeed. The chapter also discusses what they believe success means to them and what the necessary steps are to succeed. Before expanding on these explanations, a brief discussion of theoretical models is presented that explains reasons for minorities succeeding or failing in societies.

Proponents of the deficit model (Heller 1966; Holtzman, Diaz-Guerrero, and Swartz 1975; Ingle 1970; Jensen 1973) have attributed Mexican children's failure in school to cultural and developmental deficits related to the home socialization process. The inevitable recommendation is for schools to rectify the students' deficits so that they will be equal to Anglo mainstream students. Under this deficit premise researchers propose parenting courses to equip Mexican parents to encourage their children's cognitive development and to use other child-rearing practices.

The shortcomings of deficit-model research lies in the underlying assumptions that Mexican culture is inferior to Anglo culture and that Mexican parents are incapable of providing their children with the necessary competitive values to succeed in society. Based on these assumptions of deficiencies, social policies and compensatory programs were designed in the schools to address inequalities in an attempt to compensate for the supposedly missing mainstream skills (White 1973). Many of those programs have not been successful in transforming minority children's behavior to be in accordance with mainstream values.

Goldberg (1971) and Ogbu (1978) explain the failure of compensatory programs as being due to methodological problems as well as to the denial of the validity and integrity of Mexican culture by Anglo middle-class educators. Knowledge about the home socialization and native learning processes is absent in the deficit theory, which states that minority families are failures when they cannot adapt to their new environments. Such conclusions are made in the absence of formidable data about the sociocultural context of adjustment that helps to construct people's perceptions of their reality and how to participate in it.

We need to examine middle-range micro aspects of the home and family structures and the organizational system of the home in order to better understand the sociocultural context that influences differential performance of children in schools. Some anthrolinguistic and sociolinguistic literature has observed linguistic and social behavior in the home (Heath 1982; Shultz, Florio, and Erickson 1982). These studies show the linguistic socialization of children in the home and the acquisition of social rules of competence as expected by the adults in the home and the school.

Ogbu (1981a) argues that most children grow up to be competent adults in that people in a given cultural group are motivated to transmit and acquire those competencies that are necessary for them to perform cultural tasks. According to LeVine (1976) and Ogbu (1981a), the folk theory of success includes five components: (1) the range of available cultural tasks or status positions, (2) their relative importance or value, (3) the competencies essential for attainment or performance, (4) the strategies for attaining the positions or achieving the cultural tasks, and (5) the expected penalties and rewards for failures and successes (Ogbu 1981a: 420).

The above theory of success makes sense only in the context of studying the family unit since it is within this unit that we can observe the rewards and penalties associated with the acquisition of knowledge and social strategies. For example, the notions that immigrant families develop about achieving success in the United States are derived from what they observe around them, what they perceive they want, and possibly what their friends are doing in order to acquire competencies and opportunities.

Child rearing in the home is influenced by the newly acquired understanding of the importance of success in that the parents begin to encourage their children to do well in school; yet they do not know which academic competencies are essential for them to achieve success. Thus, the parents begin to see that their efforts are not rewarded if their children do not do well in school. Their personal failure (for not succeeding in the new society) may force the parents to enforce more strictly the values and culture that are familiar to them and that they recognize as important for succeeding in their own family and community.

The rapid sociocultural change experienced by minority families, especially those who have emigrated from another country, often results in the marginal status of these families and groups. The process that families experience in this transition involves intrinsic values and perceptions of oneself and of the social environment. Such categories are largely formulated in the context of the family unit (Trueba, in press). The socialization process that Trueba discusses is a protracted one within the nuclear and extended family that includes adults and children. This process of projecting meaning to one's surroundings consists of the acquisition of language, knowledge, perceptions, and competencies that are necessary for the family's survival and identification within their community and group. This understanding of the family as a primary socializing unit is the basis of the analysis in this study.

THE STUDY

The specific questions posed in the part of the study presented here are:

1. How do these three families view the role of schooling for their children?
2. What do they consider to be important competencies in attaining future goals?

My data presents a thin slice of the macroperspective by focusing on the day-to-day family interactions and the values that prioritize the practices that create continuity and change in a culture.

Setting

La Perla, an urban community in a Northern California city, is strategically located near the wealthy Silicon Valley, which serves as a source of low-level assembly line employment for many Mexican immigrant families. La Perla is of particular anthropological and educational research interest because of the high Mexican immigrant population. According to the 1980 Census, the total Hispanic group in La Perla comprised the largest minority group, at 40.27 percent. Adults in the community are at the lowest socioeconomic status, and the Mexican children in the school district score at the lowest percentile on the state achievement tests in spite of many supportive programs such as bilingual education and adult literacy programs.

When we speak of La Perla as predominantly a Mexican community, it is not to categorize it as a homogeneous group, since the 40.27 percent of the Spanish-speaking people actually represents a widely diverse heterogeneous population within the general classification of Mexican. We have ethnohistoric data, as well as other ethnographic interviews, which reveal different perceptions of Mexicans based on their own sense of ethnic identity.

Recently arrived Mexican immigrants identify themselves as Mexicans and consider other people of Mexican descent who do not speak Spanish as Chicanos. Chicanos are perceived as people who are born in the United States or who have resided in the United States for many years and have adopted many Anglo values and lifestyles and have lost the practice of speaking Spanish and observing Mexican customs. Recent Mexican immigrants often blame Chicanos for the oppressive socioeconomic conditions, assuming that these conditions are due to the Chicano's unwillingness to work hard. For many Mexicans, the term Chicano and "Cholo" are synonymous. Cholos are male youths (Cholas are female youths) who wear khaki pants, head bandanas, and loose-fitting Pendleton shirts. Many of the youths are school truants or dropouts who spend a great deal of time standing on street corners or in parking lots. Mexicans resent this group of Mexicans because they feel that their behavior stigmatizes other Mexicans.

Mexican-Americans are generally identified as the group of Mexicans who have had roots in the United States for many generations or who have immigrated legally and have become United States citizens. This group prides itself on having learned English well enough to obtain a full-time, secure, middle-income position. Some people who identify themselves as Mexican-Americans no longer speak Spanish, nor do their children. Some Mexican-Americans consider themselves more capable of living in the United States than recently arrived Mexicans. They express concern that many recent Mexican immigrants are "lumpen proletariat" (poor people belonging to the criminal element). Another criticism of recent Mexican immigrants is that they take jobs belonging to Mexican-Americans or Chicanos simply because they speak better Spanish. The same complaint is expressed about the recent Latin American immigrants. Mexican-Americans sometimes identify themselves as Chicano, particularly on issues surrounding political organizations that have to confront the white establishment.

Mexicans who identify themselves as Chicanos socially and politically are relatively few in La Perla. This category usually includes the high school youth who work in the community center as well as other young professionals who studied away from La Perla and returned to work in advocate positions for the community center. Some Chicanos felt that on some issues, such as bilingual education, certain Mexican-Americans have been unsupportive because they do not want to identify themselves as Mexican.

Although Mexicans in La Perla identify themselves as they choose, they may be perceived differently by other Mexicans who view certain values and characteristics as peculiar to certain groups. For example, one family identifies itself as Mexican-American, but other families on the same block who also identify themselves as Mexican-American view this family as Chicano because of the type of dress the children in the family wear. Thus, the items that people claim as their badges of identity are variable and interchangeable and are contingent upon other people's perceptions of them.

Methodology

Features of this study of the family unit and parent perceptions of schooling are part of a larger study (Delgado-Gaitan 1983). Ethnographic interviews and observations were the primary sources of data collection. Demographic data were also collected about language use and social relations in the church and community agencies, including the schools. I also became a substitute teacher to get better insight into the educational programs for Mexican students.

The three families selected for this study all lived within two blocks of one of the schools where I observed and substituted. At Oakgrove School I began a relationship with a group of first- second- and third-grade children who played together during recess. Interviews with the parents proceeded smoothly once I began accompanying the children to their homes. My affiliation with the schools made my entry into the homes easier since the parents saw me as a teacher.

My first visits with the children and the parents in the home occurred in the spring. Approximately one year of observations and informal interviews were conducted prior to the formal interviews with the parents, teachers, and children. The interviews with the parents and children dealt with (1) educational goals for their children, (2) their views and attitudes toward the school, (3) their meaning of education, (4) their concept of how to achieve their goals, (5) the values that they perceived would help them obtain success for their children, and (6) the home practices that they felt prepared their children to achieve.

The adults and the children spoke only Spanish in the home. The interviews, which lasted between one and three hours, were therefore conducted in Spanish. The variation in homes can be seen in the varying degrees of data offered by the informants. Some adults were particularly detailed in their discussion of questions while others were quite brief in their responses during the ethnographic interviews. Audio recordings were made of the final interviews, since, by that time, parents and children felt comfortable and trusting around me. The build-up of trust and rapport with the families came about through personal services I provided and the interpersonal relations that developed in the process. The result was frankness and openness on the part of the families in the data-collection process.

Configurations of Data and Analysis: At Home with the Kids

The data presented in the subsequent section presents a profile of the Islas, Reina, and Salas families, with a focus on the parents' experiences in their role as supporters of their children's careers. The key unit of analysis is the family. Through discourse analysis I examine how parents' perceptions of their role in the home compares and contrasts with the role of the school.

ISLAS FAMILY

Home Environment

The Islas live in a four-family apartment building on Bolero Street. Five members of the Islas family reside in a one-bedroom unit for which they pay $300 monthly. Three single-bedroom apartments are on the second level over the carports and one is on the lower level. A small patch of grass surrounds a single tree next to the driveway. The Royal Electronic Plant is located across the street on Bolero Street, and a tool and die garage is across on Miranda Street. Industry and apartments surround the apartment on one side, and a single dwelling is on the other.

The Islases have lived in this apartment for seven years. Ten years ago Mr. and Mrs. Islas emigrated from Mexico. Mr. Islas is from Apatzingán, Michoacán, and Mrs. Islas is from Tijuana. All of the three children were born in the United States. Pedro is nine, Yolanda is seven, and Sabrina is one and a half.

Both Mr. and Mrs. Islas work, although Mrs. Islas is frequently unemployed. When employed, she makes dry flower arrangements in a company in Vista Mar on the day shift. Mr. Islas has the graveyard shift at Mott Engineering Manufacturing, Inc., in Rincon. In addition, he is often called to do gardening for private parties on Saturdays. Both adults alternate caring for the children since Mr. Islas stays home during the day and Mrs. Islas stays home in the evening. During the school year Sabrina is the only one at home with the father, but in the summer all three children are home during the day.

Children's Activities

The day begins at the Islas' apartment about six-thirty, when Mrs. Islas awakes to feed Sabrina. Pedro and Yolanda awaken shortly afterward. They dress, wash, and then go into the kitchen. If the mother has left for work, Pedro assumes responsibility and pours Yolanda and himself a glass of milk and then sets two bowls and a box of cereal on the table. When Mrs. Islas is home she takes responsibility for the breakfast while Pedro watches Sabrina. The father sleeps in if the mother is home since he works the graveyard shift; otherwise, he gets up and watches the baby.

At eight, Pedro and Yolanda walk to Oakgrove School, which is one block down Bolero Street. Nora often joins them since she lives next door. Many children from other apartments on the same block walk to school at the same time. Pedro walks ahead of Yolanda when she stops to talk to her friends.

The Islas children do not always walk home together even though they get out at the same time. Pedro never stops off anywhere, while Yolanda sometimes stops at her friend's apartment, although they are both expected to go straight home. When they arrive Mr. Islas is in the house with Sabrina. Pedro and Yolanda may stay inside, depending on the weather. A popular afternoon activity is watching "Batman" on television. Efrén, who lives two apartments away, often visits Pedro. If Mrs. Islas is home she watches her soap opera in Spanish as she crochets dresses for Sabrina. The boys go to Efrén's house to watch television. Yolanda either stays with her mother and Sabrina or visits Nora next door.

If the Islas children choose to go to church on Sunday, the "Movimiento Familia" group in Sacred Heart Church becomes their primary activity. The remainder of the day is spent watching "Siempre en Domingo," a variety program in Spanish. On Sunday the children play indoors and outdoors around the apartment.

Home is the pivotal point of the Islas' activities. Limited financial resources preclude family outings and other activities. Their primary involvements seem to be with one another as they conduct their daily routines to maintain a cohesive family structure. Their neighbors, the Reina family, are good friends and assist the Islas family by providing financial or employment information. Occasionally, the Reinas buy Pedro and Yolanda small toys. For example, on the Fourth of July, they bought fireworks for both the Islas and the Salas children.

Parents' Expectations of Children's Responsibilities

If Mr. Islas is home alone with Sabrina, Pedro is usually expected to stay in the apartment to help care for his baby sister. When Mrs. Islas is working, neither Pedro nor Yolanda is allowed to leave the apartment complex until Mrs. Islas gets home.

When Pedro arrives home from school, he is sometimes expected to run errands to Esperanza's (the market) for groceries if the need arises. At other times Mr. Islas drives to the store while Pedro watches Sabrina. When both of the parents are away from home, they expect the children to stay inside. Pedro is entrusted with the responsibility for the children when left alone with his two younger sisters.

Pedro receives more of the assignments, and Yolanda is rarely expected to assume much responsibility around the house when Pedro is present. Her mother often complains about her irresponsibility and her inability to carry out tasks as instructed. Yolanda cringes and sits quietly when her mother criticizes her for not being capable. Her eyes fill with tears that are never quite released. Because Yolanda depends on others, her mother scolds her. For example, she seldom prepares herself something to eat, instead expecting her parents or Pedro to do it for her. Mrs. Islas despairs because of her daughter's lack of self-reliance.

Yolanda, however, does not see herself in the same way as her mother sees her. She in fact helps out by doing housework and running errands to *Mario's,* although Yolanda admits needing help to run the errands. Yolanda also agrees that most of the time she dislikes having to do any work around the house and prefers to play with her friends, Herlinda and Nora.

Conversely, the parents perceive Pedro as more serious and reliable than Yolanda since he apparently complies with the responsibility bestowed on him. Pedro is somewhat soft-spoken and gives a great deal of thought to work assigned to him. This is not to imply that Pedro prefers work over play, because "hanging out" with Efrén, Nora, and Yolanda are frequent scenes around the apartments. Their daily routine of housework and play varies minimally on weekends.

The Islas children are responsible for sweeping, washing dishes, and making beds. These tasks have to be done before the children leave for school. Other tasks, such as running errands to the store and helping Mrs. Islas at the laundromat, can only be performed after school. Neither parents nor children ever mention that taking care of younger siblings is a chore; yet older children are always looking after younger siblings. One explanation for this is that families consider being with each other a natural part of family interaction. Children, therefore, do not resent child care as much as other tasks. Often Yolanda and Pedro are left alone to care for Sabrina.

Yolanda and Pedro are quite aware of their tasks and responsibilities since they are frequently reminded of them. Yolanda says that she dislikes dishwashing, and she also disobeys the standard rule to request permission to leave the house. When her friends invite her to visit their houses Yolanda goes without permission because she is afraid of not receiving consent if she asks her parents. Pedro, on the other hand, recognizes that he is very responsible and gets angry when Yolanda defies him. Yolanda resents being criticized by her elders; she insists that the reason she does not do as much as Pedro is that the tasks are difficult. Clearly, every member of the Islas family is aware of the routine chores for which the children are responsible. In addition to knowing "what" to do, the children are also expected to understand "how" to accomplish their tasks: for example, they should help each other, respect each other, and not fight.

According to the parents, Yolanda and Pedro frequently fight about money. Yolanda helps herself to the money Pedro saves. His accumulated earnings come from quarters he gets when he runs errands. Although she promises to replace the money, Pedro challenges the fact that she takes his money. He angrily confronts her. Mrs. Islas intervenes and sometimes spanks them for creating a disturbance. Most of the time, however, the children respond to a sharp "¡Ya apláquense!" (Enough, settle down!).

Schoolwork

The Islas children assist each other in some homework tasks, such as reading and writing. It is interesting to observe how Yolanda and Pedro share work when they obtain an old storybook and a wrinkled piece of paper. Yolanda teaches Pedro to read. She is in the first grade and he is in the third. In turn, he occasionally assists Yolanda in addition and subtraction because his math skills are more developed. The following event illustrates how Yolanda and Pedro work together to read a book:

YOLANDA: [Sits on the floor with a single sheet of paper drawing dolls and practicing writing her name.]

PEDRO: [Turns off the television, goes into the bedroom and brings out a pencil and a thin book, *Gato y Perro*.]

YOLANDA: Oh, déjame ver el librillo. (Oh, let me see the book.)

PEDRO: No, yo lo traje. Tú tienes tus monas. (No, I brought it. You have your dolls.)

YOLANDA: [Goes to sit next to Pedro on the couch and begins reading the book aloud.]

PEDRO: [Points to a word.] Esa palabra, ¿qué es? (What's that word?)
YOLANDA: Bajo. (Under.)
PEDRO: Oh, bajo de la c-c. (Oh, under the b-b.)
YOLANDA: Cama. (Bed.)
PEDRO: Oh, cama, gato, gato. (Oh, bed, cat, cat.)
YOLANDA: [Takes the book and reads the page to Pedro.]
PEDRO: [Reads the page aloud at the same time Yolanda reads it to him.
He repeats the words right along with her.]
YOLANDA: [Continues reading.] Si, no haré un b-b. (Yes, I won't make a b-b.)
YOLANDA: Bola. (Ball.)
PEDRO: Oh, bola de gato, lo haré, lo haré. (Oh, cat's ball, I'll do it, I'll
do it.)
[There is unintelligible stumbling.]
YOLANDA: [Takes the book.] —Miau, miau. Sí, bá-ja-te. (Yes, g-e-t d-o-w-n.)
PEDRO: [Repeats the words as Yolanda reads.] ¡Ya lo sé! ¡Ya lo sé. Dame
el libro. ¡ Mira cómo se hizo rosca el perro! (I know it! I know
it! Give me the book. Look how the dog curled up.!)
YOLANDA: [Looks on.]
PEDRO: [Flips through other pages and comments on the pictures.]
YOLANDA: Yo lo quiero leer. (I want to read it.) [She grabs the book from
Pedro and begins reading aloud.]
PEDRO: [Mouths the words as Yolanda reads.]
YOLANDA: Ya lo lei—toma. (I've read it—here.)

Although Yolanda mispronounced a few words as she read to Pedro, her fluency made it easier for Pedro to get a sense of continuity and reinforcement as he read along with Yolanda.

Mrs. Islas admits to feeling very good when the children work together harmoniously. She also feels encouraged that Pedro can improve his reading if he gets help. Yolanda and Pedro's reading practice sessions are unrelated to homework lessons from school since assignments are infrequent.

The Islas children contribute to the routine of the household by performing chores around the house. The parents impose a code of conduct which reinforces obedience and collaboration. Mrs. Islas comments: "Estos niños necesitan aprender a trabajar—si no, salen flojos sinvergüenzas y no consiguen un buen trabajo" (These children need to know how to work—if not, they will be lazy good-for-nothings and they will not get good jobs).

The Islases' Views on Schooling

Mr. Islas's views. Many interviews were conducted with Mr. and Mrs. Islas regarding their perceptions of the school, their children's education and their own role as supporters. Through extensive observations, I was able to understand Mr. Islas's reluctance to respond to the interview questions. Mrs. Islas also explained that Mr. Islas was illiterate in both languages and that he felt most inadequate in discussing anything concerning schools. With that piece of information, it became clear what type of indirect questions would safely encourage Mr. Islas to speak about his attitudes and views in subsequent interviews. As predicted, Mr. Islas confided that he expected Pedro and Yolanda to do well and to help around the house without fighting.

[Mr. Islas—MR I; Interviewer—I]

    I: ¿Usted piensa que es importante que los niños aprendan a leer y escribir? (Do you think that it is important that the children learn to read and write?)

MR. I: Pues sí, cómo no. Así no tienen que andar pidiéndole favores a nadie. Yolanda sabe leer mejor que Pedro. Nos dicen en la escuela que a él se le dificulta leer pero sabe las matemáticas. (Of course; that way they don't have to run around asking favors from anyone. Yolanda knows how to read better than Pedro. They tell us at school that he has difficulty in reading but he knows mathematics.)

    I: Cuando ya estén los niños grandes, ¿qué tipo de trabajo le gustaría que consigan Pedro y Yolanda? (When the children are grown up, what type of work would you like them to be able to have?)

MR. I: Pues lo que puedan conseguir, yo creo. No sé, porque no sé lo que quieren ellos ser. No más que no andar como los Cholos de vagos. (Well, whatever they can get, I think. I don't know because I don't know what they want to be. As long as they don't end up like the Cholos, as bums.)

    I: ¿Usted piensa que alguien que sabe hablar y leer y escribir el inglés tiene más oportunidad de conseguir empleo? (Do you think that someone who speaks, reads and writes English can have better employment?)

MR. I: Yo creo que sí porque allá donde trabajo yo de jardinero, yo no sé el inglés, pero hay otros mexicanos que sí saben inglés y me parece que ellos podían conseguir mejor trabajo. Yo estoy allí porque no me piden papeles, pero los niños son cuidadanos y ellos tienen derechos que nosotros no tenemos. Y sabiendo inglés van a poder conseguir mejor empleo, ¿no cree? (Yes, I think so because where I work as a gardener, I don't speak English but there are other Mexicans that do know English and I think that they should be able to get a better job. I'm there because they don't ask me for papers but my kids are United States citizens and they have rights that we don't. Knowing English would help them get better employment, don't you think so?)

    I: ¿Usted piensa que es suficiente saber el inglés para poder conseguir buen trabajo? (Do you think it is sufficient for someone to know English in order to get a good job?)

MR. I: También saber trabajar en lo que escogen. (Also to know how to work in what one chooses.)

I: ¿Y cómo aprenden lo que deben saber para el empleo que escojan? (And how should they learn what they should know for the job that they choose?)

MR. I: En la escuela deben de aprender, ¿que no? Nomás que a veces los chiquillos no quieren trabajar. Prefieren andar ahí de vagos, nomás jugar. (They should learn in school, right? Except that these kids don't want to work. They prefer to run around and play.)

I: ¿De cuál otra manera pueden Yolanda y Pedro aprender una carrera de trabajo? (What other way could Yolanda and Pedro learn a career?)

MR. I: No sé. (I don't know.)

I: Por ejemplo digamos que Yolanda quiere ser secretaria, ¿cómo alcanzaría su deseo? (For example, let's say Yolanda wants to be a secretary, how do you think she could learn to do it?)

MR. I: Será en la escuela secundaria, ¿no? Mi hermano dice que su muchacha mayor está aprendiendo a escribir a máquina en la escuela. Yo digo que si quieren, allí pueden aprender. (Probably in high school, right? My brother says that his older daughter is learning to type at school and I guess if they want to, they can learn there.)

I: ¿De qué manera piensa usted que pueden ustedes como padres ayudarles a los niños aquí en la casa para que puedan aprender mejor? (In what way do you think that you could help your children here at home to be able to better learn what they need?)

MR. I: Yo creo que su mamá les puede ayudar a leer con que sea en español. Nomás que a veces los niños se hacen flojos y dicen que los maestros no les dan tarea; así es que su mamá no les puede ayudar aunque quiera. (I think that their mother can help them learn as long as it's in Spanish. Except that sometimes the kids get lazy and they say that the teachers don't give them homework; so their mother cannot help them even if she wants to.)

I: ¿Qué opina usted sobre la escuela? Le están enseñando a sus niños lo que deben aprender? (What is your opinion of the school? Are the teachers teaching your children what you think they should learn?)

MR. I: Yo creo que sí. Nomás que a veces que vamos a hablar con las maestras, dicen que los chiquillos no van bien. Yo digo que es porque se la pasan jugando. (I think so, except that sometimes when we go to talk to the teachers they tell us the kids aren't doing well. I think that it is because they want to play.)

Mr. Islas appears to have some faith in the function of school to instruct Yolanda and Pedro in their pursuit of a career. It also seems that he sees the children as fully responsible for their success and that the one way they could be more successful is to spend less time playing and goofing around and more time studying. Although Mr. Islas is not knowledgeable about the specific pragmatic steps necessary for his children to achieve their goals, he is convinced that their United States citizenship and English-speaking ability are advantages that he does not have. According to Mr. Islas, his children have a choice as to the type of work they want to do. However, he sees his role as limited since he defines support in the home in terms of academic assistance, which only his wife, who is literate in Spanish, is partly capable of providing.

Mrs. Islas's views. Mrs. Islas, however, expresses different perceptions from Mr. Islas. She felt that she should be very active in making sure that Yolanda and Pedro get to school in the morning and that they are reminded to behave in school and come home directly from school to take care of their baby sister, run errands, or wash dishes. Mrs. Islas claims that she tries to discipline the children so that they are obedient and respectful not only at home but in school. Her expectations are sometimes overshadowed by the children's insistence on doing as they wish against her rules. On those occasions, Mrs. Islas attempts to regain control by yelling at them to do as she requests. Sometimes, when she becomes too frustrated by the children, she gives up trying to control them. She was observed numerous times throwing her hands up in despair.

[Mrs. Islas—MRS. I; Interviewer—I]

MRS. I: A mí me parece que los niños tienen que decidir por sí mismos lo que quieren ser cuando crezcan porque ellos tienen que hacerlo. Lo único que yo quiero es que puedan conseguirse un trabajo seguro, no como nosotros que andamos aquí y allí. Pero estos chiquillos no les gusta trabajar. Por ejemplo, esta Yolanda quiere que todos le hagan todo. Ella no levanta un dedo para nada aquí en la casa, per sí sabe leer mejor que Pedro. Me dicen que ni en español ni en inglés puede leer. Así no se puede en este país. Hasta yo estoy yendo a clases de inglés aquí a la escuela, a ver is me entra algo. Pero los chiquillos me tienen que ayudar. (It seems to me that the children have to decide for themselves what they want to be when they grow up because they're the ones who have to do it. The only thing I really hope for is that they get a secure job, not like us who move from one job to the next. But these kids don't like to work. For example, Yolanda wants others to do everything for her. She doesn't lift a finger for anything around the house, but she does know how to read better than Pedro. They tell me that he cannot read either in Spanish or English. This is no way to survive in this country. I am even going to English classes here at the school to see if something will stick, but the kids have to help me.)

I: ¿De cuál otra manera les ayuda usted a que tenga éxito en la escuela? (What other way do you help your children to succeed in school?)

MRS. I: Yo siempre les digo que pongan atención y que no se la pasen jugando, porque, ¡ay!, cómo les gusta jugar. Y es todo. Pues, ¿qué más puede hacer uno? Ellos son los que deben de aprender, pero, ¡tienen una cabeza más dura! (I always tell them to pay attention and not to goof around because they sure like to play. And that's all. Well, what else can one do? They're the ones who have to learn, but they sure have a hard head!)

As with Mr. Islas, Mrs. Islas did not have definite plans for their children's future, but she did hope they would be able to get secure jobs so that they would not have to be laid off continually as she and Mr. Islas had been. Additionally, Mrs. Islas knew that even though she could not assist them with their homework because of her limited literacy, she made sure to remind them of the values of discipline and obedience that she felt were necessary for them to succeed in school. Both Mr. and Mrs. Islas seemed to place most of the responsibility for learning on the children. In their view, if the children did not succeed, they were to blame for not "trying" or for "playing around" instead of working. At times, a "lack of understanding" on their part was also blamed for the reports of underachievement, especially for Pedro's inability to read.

REINA FAMILY

Home Environment

The Reina family members include Mr. and Mrs. Reina, Nora (eight years old), and Laura (three years old). They immigrated to La Perla four years ago from Apatzingán, Michoacán. Mrs. Reina's parents, who immigrated ten years before, assisted them financially. The Reinas own a piece of property in Apatzingán. Prior to coming to La Perla, Mr. Reina studied in a school equivalent to an American high school; Mrs. Reina attended only the equivalent of elementary school. Much of her time was spent working on her family's ranch outside of Apatzingán. At fourteen she married Mr. Reina and had Nora very shortly afterward.

Nora was born in Mexico and Laura was born in La Perla. They have lived in the same apartment since they arrived. Both Mr. and Mrs. Reina worked the day shift on the assembly line at Mott Manufacturing. He complained about being overworked and underpaid, so he was fired, and Mrs. Reina left in solidarity with him. They both remained unemployed for over a month until Mr. Reina found a temporary job on the assembly line at Royal Industry in Marina shortly before Christmas. By February, Mrs. Reina was employed in the same company. She works the day shift and he goes in on the night shift. Since getting their new jobs, the Reinas have changed their routine at home.

Children's Activities

Nora leaves for school after her mother leaves and before her father wakes up. Laura and her father sleep a little later. Nora's mother leaves a bowl of cereal out for her but she is responsible for dressing and combing her long dark hair. On rare occasions her father gets up to assist her.

After school Nora rushes home to be there before her father leaves for work. Nora is now old enough to care for Laura, her sister. In the earlier part of the year the girls were not allowed to stay alone in the apartment. They had to go everywhere with their parents, but after Nora turned eight, the girls began to stay by themselves for a half hour or so between the time Mr. Reina left for work and Mrs. Reina returned.

Nora invites Yolanda to stay with her and Laura inside the apartment, then locks the door and they dance and play records. Watching cartoons is also a popular pastime. Nora makes certain that Laura does not hurt herself, so she keeps an eye on her while she plays with her friends. Once Mrs. Reina arrives the girls are allowed to leave the house.

Yolanda Islas is Nora's best friend; they play and go to school together. They exchange clothes and shoes. Since Nora has many more clothes than Yolanda, she lets Yolanda wear her things. Because the Reinas enjoy a slightly better financial position than the Islas family, the Reina girls are taken on more recreational outings than are the Islas children. When the weather is good, the Reinas make frequent trips to the San Jose flea market. Clothes and produce items are purchased at the flea market. The family spends the greater part of the day shopping before they come home. Oftentimes the Reinas drive from the flea market directly to Mrs. Reina's parents' house in Marina.

Extended-Family Relationships

The Reinas have a very close relationship with Mrs. Reina's mother. Mrs. Reina, being the oldest daughter, assumes a great deal of responsibility for her fifteen-year-old sister and her brothers, also in their middle teens. Many weekends and weekday evenings are spent at Nora and Laura's grandmother's home. Laura and Nora play records and dance with Berta, their teenage aunt. At other times they play with the neighbors' children. Regardless of the activity, Nora and Laura recognize their grandmother's house as their house too.

Maintaining close familial relationships and meeting the obligations of raising two children require great care and time on the part of the Reinas. Mr. Reina states his viewpoint regarding his priority:

Aquí en este país tiene uno que tener mucho cuidado con su familia porque hay mucha droga y las escuelas no hacen nada para prevenir que los muchachos no usen las drogas. Nosotros no queremos que nuestras hijas se porten

así como esos Cholos en las calles. Así es que uno tiene que estar enseñándoles
lo bueno siempre.

(In this country one has to be very careful with the family because of the
drugs. The schools do not do anything to prevent these young people from
using drugs. We don't want our daughters to run around like Cholos in the
streets. So we always have to be teaching them what is right.)

According to Mr. Reina, teaching correct values to the children is the most
important function of the family.

Parents' Expectations of Children's Responsibility

The Reina children, Nora and Laura, experience a slightly different set of
expectations in their home from those experienced by the Islas children. Mr. and
Mrs. Reina feel that eight-year-old Nora should not have to do much work at
home since the one-bedroom apartment is small. During the earlier few months
of the study, Nora's tasks required minimal responsibility. The most that Nora
had to do was wash dishes occasionally. Because the girls were never left alone
without supervision, Nora was seldom responsible for child care.

Before the year of this study ended, Nora had begun to wash dishes voluntarily, although her parents expressed concern that she might cut herself with glasses
or knives. Her parents, however, did not require her to do much work around
the house. The most that was expected of Nora and Laura was that they not mess
up the house, or as Nora said, "No debemos de hacer travesuras" (We are not
to be mischievous).

A new job for Mr. and Mrs. Reina at Royal Industries meant a turning point,
with new chores for Nora: she had to assume added responsibility for Laura.
During the time of the study Mr. and Mrs. Reina worked opposite shifts on the
assembly line. There was a half-hour gap between the time that Mr. Reina left
for work and Mrs. Reina returned home. During this half hour, Nora was
instructed to stay inside and care for Laura. Nora, then, had to obey a standard
rule, that is, to come home without delay. When Mr. Reina left for work, Nora
usually called Yolanda to baby sit with her.

Nora accepts her responsibility seriously and when caring for Laura is strict
with her and expects her to sit still. Nora prefers Laura to observe but not to
participate in her activities. Consequences for failing to perform her tasks are
clear to Nora. Her father spanks her if she steps outside the apartment before her
mother arrives. In Nora's words: "Estoy aprendiendo a cuidar la casa" ("I'm
learning to take care of the house"). Mr. Reina admits, "Quiero que aprendan
a obedecer—si obedecen, les compro todo lo que quieren, pero is no me obedecen,
entonces ya saben que les pego y no les compro lo que quieren" ("I want them
to learn to obey—if they obey I'll buy them whatever they want. But if they don't
obey, I'll spank them and won't buy them what they want").

The Reinas's Views on Schooling

Mr. Reina's views. Mr. Reina expressed his disapproval of the schools in the United States since many children end up on drugs and are undisciplined after going through the schools.

[Mr. Reina—MR. R; Interviewer—I]

MR. R: Me gustaría que mis hijas aprendieran alguna profesión que sea decente. Allá en Michoacán una muchacha bilingüe tiene buenas oportunidades, por eso creo que voy a llevar a las niñas, pues toda la familia, a Michoacán para que ellas terminen su educación en México. Tan pronto como termine mi esposa en su trabajo y la desempleen, nos vamos. Porque aquí en las escuelas secundarias es un peligro para jóvenes. Las niñas pierden el respeto a sus familias y andan ahi como Cholas. Las escuelas en México son pobres pero por eso se aprecia la educación. Aquí [en los Estados Unidos] las escuelas son ricas, tienen todas las materias y todavía no pueden controlar a los estudiantes. No sé en qué consiste eso.

También en este país sufre mucho el mexicano. Trabaja y trabaja sin tener nada. El mexicano hace trabajo que ninguna otra raza quiere hacer. Es trabajo dura y siempre nos tratan como extranjeros sin ningunos derechos mientras que otros refugiados de otros paises entran con todos los derechos y oportunidades que el mexicano no recibe en toda su vida aquí.

(I would like to have my daughters learn some profession that is decent. In Michoacán, a bilingual girl has good opportunities; that is why I want to take the girls to finish their education in Mexico as soon as my wife finishes her job and gets laid off. Here in the schools, it is dangerous for young people. The girls lose respect for their families and they run around like Cholas. The schools in Mexico are poor but that's why people appreciate their education. Here [in the United States], the schools are rich, they have all the materials and still they cannot control the students. I do not know why that is the case.

Also, in this country Mexicans suffer a great deal. They work and work and still have nothing. Mexicans do work that no other ethnic group of people wants to do. The work is hard and still we are treated like foreigners without any rights while refugees from other countries enter with all of the rights and privileges that the Mexican is not granted in a lifetime in this country.)

I: ¿Qué es lo más importante que aprendan las niñas para que tengan éxito en sus estudios y en su carrera? (What is the most important thing that your daughters can learn in order to be successful in their studies in their career?)

MR. R: Pues hay muchas cosas que deben ellas de saber. Primeramente, deben de saber los dos idiomas porque el español no se les debe de olvidar. También las niñas tienen que estudiar y aquí veo que a las maestras no les importa. No mandan tarea con los niños; luego vamos a hablar con ellas allá en la escuela y nos dicen que Nora va bien y se porta bien pero que podría estar más adelantada. Pues cómo no, pero ¿qué esfuerzo hacen ellas para adelantar a los estudiantes? No tienen ningún control.

(Well, there are many things they should learn. First they should learn the two languages because they should not forget the Spanish language. The girls should also study and here I do not see the teachers sending homework with the children, and when we go to talk with them at school, they tell us that Nora is doing well, and that she behaves nicely, but that she could do more to get ahead. Well, of course, but what effort are they making to help the students get ahead? They have no control.)

I: ¿De qué manera pueden ustedes como padres ayudarles a los niños aquí en la casa para que se adelanten? (In what way can you as parents assist your daughters here at home so that they can get ahead?)

MR. R: Yo como padre aconsejo a las niñas pues ahorita no más a Nora, porque Laura todavía es chica, que trabaje en la escuela y que le ponga atención a la maestra. Yo digo que uno les debe de hacer entender que es importante que estudien. Yo ya no puedo estudiar porque estoy muy cansado y luego cuesta para dejar a los niños con quien los cuide mientras uno va a estudiar. Pero ellas lo deben hacer porque es gratis.

(As a father, I counsel the girls. Well, right now it is only Nora, because Laura is still young, but I tell her to work and listen to the teacher. I think one could help them understand the importance of studying. I cannot study because I am tired and it costs money for us to leave the girls with someone while I go to study. But the girls should do it because it is free.)

Mr. Reina also wanted his daughters to have a career in which they could work in an office. Such jobs, according to Mr. Reina, would mean that the girls would not have to work as hard as they have worked. This parent anticipated expensive education costs for his daughters and cited financial difficulties as a possible limitation on their daughters' professional training in the future.

Mrs. Reina's views. Mrs. Reina's views of the system were not as pointed as those of her husband, and she explained that she married at age fourteen and had her first daughter, Nora, at age fifteen, which precluded her attending much school. Mr. Reina, on the other hand, completed high school in Mexico. Mrs.

Reina believes that her daughters should not be burdened with household responsibilities since the children are still rather young. Mrs. Reina offers her views regarding school.

> [Mrs. Reina—MRS. R: Interviewer—I]
>
> MRS. R: Yo creo que deben de portarse bien y ponerle atención a la maestra, ¿no? Yo digo, porque no sé exactamente que es lo que deben de hacer en la escuela.
>
> (I think children should behave well and pay attention to the teacher, right? I would think, but I do not know exactly what they are supposed to do in school.)
>
> I: ¿Qué piensa usted que deben los niños de aprender en la escuela? (What do you think children should learn in school?)
>
> MRS. R: No sé. Yo quiero que aprendan inglés pero que no se les olvide su idioma porque la van a necesitar. (I don't know. I would like them to learn English and not to forget their own language because they will need it.)
>
> I: ¿Qué tipo de trabajo le gustaría que consiguieran sus niñas en el futuro? (What type of work would you like your girls to get in the future?)
>
> MRS. R: No sé, yo creo que algo que ellas quieran hacer. Mi hermana ya comenzó a vender en una tienda y le va bien. (I don't know. I think that it should be something they want to do. My sister has already started working as a salesperson in a store and she is doing fine.)
>
> I: ¿Le gustaría que Nora trabajara en una tienda como está haciendo su hermana? (Would you like Nora to work in a store like your sister is doing?)
>
> MRS. R: Sí, si quiere ella. (Yes, if she wants to.)

Mr. Reina has a wide vision of the socioeconomic condition of his family in the United States. He perceives his role as a parent as one of providing his children an environment that would maximize their opportunity to learn. He also sees his role as a counselor; respect and good behavior are the fundamentals proposed by Mrs. Reina. Both of the Reina parents value bilingualism for their children. Mrs. Reina did not express high expectations for their daughters' career possibilities, while Mr. Reina sees that it is possible for Nora and Laura to get white collar positions if they are well prepared by the schools. He sees that schools in the United States create more problems than they do good for the students because of their permissive standards. Mr. Reina has a clearer idea of the steps necessary to achieve the desired goal. Mr. Reina fears that financial limitations may be a deterrent if education gets too costly in future years. His theory of the process required for the childrens' success appears to be in accordance with what he has seen other Mexican girls accomplish. He considers the necessary financial and pragmatic steps that are needed as well as the consequences. Both parents recognize their literacy limitations as they talk about their role at home relative to their childrens' schoolwork. However both parents see themselves as helping the children practice self-discipline and respect. These behaviors appear important to the school success of these children and as a way of preventing association with Cholo peer groups.

SALAS FAMILY

Home Environment

The Salas family lives next door to the Reinas. Mr. Salas is a cousin to Mr. Islas. The Salases emigrated four years ago from a ranch outside of Apatzingán, Michoacán. Efrén, age eight, was born in Mexico, while Andrea, age three, and Maria, age one, were born in La Perla. They have lived in this apartment complex for only two years.

The one-bedroom apartment is less than adequate for the five-member family. Part of the front window was broken and a few months passed before the owner replaced it. A wall and ceiling damaged by running water and a leaky faucet inside the apartment also await the owner's attention. One month the building was sprayed for roaches while the families were inside. Roaches were literally dropping from the ceiling and falling on Maria, who slept on the floor. Only two broken couches and the television sit in the living room. A table and two chairs are in the kitchen.

Materially, the Salases have not acquired much in the four years they have been here. Their inability to purchase furniture may be due to the employment problems they have encountered. Often, both Mr. and Mrs. Salas are unemployed at the same time. Because they lack technical skills, they are limited in the type of work they can perform. Because their car has been broken down for some time, they are less mobile than the families with cars. These conditions prevent them from establishing more comfortable living arrangements. Because of their constant financial instability, their diet is restricted: beans, corn tortillas, and milk are often the only foods consumed. The family also cannot afford a telephone or a birthday cake for the children's birthdays. Efrén's birthday passed unnoticed because he did not tell any of his friends. His family could not afford to celebrate it.

Children's Activities

Efrén spends a great deal of time inside the apartment even when the other children are outdoors. He openly complains that people ridicule him because of his burned face. Three years ago a young playmate of Efrén's set him on fire as they played with matches. His face and parts of his body are badly scarred. Efrén also complains that Yolanda and Nora tease him because he does not comb his hair. Their conflict is ongoing because he calls the girls offensive names. Part of the time, however, Efrén is included in group activities around the apartment complex and on the street. He is extremely sensitive about his physical appearance and emotionally shies away from situations that prove painful.

Meeting their daily survival needs is the primary task of the Salas family. Through their efforts and those of Mr. Islas and other friends, the Salases struggle for existence. Mrs. Salas says she lives for the day that her husband's lawsuit, which will grant them money that is rightfully theirs, will be resolved. She already has plans to move from the apartment into a more spacious and cleaner house.

Parents' Expectations of Children's Responsibility

Efrén reluctantly accepts many of the tasks assigned to him by his parents. Since he is the oldest child, he must help to care for his two younger sisters, Andrea and Maria. Mr. Salas's work demands long hours away from home. Many evenings and weekends are spent playing with his band, "Venus." As a composer and singer in the band, he must invest a great deal of time in rehearsals. During weekdays, Mr. Salas works at a food-packaging company. Mrs. Salas occasionally works part-time in the same company as her husband. When she works the two girls stay with a neighbor and Efrén goes to school. When she is laid off, Mrs. Salas takes Andrea to Oakgrove preschool daily. The parents expect Efrén to help around the house by doing chores. Mr. Salas considers Mrs. Salas responsible for managing the home and reminds Efrén to assist. Mrs. Salas comments that although their three-room apartment does not require extensive care, cleaning up after the younger children is constant work.

Mrs. Salas complains that Efrén does not accept direction from her as willingly as he does from his father. Efrén undermines his mother's authority at home when he is requested to do a chore. She is forced to nag him before he takes action. Going to the store for errands is his favorite activity because he is usually compensated with a dime or a quarter for sunflower seeds. If Pedro accompanies him to the store, Efrén shares his candy or seeds, but he rarely accepts what others have to share. Sometimes the children invite Efrén to go to McDonald's; he immediately says, "no, no tengo dinero" (No, I don't have any money). Pedro or Herlinda offer to share their money and he says, "no quiero que me compren ustedes" (I don't want you to buy for me). If his mother overhears this conversation, she may offer him a few cents and encourage him to go. Eventually he accepts, but only with constant prodding. His anxieties about money persist up to the counter: Efrén insists, "Yo quiero algo que no cueste mucho" (I want something that doesn't cost a lot). He is overly careful not to impose on others.

Mr. and Mrs. Salas value certain standards for Efrén similar to those held by the other two families. Efrén should be obedient, respectful, and helpful around the house while sharing equally with his sisters' friends. Mr. Salas emphatically states, "Todos tienen que ser parejos. Que no perjudiquen a nadie. De desear más son malas costumbres" (Everyone has to be equal. Not to hurt anyone. It is bad manners to want more).

At times Efrén assists Mrs. Salas with dressing and feeding his younger sisters. The rest of the time he watches television or draws pictures. His illustrations show great artistic potential. Efrén complains that his sisters tear up all his work and that he doesn't have much private space. On one occasion he checked out a book from the library and hid it so that his sisters would not tear it up. He hid it so well that he had to pay late fees at the public library because he forgot where he put the book. Efrén prefers to be alone more than the other children. He stays inside, oftentimes to avoid confrontation with those who tease him or pick on him. The children (Herlinda, Nora, Yolanda) claim that they enjoy teasing him because he gets angry, but they like him.

The Salases explain their socioeconomic condition as a motive for training Efrén to help around the house, since Mr. Salas's work is very time consuming. Efrén is expected to be resourceful and learn to get what he needs. When he needs help with something he goes to Pedro. Efrén's parents encourage him to do his chores in a dutiful spirit.

The Salas's Views on Schooling

Mr. and Mrs. Salas's views.   The Salas parents feel strongly about the need for Efrén and his younger sister to learn in school. Mrs. Salas, however, expresses that she feels frustrated that Efrén does not listen to her.

[Mrs. Salas—MRS. S; Interviewer—I]
> I: ¿Qué es lo que usted piensa que Efrén no escucha? (What is it that you feel Efrén does not listen to?)
>
> MRS. S: Yo le digo que se porte bien con sus hermanas, pero a veces se enoja mucho con ellas y las hace llorar. Dice que ellas le rompen sus libros y luego él se los esconde y ellas los encuentran; y así se la pasan. (I tell him to behave with his sisters but sometimes he gets angry with them and he makes them cry. He says that they tear up his books and then he goes and hides their books and they find them; and this way they go on.)
>
> I: Yo veo que usted va a llevar a su niña a la escuela en las mañanas. ¿Usted ayuda en las clases pre-escolares? (I see that you take your daughter to school in the mornings. Do you help in the preschool?)
>
> MRS. S: Si, a veces cuando no estoy trabajando les ayudo allí con los niños. Voy a jugar con los niños con esos juguetes que les tienen allí. (Yes,

sometimes when I'm not working, I help them there with the children. I go to play with the children with those toys that they have there for them.)

I: ¿Usted también se ocupa en la clase de Efrén como con Andrea? (Do you also work in Efrén's class the way you do with Andrea?)

MRS. S: No, a veces sí me mandan decir que vaya pero no para ayudarles. Dicen que él va bien, nomás que tiene dificultad en leer por cuestión de que no se le entiende cómo habla. No pronuncia bien y le dan lecciones especiales para hablar mejor. (No, sometimes they send me notices to go but not to help. They say that he is doing well, except that he has a lot of difficulty in reading because they can't understand his speech. He doesn't pronounce well so they give him special lessons to speak better.)

I: ¿Qué tan importante piensa usted que es la escuela y educación para los niños? (How important do you think school and education is for children?)

MRS. S: Muy importante. Tienen que aprender todo lo que puedan para que consigan un trabajo bueno y seguro. ¡Ay!, porque como estamos nosotros aquí a veces ni tortillas podemos comprar. Ojalá que ellos puedan aprender él inglés y así se van ayudando. (Very important. They have to learn all they can in order to get a good and steady job. It's necessary because like we are now here sometimes we can't even buy tortillas. I hope that they can learn English and that way they can help themselves.)

I: ¿Qué tipo de trabajo le gustaria para sus niños en el futuro? (What type of work would you like to see your children get in the future?)

MRS. S: Pues eso depende de ellos. Yo no sé. Fíjese, nosotros nunca estudiamos en México porque éramos pobres. Siquiera mi esposo puede cantar y sabe tocar en la orquesta. Le pagan pero no muy bien. Y yo no sé más que el trabajo de las casas y en las fábricas así cuando me llaman.
(Well that depends on them. I don't know. Look, we never studied in Mexico because we were poor. My husband at least sings and knows how to play in the band. They pay him but not very well. And I don't know anything but housework and factory work—when they call me.)

I: ¿Hay algunas posiciones o trabajos que podrían conseguir los niños? (Are there any positions or jobs that the kids would be able to get?)

MRS. S: Pues con que ellos estén contentos y puedan trabajar. . . . (Well, as long as they are happy and can work. . . .)

Mrs. Salas did not offer any views about direction of their children's future success other than to state that they should go to school. Mr. Salas, however, firmly stated that he expected Efrén to learn to be a good person first, to share, to be equal and fair with others, then to pay attention to the teachers in school because they are there to help and to teach.

[Mr. Salas—MR. S; Interviewer—I]

I: ¿Qué tipo de trabajo le gustaria para Efrén y las niñas en el futuro? (What type of work would you like for Efrén and the girls in the future?)

MR. S: Pues para mi hijo yo digo que sepa hacer algo útil como mecánico o algo así y que se compre un tallercito para que componga el carro de su padre. (Well, for my son I would say that he should do something useful like being a mechanic or something like that and to buy a small car-repair shop to fix his father's car.)

I: ¿Cómo piensa usted que se debe de preparar Efrén para poder llegar a tener su negocio? (How do you think that Efrén should prepare himself in order to have his own business?)

MR. S: Yo le digo a mi hijo que se aplique y aprenda el inglés y que sepa las matemáticas para que no lo hagan tontón, y de allí pues él tiene que ser justo con otros. Compartir con todos. Aquí en la casa hasta cuando hay una naranja yo les digo que se corta y se reparte en todos. (I tell my son to discipline himself and learn English and mathematics so that no one can make a fool of him. From there on, well he has to be honest with others and share with others. Share with everyone. Here at home even when we have an orange I tell them to cut it and distribute it among everyone.)

I: ¿Cómo ve usted que va Efrén en sus estudios? (How do you see Efrén doing in his studies?)

MR. S: Yo nomás hablé con la maestra cuando nos llamó a su mamá y a mí para darnos el reporte de Efrén y nos dijo que tenía problemas con el inglés porque no habla claro. Pero mi hijo aprende bien y ya sé que a veces yo no soy tan fuerte con ellos como debo de ser porque si él quiere quedarse a ver televisión en la noche, yo no le exijo que se acueste. Luego, en la mañana, el pobre está cansado y no puede estudiar en la escuela.

(I only spoke to the teacher when she called his mother and me to give us a report about Efrén, and she told us that he had problems with English because he doesn't speak clearly. But my son learns well and I already know that I am not as strong with my children as I should be, because if he wants to watch television at night, I don't insist that he go to bed. Then, in the morning, the poor child is too tired to study in school.)

I: ¿De qué manera apoyan ustedes a los niños para que tengan éxito en sus estudios? (In what way do you support your children to be successful in their studies?)

MR. S: Aquí en la casa su mamá y yo aunque no les podamos ayudar con la tarea en inglés cuando la traen, mi esposa los lleva a la biblioteca para que escojan libros. Pero aquí en la casa hacen pleito con sus hermanas que están chiquillas porque le agarran sus libros. Y también tiene que sea bien educado, que le ayude a su mamá con las otras niñas y con la limpieza y que sea respetuoso. No quiero que ande allí como esos que les llaman Cholos que son flojos. (Here at home their mother and I even though we cannot help with their English homework when they bring it, my wife takes them to the library to pick out books. But here at home he fights with his sisters who are younger because they take his books. And also here at home we tell him to be well behaved by helping his mother with the girls and the housework, and to be respectful. I don't want him to run around like the so-called Cholos, who are lazy.)

Mr. and Mrs. Salas agree on the importance of education for their children although they focus their responses on Efrén. Mrs. Salas is aware of the importance of learning English and of being well behaved. Mr. Salas holds certain expectations for Efrén to own his own mechanic's garage and he, along with Mrs. Salas, encourages Efrén to go to school and do well, especially in English and mathematics. The father jokingly says that he should open up a garage to fix his car. This is realistic to the extent that Mr. Salas' car is usually broken. Their responsibility as supporters in the home is primarily viewed in terms of emotional and moral support, and to a limited extent, to act as resources by taking Efrén to the library. It appears that even though the school reports show Efrén to be experiencing difficulty in his schoolwork because of his speech, Mr. Salas has strong faith that his son learns well and will succeed. Mr. Salas admits to their negligence about getting Efrén to bed early. One of the strongest characteristics in the Salas home appears to be the parents' high hopes that their children can do something productive as well as be economically secure, and their faith that Efrén can learn and achieve. The parents place a great deal of emphasis on their children's cooperative and respectful behavior. They encourage Efrén to study in school and to overcome his academic difficulties.

CONCLUSIONS AND IMPLICATIONS OF FINDINGS FOR SCHOOL

The three families presented in this chapter offer diverse theories about the importance of schooling for their children as well as their views about the way they can achieve success. Each family has its own socioeconomic history as well as its own social organization in the family. Individual and cultural child-rearing techniques contribute to the parents' perceptions of success. The major points that we can conclude about these families are summarized here. First, household tasks, such as caring for siblings, running errands, and housecleaning, reveal the responsibility that these children are expected to learn, as well as the families' values or conduct. Second, parents expect children to work cooperatively with one another and to respect adult authority. Third, parents expect their children to do well in school by doing whatever the teachers expect. Fourth, some of the families shared specific types of occupational expectations for their children. The occupational expectations were beyond those met by the parents. Fifth, except for the Salas parents, the parents were unaware of what was required for their children to succeed, except that they all felt that learning English and staying in school were necessary for their children's success. Sixth, occupational success was seen as an alternative to the street culture of Cholos, which parents rejected. Finally, we need to recognize that the parents' folk theory of success is based on their own failure to achieve an integral place in society, their desire to prevent their children from experiencing the oppression that they have known, and to provide for their children a well-defined direction for achieving professional, high status positions in society.

While these families show a great deal of concern to maintain their cultural values of respect and cooperation and their Spanish language, we also see their urgency in having their children learn English and any other competencies that will lead to success. These families view the acquisition of new skills for their children as not only essential for entry into the work force but as a deterrent to the subculture of the Cholos. In the data, we see that their cultural values and practices can coexist with the new competencies that the school teaches.

These conclusions about the families' folk theory of success points us in new directions with respect to educational social reforms. A specific area of focus for implication is the fifth point in the conclusion, which states that for the most part, parents, in spite of their desire to have their children achieve, do not know the precise steps that they should take to advise their children about a particular career. Through parent education classes, these families can be taught facts about career opportunities for which their children can plan, thus allowing the school and the home to be more congruent in an effort to provide more systematic direction and opportunities for Mexican children to obtain successful positions in society.

Parents' folk theories of success provide their children with the necessary cultural values of integrity and discipline. It is the responsibility of the schools and community centers, however, to instruct parents, beginning in the early years, about the requirements of the system and the competencies that children are expected to acquire.

CHAPTER 8

Towards a Psychosocial Understanding of Hispanic Adaptation to American Schooling[1]

Marcelo M. Suarez-Orozco

This chapter reports findings from ethnographic research considering the psychosocial contexts of learning in bilingual classrooms. Preliminary findings strongly suggest that there exist important differences to be explored in the school adaptation of the various Hispanic-American groups (see Suarez-Orozco 1986; National Commission on Secondary Schooling for Hispanics [NCSSH] 1984; Davis, Haub, and Willette 1983). Indeed, I would contend that the challenge to the next generation of scholars working on questions relating to Hispanic functioning in the United States will be to systematically explore the finer distinctions emerging from careful study of the various Hispanic groups residing in this country.

In this chapter I explore, in the comparative tradition of anthropological research, some key issues relating to the school functioning of two distinct Hispanic groups: Mexican-Americans, that is, individuals of Mexican ancestry born in the United States, and recent Central American immigrants. Much research is now available on the schooling of Mexican-Americans (see below). Indeed, the bulk of research considering the problematic aspects of Hispanic school adaptation has this population as its source. Conversely, there is yet to appear a successful interpretation of the adaptation of more recent immigrants, from troubled Central American nations such as El Salvador, Guatemala, and Nicaragua. Yet the last five years has witnessed an impressive and continuous flow of immigrants from such nations to the United States (Suarez-Orozco 1986; La Feber 1984; Mohn 1983).

Below, I consider certain key issues facing these populations in schools and their different responses to schooling. I will explore the theoretical significance of these differences in the context of specifically juxtaposing two complementary approaches to the study of minority school functioning: DeVos's psychosocial model of ethnic adaptation and minority status in plural societies (DeVos 1980, 1982, and 1983), and Ogbu's cultural-ecological approach to the study of minority adaptation to schooling (Ogbu 1978, 1981a).

THE PROBLEM OF HISPANIC SCHOOL FAILURE

The problematic school performance of Hispanic-Americans has been amply documented in the scholarly literature (for recent overviews see Lefkowitz 1985; NCSSH 1984, vol. 1; Brown, Rosen, Hill, and Olivas 1980; Fernandez and Marenco 1980; Carter and Segura, 1979; Benitez and Villareal 1979). Brown et al. report that nationwide, Hispanics aged fourteen to nineteen are *half* as likely as non-Hispanics to have completed high school. They also report that only 34.3 percent of all Mexican-Americans aged twenty-five or older completed high school (Brown et al.: 22), compared to 67.1 percent of the non-Mexican-Americans in the same age group. Similarly, Knowlton (1979) reports that in the Southwest only 60.3 percent of the Mexican-American youth graduate from high school (compared to 86 percent of Anglo-American youth).

Maestas (1981) reports that Mexican-American children performed significantly lower on a number of achievement scales ranging from measures of reading achievement to participation in extracurricular activities. Ogbu (1983b:1–2) found in Stockton, California, that Mexican-American students performed well below not only Anglo students, but also below immigrant minority students, including Chinese, Japanese, and Filipinos. More recently, NCSSH (1984) reported that nationwide 47 percent of Mexican-American and Puerto Rican students who enter high school never finish, compared to 17 percent of Anglo students (NCSSH 1984: 10). (See also Lefkowitz 1985:2–11.)

Brown et al. (1980:68) note that although Hispanic and Anglo students nationwide reported spending about equal amounts of time on their homework, Hispanic students tended to receive lower grades than did Anglo-Americans. For example, only 3.7 percent of all Hispanic high school seniors received straight *A* grades, compared to 10.4 percent of the Anglo population. (See also Benitez and Villareal 1979 and Carter and Segura 1979.) In brief, there is ample evidence to cause concern over the problematic performance of Hispanic students in American schools.

Upon close scrutiny, we find certain heuristically important differences in educational functioning among the various Hispanic subgroups: Mexican-Americans, Cuban Americans, Mainland Puerto Ricans, and "Other Hispanic," that is, of Central and South American origin. Yet, I would like to emphasize that more research is needed in the area of Hispanic subgroup variability.

As of yet the record suggests that mainland Puerto Ricans and Mexican-Americans tend to lag behind Cuban Americans and Hispanics of Central and

South American origin. According to some measurements these differences are rather marked. For example, NCSSH reports that whereas nationwide 21.15 percent of Mexican-American sophomores dropped out of school in the year 1982, only 11.4 percent of students of Central and South American origin dropped out of school that same year (NCSSH 1984, vol. 2: 57). Likewise Brown et al. report that "Puerto Rican and Mexican-Americans had much higher non-completion rates [in High School] than the other Hispanic subgroup" (1980: 101). (For a similar finding, see Davis, Haub, and Willette 1983: 29.)

In the first phase of our two-year-long ethnographic research among Mexican-American students in an industrial center of Northern California, we encountered reports, similar to those found in the scholarly literature, from concerned parents, community leaders, teachers, staff, administrators and school officials: Mexican-American students were performing alarmingly below standards on a number of academic measures. As our research progressed, we became puzzled by the apparent fact that few recent immigrants from Central America at the school site shared the same problems.

The recent arrivals had their own specific problems and concerns, most often relating to the war they had left, physically if not psychically, as most of them remained deeply concerned about the fate of the relatives and friends remaining in the midst of the violence (Suarez-Orozco 1986). As the research progressed it became clear that the issues facing Central American immigrant students were quite different from those of our larger, Mexican-American, sample. This posed a number of important theoretical questions. First, are there indeed documentable differences in the patterns of school functioning between United States-born students of Mexican ancestry and immigrant Hispanics from Central America? If such differences do exist, what can they reveal about minority schooling and the problem of minority nonlearning in plural societies?

Armed with such questions in mind, notebooks, tape-recorders, and complete ignorance about Central American immigrants in the United States, I began the second part of my research. In order to explore these issues systematically, I conducted a year-long ethnographic study of the adaptation to schooling among recent immigrants from Central American nations. The research began with participant observation at two school sites with a high concentration of Central American students. After that period of about four months, excited by what the ethnographic record was suggesting, I began an in-depth study of the psycho-pedagogical adaptation of fifty students.

In the next section of this chapter, I explore certain key schooling issues facing a Mexican-American population in a West Coast inner city. I dissect an interactional sequence with tools borrowed from the work of John U. Ogbu and George A. DeVos. The complementary approaches of these two scholars are used to examine the structural *and* psychological factors mediating school problems among certain minority students. Subsequently, I turn to a brief analysis of the key issues facing new arrivals from Central America.

INEQUALITY, SENSITIVITY TO ENCOMPASSING DISCRIMINATION, SELECTIVE PERMEABILITY, AND SCHOOL FAILURE: A PLEA FOR PSYCHOSOCIAL SEMIOTICS

The following "key incident" (Erickson 1977: 61) was recorded in a fourth-grade classroom. It is of significance because it relates to subsequent developments in the classroom. It also illustrates the perspective that might be gained by relating macrostructural considerations (Ogbu 1974, 1978) to specific interactional sequences in the classroom to more fully explore the educational strategies of minority students with enduring school problems (DeVos 1978, 1980).

It was election day in the fourth grade. The children, seventeen Mexican-Americans, nine "whites" and two blacks, sat quietly at their desks facing "Mrs. Lark." In English she said: "We will now elect two people to the Student Council. I want you to think hard about the nomination . . . This is democracy, the election is very important and we all participate. I want you to think who is the most important person in the classroom to represent the grade . . ." Mrs. Lark continued, "Whoever wins will meet with Ms. Lomas [another teacher] during lunch to . . ." At this juncture she was interrupted by Mary, a monolingual English-speaking Anglo student. Mary said in a whiny tone [without first putting her hand up and waiting for the teacher to call her name, as grade rules explicitly require], "You mean I'll miss lunch?" She was expressing a certainty that she would be nominated and that she would win the election and therefore would have to meet with Ms. Lomas during lunch hour. Mrs. Lark replied in an apologetic tone, "well, you'll meet after lunch . . ." No other child up to now had spoken a word.

Mrs. Lark, in an authoritative tone, continued, "Election time is serious time [pause] and I want you to think of the most important person in the class. Then I want you to put your hand up and one by one say 'I nominate so and so to represent our grade in the Student Council.' "

Mrs. Lark then inquired, "Do I hear any nominations?" Mary stood up [not putting her hand up and not waiting to be called] and said "I nominate Mary K. [herself] to represent our grade in the Student Council." Manuel, a bilingual Spanish-English speaker, immediately asked, "Is that legal?" Mrs. Lark dismissed him with a sharp "Of course." She then wrote "Mary" in the middle of the black board.

Rogelio, a Spanish-speaking Mexican-American child with limited English knowledge, put his hand up. Mrs. Lark called upon him. Rogelio stood up and in his characteristic soft voice just said "Pedro," and not the required "I nominate Pedro M. to represent our grade in the Student Council." Mrs. Lark looked over his head and addressed the class at large, obviously referring to Rogelio's nomination: "the person has to be outspoken!", referring to the fact that Pedro is a very shy, very limited, English speaker.

Mrs. Lark then looked at Rogelio impatiently. He repeated very softly "Pedro." Breaking eye contact with Rogelio, Mrs. Lark again addressed the class at large in her more pedagogical tone, saying, "remember it has to be a good, outspoken citizen to represent D-3," for the second time implicitly vetoing Rogelio's choice. Pedro, who had been petrified at his desk ever since his name first came up, now turned red. He kept his head down and stared at the floor. Mrs. Lark turned again to Rogelio, who was now clearly embarrassed by the misunderstanding. She pushed him: "So . . . who do you want to nominate?" Rogelio turned red, dropped his eyes, and whispered simply, "no." Mrs. Lark wrapped it up quickly, concluding, "So you withdraw your nomination?" Rogelio did not answer. He sat down. The election went on, no other Mexican-American child was nominated and thus none was elected. Mary won the election.

Subsequent to this incident, Pedro and Rogelio remained unusually quiet and inactive for the rest of the school day. For example, an examination of the ethnographic record indicates the following:

1. Neither Pedro nor Rogelio volunteered to answer any of the questions posed to the class for the rest of the day.
2. Neither Rogelio nor Pedro volunteered the ever-sought-after task of passing out books or assignment sheets for the teacher, although such opportunity arose four times later on that same day.
3. In a subsequent reading period with Mrs. Lark they did not follow the reading but rather sat quietly at their desks and avoided making eye contact with the teacher as much as possible.

I chose to present this interactional incident as, in my estimation, it clearly articulates a pattern that recurs in the American classrooms I have been studying for the last three years. Rather than viewing the classroom as a mere mirror of society, I argue that the classroom can be analyzed as a stage, articulating and enacting various cultural texts that directly affect the adaptive strategies of minority students. In this sense, I treat the classroom more in the fashion Lévi-Strauss treats a Bororo myth or Geertz treats the Balinese cockfight; that is, as a "semantically layered" representational system simultaneously enacting a number of basic cultural scripts. In the previous "key incident," shared Anglo cultural fantasies of equal opportunity ("we all participate"), and concrete barriers are given form and life, at once displayed for all to learn. The "total lesson" is "this is [a] democracy," "we all participate" but kindly take note who belongs to the "we" category and thus gets elected for certain jobs.

John Ogbu (1974, 1978, 1981a) has pleaded that such microscopic classroom interactions be related to wider forces in the encompassing sociocultural atmosphere. Ogbu, in fact, advocates a "cultural ecological" approach to the problem of minority school failure. Ogbu argues that poor school performance is a syndrome usually associated with a specific kind of minority status, what he calls "castelike minorities" (Ogbu 1978: 11–42). Ogbu identifies castelike minorities as groups originally incorporated into a society against their will, who have been exploited and depreciated systematically over generations through slavery (blacks in the United States) or colonization (Mexicans in the Southwest after the Anglo colonization of the Mexican territories). According to Ogbu, these minorities were historically relegated by virtue of birth to the lower niches of the economic-opportunity structure. He argues that they faced a "job ceiling" above which they could not rise regardless of talent, motivation, or achievement. As such, education was historically irrelevant to their social reality. For heuristic purposes, these minorities are to be differentiated from *immigrant minorities* such as Salvadorians, Guatemalans, and Nicaraguans in the United States.

According to Ogbu, the two minorities differ in that castelike minorities must operate in an encompassing social context in which *there is a basic continuity in a long history of instrumental and expressive exploitation and depreciation by the dominant group.* This poses unique questions regarding employment opportunities and thus schooling. Briefly, castelike minorities traditionally inhabit the lowest-paying and most undesirable labor sector. Such minorities invariably reflect in their world view different aspects of the genre of depreciation. Or, to put it in slightly different terms, people know and are affected by the knowledge that they have been systematically depreciated for generations. Such "remembrances of things past," continued depreciation, and contemporaneous barriers to upward socioeconomic mobility permeate how people view their "place" in society and the role of schooling for their future.

On the other hand, immigrant minorities in the broadest terms "choose to," or anyway do, leave their original environment, presumably with the intention of entering a more self-advantageous social realm. In this sense, immigrants and castelike minorities differ in their earlier experiences vis-à-vis the majority population. Whereas castelike minorities came into contact with the majority population as a dominated group, immigrants chose to join a new social order. Such immigrants are obviously free of a history of depreciation over generations in the new social environment. This is certainly the case of Salvadorians, Nicaraguans, and Guatemalans entering the United States today. There is no history, not directly observable anyway, of Anglo exploitation and depreciation of Salvadorians, Nicaraguans, or Guatemalans. Free from such experiences, my Central American informants seem to have inebriating beliefs about the nature of their possibilities in the United States through education. Perhaps the most common quasi-formulaic phrase offered to me was, "En los Estados Unidos estudiando uno puede llegar a ser alguien" ("In the United States you can become somebody by studying") (Suarez-Orozco 1986).

Ogbu has suggested that castelike minorities such as blacks, Mexican-Americans, and Native Americans in the United States fail in school because school has traditionally failed them. Or, to put it differently, school failure may be understood as an adaptation to the barriers ("ceilings") limiting posteducational rewards in the labor marketplace. In short, the jobs requiring education have not been traditionally open to castelike minorities. Keenly aware of such posteducational barriers, many minorities come to view education as irrelevant or worse (see Matute-Bianchi 1985). That is, for minorities like blacks and Mexican-Americans in the United States, Burakumin and Koreans in Japan, formal education has yet to emerge as a viable instrumental route giving adequate posteducational rewards.

The research of Goho and Smith (1973) indicates that such a job ceiling continues to limit the posteducational rewards available to Mexican-Americans. They compared the earning patterns of Anglo-Americans and Mexican-Americans in relation to the relative influence of higher education in each case. They found that Mexican-American college graduates earned less money than Anglo-Americans with the same educational credentials. Furthermore, Mexican-Americans with one to three years of college earned only 10 percent more than those individuals with just a high school diploma. In short, formal education is not an investment that pays acceptable revenues to members of certain minorities.

Faced with such barriers, minority students formulate beliefs regarding schooling which are often in opposition to those of the mainstream culture (see Ogbu and Matute-Bianchi 1986; Matute-Bianchi 1985). Many adolescent Chicanos indicated outright that formal education was no avenue for them "to make it" in society (Ogbu 1981a:413–429; Matute-Bianchi 1985). One informant pointed out, as evidence of the irrelevance of schooling to the reality of minority young men in the inner city, the case of an older cousin, who was a good student, "always went to school," finished high school with good grades and was at the time unemployed.

A key variable to consider in discussions of castelike minority responses to formal schooling is related to the *expressive dimensions of exploitation.* This aspect of exploitation is a dimension of the problem which Marxist critics rarely bother to explore (see DeVos 1984). However, in the context of exploitation, the dominant group commonly dumps its "psychological garbage" on certain minorities, often to rationalize institutionalized inequalities.

For example, collective Anglo fantasies include folklore motifs relating to the hyperphallic, hypersexual, and intellectually inferior black; the lazy, dumb, superego-less Mexican, and so forth. More than once I was astonished when teachers articulated these and other folkloristic fantasies in so many words in my very presence. For example, one substitute Anglo teacher who had never before taught in a minority high school was pleasantly surprised when, during the lunch period, she returned to her car to find all four hub caps were still intact. As she said, "I thought the Mexican kids would steal them." Another teacher stated with some certainty that she expected a large percentage of her fourth grade minority students to end up in prison. Students do become aware of such attitudes. One student confided with some sense of frustration: "No matter who gets in trouble they always blame the Mexicans."

In such an atmosphere, minority students come to experience formal schooling not only as irrelevant, but worse. The traditional educational system, run by Anglos, becomes psychologically "a threat" to one's sense of ethnic belonging.

When schools become a stage for enacting the inequality and depreciation in the encompassing social structure, as our examples illustrate, success in school may induce what DeVos (1978:7–24) has termed a state of "affective dissonance." In such a context, success in school may be dangerous, a symbol indicating a wish to "pass," a wish to leave one's peers, one's ethnic group.

Rather than viewing the school as a ladder up the social stratification, Fernandez and Marenco (1980) show that schooling among castelike minorities is indeed *experienced* as one further tool of the dominant group to maintain the inequality of the status quo. Many times Mexican-American parents complained to me that the schools were not teaching their children, that they used the same outdated books year after year. Romo (1984) found that for Texas Chicano families, "Their own school experiences reinforced negative perceptions of school interactions and sensitized them to prejudices and discriminations. Of all families interviewed, Chicano parents expressed the most alienation from schools" (1984:- 646). In Lévi-Straussian dialectics, the narratives of these parents relating to schooling stand in binary opposition to the "llegar a ser alguien" ("to become somebody") motif I found among recent Central American immigrants.

THE PSYCHOLOGY OF SCHOOL FAILURE

Yet the persistent question is, How precisely do macro-environmental considerations, such as class and race stratification, and so forth, directly affect the classroom performance of a child? How do "job ceiling" and "expressive exploitation" actually affect a child's strategies in the classroom? What are the psychological mechanisms that in such cases govern learning and nonlearning in the classroom?

Recently, I outlined an approach to the study of the classroom that permits us to document the classroom enactment of the job ceiling and depreciation found in the encompassing social structure. This, and other recurrent degrading lessons enacted every day in the classroom (as well as in the media, the neighborhood, and in some cases even in the household), have concrete psychological consequences affecting the specific course of adaptation to schooling. Following the incident reported earlier, two of the dramatis personae avoided engaging in any of the subsequent learning tasks presented in their classroom. DeVos's (1980) model of human psychological functioning illuminates the dynamics of minority nonlearning. Whereas Ogbu's (1974, 1978) model addresses educational problems across groups of people in reference to macroscopic sociohistorical processes, DeVos's model allows us to cross over to explore the individual's ongoing reactions to such forces.

Briefly, DeVos (1980:101–124) suggests that human psychological functioning be heuristically conceived as analogous to the biological cell. Three basic functions govern the development of the human ego: (1) intake, (2) exclusion (or boundary protection), and (3) expulsion. These mechanisms are universal, and in their most primitive forms they have been called introjection, denial, and projection. More mature traces of these mechanisms are also found in well-adjusted adults. Intake develops into a mature capacity for empathy, exclusion facilitates concentration, and expulsion leads to a capacity to objectify thinking.

The human ego, as a biological membrane, selectively permeates the inflow and outflow of experience. Toxic stimuli are prevented from permeating the organism. Toxicity in the encompassing environment leads to an increasing rigidity of the protecting membrane. Learning in the classroom, as in any other context, depends on the harmonious functioning of this mechanism. In Piagetian terms (Piaget 1930; Piaget and Inhelder 1969), in order to achieve a creative tension between accommodative and assimilative processes, the inflow-outflow mechanism must operate optimally.

DeVos (1978:7–24) has called this rigidity a process "selective permeability." That is, certain stimuli will not penetrate the membrane. Repeatedly facing such pedagogical incidents as the one outlined in the present study, disparaged minority children in the classroom freeze their ego membranes, not allowing certain stimuli to penetrate them. In short, they "just can't learn in school." Or, they "learn not to learn." Analysis of ethnographic materials indicates that following such discriminative, toxic lessons, children become paralyzed, avoiding subsequent learning engagements. Of course, the children are learning a great deal. They are learning their place in the society. Children learn what is expected of them and in too many cases also learn to comply with the collective expectations of school authorities. What can a student learn from a teacher that expects him or her to end up in prison? Thus, the increased relevance of the peer group and the emergence of countercultural activities often further remove youngsters from the school's stated agenda.

DeVos's model seems to explicate the much-discussed issue of alienation from school found among some Mexican-American and Puerto Rican students (see Romo 1984; NCSSH 1984, vol. 1.). The research of Fernandez and Marenco (1980), Matute-Bianchi (1985), Ogbu and Matute-Bianchi (1986:111–142), also suggest that DeVos's generalizations apply well to key interpersonal relations facing Mexican-Americans in schools.

These scholars argue that many Mexican-American students view and *experience* the schooling system as a tool of the majority population to maintain the inequality of the status quo. Tests, for example are viewed by many not as legitimate tools for evaluating learning patterns, but as instruments devised to keep students at lower levels. Romo (1984) found a pattern of alienation from school among Chicano families in Texas. She concludes that compared to *immigrant* Mexicans, "Chicano parents expressed the most alienation from schools" (Romo 1984:646).

This last issue again suggests that there are heuristically important differences in the schooling experiences of recent arrivals from Mexico and Central America and Mexican-American students. I next explore certain key issues among a population of recent arrivals from war-torn Central America.

IMMIGRANT HISPANICS: SALVADORIANS, NICARAGUANS AND GUATEMALANS ADAPT TO CHANGE

During the last five years an unprecedented number of immigrants from troubled Central America have entered the United States (see La Feber 1984 and Mohn 1983). For reasons of space, I can only report certain findings specifically related to schooling. At two school sites, containing a total of over five hundred recent Central American arrivals, teachers generally agreed that, as a group, they were "good students." For example, the majority of my teacher-informants reported that Central Americans were more motivated, put forth more effort, studied harder, and earned better grades than black students. Also, teachers reported that the new arrivals were more respectful than either Anglo or other minority students. Less subjective measurements suggest that the teachers' impressions regarding discipline were accurate. For example, at both school sites the recent arrivals were grossly underrepresented in the numbers of school suspensions and other citations for disciplinary problems (Suarez-Orozco 1986).

The Central American students were learning English at a fast pace—so fast that in one school a teacher complained that they were kept artificially in English as a Second Language (ESL) classes much longer than they should have been, due to lack of space in regular English classes. The school's English Department had no room for them, so they were held back at a lower level. This was a universal complaint reported by the students themselves. The students said they wanted to take harder, more advanced classes, but the school officials would not let them. To give a single example, in an English development class of sixteen Central American students, nine students earned A's, six earned B's, and one student earned a C. The teacher pointed out that six of these students should have been moved to a more advanced level of English.

It was impressive to note the achievement motivation of recent Central American students. Their wish to learn, especially to learn English, and to do well in school, emerged over and over again in conversations with students. The teachers confirmed our impressions that the students were highly motivated. Five of my fifty high school informants went on to enroll at very prestigious West Coast universities. I further tested the achievement motivation of students systematically by means of the Thematic Apperception Test. These results confirm the presence of a rather robust achievement motive among the recent arrivals. Other publications provide a full report of these findings (see Suarez-Orozco 1985, 1986).

Ethnographic research among recent arrivals from Central America indicates that their adaptive strategies to schooling were indeed different from that of minorities with a long history of degradation in an Anglo milieu. Central Americans as a group are trying very hard to learn in schools, although many carry with them the tragic legacy of war and misery in their native lands.

For example, only 30 percent of my informants were in the United States residing with their entire nuclear family. Therefore, 70 percent (thirty-five out of a sample of fifty students) had one or more members of their nuclear family still residing in a war-torn Central American nation. Some, particularly the young men, were living with distant relatives in the United States in order to avoid military service and the war back home. In some cases, parents used their life's savings to send the children to the safety of the United States. This placed a particular psychological burden on these students: the motivation to achieve in school becomes fueled by a personal concern to help the less fortunate folks back home (see Suarez-Orozco 1986).

A peculiar form of guilt over parental or familial suffering (for making efforts to send them out of their countries) became intertwined with a need to achieve, to do well in school in order to repay parents by "llegando a ser alguien" ("becoming somebody"). Perceptions of opportunities not previously open to them in their homelands emerged as the new immigrants resettled in the affluent society. Many of these students felt psychologically driven to study, to take advantage of new opportunities in the United States, and to earn dollars to help their parents and siblings out of war and misery. A Nicaraguan student was sent to the United States to live with an uncle to avoid military service and the "contra" war. His less fortunate sister was drafted to participate in picking the coffee crop. His guilt over her suffering came up over and over again in discussions and psychological tests. After school he worked part-time to save money to buy her way out of Nicaragua into the United States. He received an $A-$ record in school during his first year of North American schooling. He applied to college to study computers, to get a good-paying job in order to help his family back home. He had no doubts that there were so many "oportunidades" ("opportunities") in this country that he would get ahead.

José, Estela, and Pedro had stayed in their native Guatemala with their maternal grandmother when their mother left on the uncertain journey to the United States alone, escaping misery and a drunken, abusive husband. Some years later, when she found sufficient security, she brought her children to be with her. When I first met them she worked as a maid Mondays through Saturdays. She immediately enrolled her children in school upon their arrival. She wanted them to become educated and one day "be somebody," as she put it. All three of her children made the school's honor roll during their first year of American schooling. The two boys worked a paper route before school each morning to help their mother with the bills. Their dream was to learn English well and enter a profession that would make their sacrificing mother proud of them and that would enable them to help her financially. These are the issues confronting many Central American students.

Free from a cumulative history of direct depreciation by the Anglo world, more recent immigrants from Central America can afford to take a more pragmatic view of their real, present hardships and marginality (political, economic, legal, and linguistic). For one thing, they view this state as temporary. They strongly believe that through study and hard work they *can and will* get ahead in this country. This pattern was also observed among newly arrived immigrants from Mexico (Suarez-Orozco, in press); in fact it may be part of a more general pattern that characterizes some immigrants in their adaptation to educational institutions in this country (see Ogbu 1983b).

It would be erroneous to assume that all Central Americans became "model students." Indeed, the new arrivals did face specific problems that interfered with their schooling. First, most of my informants (68 percent) worked, some full-time, while enrolled in school. They needed the money for their own subsistence in the inner city, as well as to send back home (see Suarez-Orozco 1986). All of those who worked reported that their job interfered in various ways with their schooling. Others were obviously shaken by the genocide they had escaped, yet their ongoing psychological problems went without professional help. As noted earlier, many youngsters resettled in the new land without their nuclear families. This is far from an ideal pedagogical situation. Lastly, some undocumented new arrivals did not pursue education vigorously because they sensed that colleges and universities would require them to present proof of legal residency as a basic prerequisite for entrance (see Suarez-Orozco 1986). Given these and other considerations, it is remarkable that 10 percent of my high school informants went on to enroll at major colleges and universities.

Keenly aware of the tragic conditions in their native land, recent immigrants from Central America characterized the American educational system as the *only way up:* "para llegar a ser alguien acá lo más importante es estudiar" ("to become somebody here the most important thing is to study") was a common phrase from the lips of immigrant students. As one parent put it "here in the U.S. my children will be educated, they will learn English and they will get a good office job . . . maybe even back home when the situation improves." Such values and anticipation may immunize students against the poisons of degradation they nevertheless encounter in the inner-city schools.

CONCLUSION

To conclude, a key implication for pedagogical reform of ethnographies in the "thick description" (Geertz 1973: 3–30) tradition is that, obvious as it may seem, not all Hispanic-American students are the same or face similar problems. At his return from a presidential tour in Latin America, Ronald Reagan remarked, "You'd be surprised—they are all different countries down there" (quoted in Diskin 1983: 15). He articulated a collective ignorance in this country regarding even the most basic distinctions between Hispanic Americans.

Yet, there has been an increasing influx of immigrants from Latin America in recent decades. If we are to formulate successful pedagogical programs we must sensitize ourselves and our teachers to the different social histories, present realities, and adaptive strategies of the various Hispanic-American groups.

This chapter argued that, for heuristic purposes, we must begin to systematically differentiate among the various Hispanic-American groups. A broad distinction, the one herein proposed as a first attempt, is to differentiate between those Hispanic-Americans who have experienced a long history of depreciation vis-à-vis the Anglo environment and the more recent immigrants. Then we identified a number of fundamental differences in the issues facing these two populations. We have argued that members of disparaged minorities respond to inequality by formulating conceptions regarding the educational system which further remove them from investing in learning as the "way up." Thus, we see the alarmingly high rates of nonlearning and school failure. On the other hand, the more recent immigrants from Central America considered in this study come to have great expectations of the American educational system.

The issues and strategies for coping developed by these groups are instructive to the theory of ethnic adaptation and the problem of school failure. The problems facing Mexican-Americans in inner-city schools are quite distinct from those facing recent immigrants from Central America. We have considered the psychological consequences of a prior history of Anglo depreciation over generations and further concrete barriers in the job market periodically enacted in the classroom.

Conversely, Central Americans are fleeing a situation of war and misery. *That* reality overshadows many of the current, real hardships and marginality (political, linguistic, etc.). For many, the reference point remains the tragic life of many family members back home. To their eyes, the relative advantages of life in the United States are self-evident. In this context they develop notions in which schooling emerges as the most important avenue to make it in the society, to in turn help the less fortunate relatives back home.

NOTE

1. A shorter version of this chapter was presented at the 83d Annual American Anthropological Association Meetings, in Denver, November 1984. I want to dedicate this chapter to my teachers Victoria Johnson and Donald Hansen, for their selfless devotion to the development of the next generation.

CHAPTER 9

Becoming Marginal*

Robert L. Sinclair and Ward J. Ghory

Youth who do not succeed in school become marginal learners. The strained relationship that they develop with the educational environment leads others to view them as deviant individuals, either temporarily on the fringes or more permanently out of the mainstream. The environment for learning starts to disconnect from these students who are having difficulties. As marginal learners, they fail to achieve full and satisfying involvement in the life of the school.

Too often educators identify lack of personal effort and weak academic potential as reasons that marginality persists and is seldom overcome. Yet, the assumption that the cause of the problem lies only inside the learner is counter-productive because it releases the school from the responsibility for creating an educational environment that reaches all students. In fact, the reasons for marginality often lie in the lack of quality in the interaction between the learner and the environment. We suggest that by looking closely at these interactions it will be possible to gain an understanding of why so many learners are becoming marginal. Further, we believe that this understanding is a necessary prerequisite for action that will increase learning for all youth, including those who have not been successful in the past.

In this chapter, then, we describe major sources of conflict that can create marginal relations with the school, analyze the sequence of events typically leading to marginality, identify various levels through which potentially marginal students pass, and consider the need for deliberate and constructive intervention to correct marginal behavior.

FORCES OF CONFLICT

If educators and parents discover forces that produce conflicts between students and the school setting, they are better able to respond in a manner that

*A modified verison of this chapter will appear in *Reaching Marginal Students: A Prime Priority for School Renewal,* Sinclair, Robert L. and Ghory, Ward, The National Society for the Study of Education Series on Contemporary Educational Issues, McCutchin Publishing Company, Berkeley, April 1987.

reduces marginality and increases learning. Our research suggests that four predominant forces generate conflicts between students and the school setting. First are contradictions arising when expectations differ between home and school environments. Second are tensions created when pressures of the adolescent culture are in conflict with behavior required for success in school. Third are frustrations directly related to authority figures and rules in school. Fourth are problems resulting from characteristics of the individual learner.

Contradictions Between Home and School

Parents, relatives and siblings—as primary educators—create a sustained and intense family learning environment that influences the young child's development. As school and adolescent cultures interact with the home, family members continue to filter and interpret these outside educational influences, mediating their impact on the older learner through daily actions. Parents retain a controlling role in selecting and orchestrating outside influences for their children. When families turn their considerable interpretive and screening powers to support and extend the social and academic priorities of schools, a compelling force for successful learning is in effect.

However, when a rift develops between the expectations from home and school, the learner is caught in the middle. Young people are trained in the home and in early schooling to seek and build on familiar aspects of their environments. They use established viewpoints and role models as touchstones when venturing into new emotional or conceptual territory. Although a degree of dissonance is important for stimulating problem-solving behavior, too much conflict between the messages from home and the lessons at school can leave the student uncertain over which set of signals to follow. At school, one's very language, appearance, and heredity can be subtly questioned or directly challenged. Styles of self-presentation, polished and rewarded at home, can be ridiculed and denied at school. The cues learned at home as signals that an adult really wants the child to stop and listen may not remotely resemble the cues a teacher is using. Parents' perceptions of a child's ability and their aspirations for a child's future may be quite different from the views of the teachers.

One type of conflict that can result when the home and school are working at cross purposes is illustrated by the experiences of Ramon when he was selecting colleges for continuing his education. Ramon was an above average student who at the start of his senior year ranked just below the top third of his class. His parents thought he was underachieving, while his teachers and college counselor thought he was working at his capacity. His parents demanded that Ramon apply to some of the top Ivy League colleges. However, in school he was told that applications to these schools might be a "waste of time." The counselor suggested that he apply to the state university to insure that he would be accepted. Ramon asked his parents to meet with the counselor.

The meeting of Ramon, his parents, the counselor, and a few teachers was a stormy one. The parents seriously questioned whether the school had been doing its job—to challenge an intelligent student. The school people held that the parents were expecting too much of their son. As the discussion heated, claims of racism were countered with claims of parental neglect. When the meeting ended, Ramon felt as if he had been torn apart, yet there was still no clear decision about colleges. Additional meetings eventually led to a compromise: Ramon would apply to one prestigious Ivy League college, two quality liberal arts colleges, and the state university.

Now Ramon had his turn. The dinner table became the battlefield, and the classroom became the retreat. Ramon told his parents and his teachers that he would no longer be a "spectator of his own life." Ramon refused to do homework and he seldom participated in class. Deadlines for college applications, which were rapidly approaching, served as a subject of frequent arguments between Ramon and his parents. The uncompleted college applications also seemed to contribute to lower grades and a general dissatisfaction with school. In short, Ramon's senior year was distinctly unproductive.

Finally, through prodding and assistance, Ramon completed the applications. He was accepted at the state university and placed on a waiting list at one of the liberal arts colleges. Eventually he was accepted by and decided to attend the liberal arts college. Fortunately, Ramon's experience on the margin was short-lived. Yet, for a time, he had felt that he was left alone to make sense out of the differences between the places where he lived and learned.

Pressures from the Adolescent Culture

Uncertain over their changing physical, emotional, and intellectual condition, adolescents are particularly susceptible to (and sensitive about) external attempts at direction. It is bewildering indeed to blend into one's personal style the conflicting influences of the family, the school and the youth-oriented media. Adolescents turn primarily to their friends for guidance. In small peer groups, messages from teachers, parents, and rock stars are processed through a filter of group values and standards. Many groups are remarkably stable and develop perspectives that influence members for years. To a degree, dependency is transferred temporarily from the family to the group, producing conditions in which a marvelous intimacy can grow from shared confidences, struggles, and values. The same hothouse atmosphere, however, can permit clearly marginal attitudes and behaviors to flourish behind barriers that adults find hard to penetrate. At the extreme, an entire "adolescent society" (Coleman, 1961) can operate within schools, diverting behavior into activities that conflict with school goals, and imposing conditions for recognition and respect that encourage marginal relations with school.

One case in which pressures from the adolescent peer group contributed to marginality at school involved a thirteen-year-old named Alvin. The values of Alvin's circle of friends could be described in terms of toughness, trouble, excitement, and autonomy (Labov 1972a). The group prized physical size, courage, and skill in fighting. Intelligence was gauged not in school terms—related to the collection, storage, and recall of information—but in street terms as a means of successful manipulation of circumstances and people. Similarly, verbal skills were honed through ritual insults, flirtations with girls, jokes, and storytelling—not through outside reading, assigned compositions, and class recitation.

When Alvin was first transferred to a different school, away from this group of friends, he was distant, fiercely independent, and quick to pick up the expectations and limits in the new setting. As long as he could work on his own projects at his own pace, he made gradual progress. However, when another member of the neighborhood group transferred to the same school, Alvin's behavior changed radically. Incidents of classroom outbursts, verbal defiance, and fighting escalated. Alvin's teachers lost trust in him. It was as though he felt obligated to demonstrate to his friends that he still endorsed their set of values. In the struggle for allegiance, opportunities provided by the school paled before the need to reestablish acceptance with his friends. Alvin wound up in court for assaulting another student, and withdrew from school, unable to connect.

Conflict with Authority Figures

Incidents of conflict over authority and power are probably unavoidable in high school classrooms (Waller 1932). Teachers continually exercise authority in ways that inevitably restrict and channel adolescent behavior. They set grading criteria, assign homework, monitor student attention and attendance, and inform parents of student progress. Conflicts over authority and power can be successfully minimized when students believe that the subject matter is important, recognize the teacher's ability to help them learn, and sense that they will be treated respectfully as individuals. But when the teacher is not clearly in control, when a teacher is incompetent, or when a breakdown in human relations occurs, marginality develops rapidly.

Jackie's dispute with her mathematics teacher is a case in point. Mr. Benthaus had been furloughed from the school staff two years previously but had returned for the current year to teach Advanced Mathematics to juniors. The textbook for this pre-calculus course was rigorous, requiring a great deal of elaboration on the teacher's part. While Mr. Benthaus had studied the topic in college long ago, he had never taught it.

Jackie had an average record in previous math classes and was taking this course to improve her skills. She did her homework and studied for tests. She also was employed four days a week and was responsible for many chores in her single-parent, working-class home. Attractive, irreverent, and quick-witted, Jackie was a social leader in most groups; however, the earnest math majors in this class were "not her type."

From Jackie's point of view, Mr. Benthaus was lax in classroom management and not knowledgeable in his subject. He tolerated but lamented tardiness, was unsuccessful in his bid to eliminate gum and candy, and was faced with constant off-task talking. Jackie indulged herself in all these pursuits regularly.

During the first quarter, Jackie constantly asked questions in class, worked hard, and was proud of the *B* she earned. In the second quarter she failed a test for lack of study time, but still was surprised and disappointed when she received a *D* for the quarter. She grew less vocal in class and perceived the teacher's questions about why she was not participating as badgering. Once she told him off in class, saying, "Leave me alone; I'm having personal problems at home." Mr. Benthaus had retorted, "Stop feeling sorry for yourself. I've got two jobs plus coaching, and three kids at home. Still, I have to be ready to teach you every day." Jackie was convinced, then, that Mr. Benthaus was not being professional, and was taking an inappropriate personal tack with her.

One snowy morning just before lunch, Mr. Benthaus was trying to hurry through a complex derivation that he wanted to complete before assigning related homework. Near the end of class, when he faltered, Jackie muttered, "Come on, bell!", a comment that cracked up the class and prevented the teacher from completing the derivation. Asked to remain after class, Jackie was assigned a detention for after school. But detention was called off because of snow. Mr. Benthaus waited for Jackie the following day, but she did not appear. When challenged, she said, "I'm not going to take your stupid detention." When Mr. Benthaus threatened to call her mother, Jackie retorted, "Try and reach her. She knows all about you, anyway." Then she stormed out. Mr. Benthaus avoided making one phone call, and, after two days, wrote an administrative referral for Jackie's failure to serve a detention.

By talking to each person individually and then together, the administrator engineered a face-saving compromise. However, Jackie's grades never progressed above *D,* and she did not continue with mathematics. The marginal status that had developed from a conflict related to authority came between the initially willing but average student and a difficult subject.

Characteristics of the Learner

A fourth source of possible conflict between students and conditions in schools is the individual characteristics of learners. We consider behavior in school to be the result of interaction patterns between individuals and their surroundings. This means, however, that patterns and qualities of behavior are due in part to the distinctive nature of a person. Physical and mental activities and attitudes of individuals do cause conflicts that can lead to students becoming marginal. Yet, in the positive sense, insights gained about the personality of a student can be used to restructure educational settings so that a productive connection can be maintained. Simultaneously, a plan can be implemented to correct characteristics of a learner. By working in tandem, individuals and schools can mesh so that students do not become alienated from the conditions intended to promote learning.

Conflict that can result from a deficiency in the learner is illustrated by Joan's experiences due to a learning disability. Her experiences during the first year in high school show how a proper link among the environment, the individual, and learning can resolve a problem in student behavior. Without this productive association, Joan's behavior could have been the beginning of the push to the margins.

In elementary school, the gap between her ability and her achievement became increasingly obvious. Teachers perceived her as an underachiever. In high school, she was placed in average-ability groups, and the expectations for academic performance were adjusted to her current level of achievement. Although Joan continued to work hard at meeting average expectations, she became unhappy with school. The challenge was gone and so were friends who were now in the advanced classes. She made new friends and received good grades, but a feeling of failure lingered.

The English teacher discovered that Joan's pace for reading and writing was markedly slow. Further diagnosis revealed that if Joan were asked to read or write within a set period of time the pace became even slower. The less time available, the slower her performance. It also became clear that Joan had difficulties with tests that were written on the chalkboard. Joan's oral reading was slow and jerky. The symptoms of her underachievement started to show, yet the cause remained a mystery.

Closer observation led teachers to the conclusion that mental activities and attitudes of this individual might relate to a physical problem with her eyes. As it turned out, her imbalanced eye muscles were in fact the major reason for her underachievement. When Joan became tense or tired, her eyes would wander out and she could not focus. Words would actually jump from place to place on the page and lines of words would disappear or melt into other lines. She would start to read or write and the words, in fact the total page, would blur and move up, down, and sideways. The messages to her brain would be jumbled. If she tried to speed up performance, the difficulty intensified. The imbalanced muscles also made it difficult for Joan to focus her eyes when changing her attention from one location to another. The eye problem, then, was a personal deficiency that had a negative effect on her performance. It simply took her longer than most students to read or write.

Steps were taken to change Joan's marginal status. She was prescribed proper lenses, and she did exercises at home to strengthen her eye muscles. Teachers made sure that she had sufficient time for taking tests. In some cases, Joan took an oral test to determine her achievement. She received special help in organizing for efficiency, improving study skills, and proofreading. The gap between ability and achievement closed, and feelings of success and satisfaction returned. Joan's eye problem persisted, but the educational setting was adjusted so that she was not relegated to limited learning and social dissatisfaction on the fringes.

The conflicts that result from contradictions between home and school, pressures of the adolescent culture, reactions to authority figures and rules, and characteristics of the individual have the potential for leading the student to marginality. By understanding the major forces of conflict, teachers, administrators, parents, and students can better ensure a positive resolution to problems that could be the beginning of alienation and reduced learning. Unfortunately, many students who enter into conflict with the school setting run a gauntlet of events that results in marginality in some form, eventually becoming a way of life.

SEQUENCE OF EVENTS

From school observations and discussions with marginal learners and their parents, we have identified a general sequence of events experienced by students who disconnect from productive life in school (Lemert 1951:77).[1] The events are all too familiar to teachers and parents who are working to form a productive bond between students and learning conditions in school. We are not suggesting here that all students who become marginal follow the same sequence of activities. Nevertheless, there is a pattern to the way in which students conflict with the environment and become marginal to school and home.

First Deviations

A student breaks or bends the rules, usually in a minor fashion, as a way of obtaining what he or she wants accomplished in school. For example, a student feigns illness to miss a test for which he or she is unprepared, or "borrows" a book on reserve at the library to complete an assignment at home.

Consequences—Assuming Improvement

When a minor infraction is brought to their attention, administrators and teachers tend to downplay or even ignore the problem. At most, light penalties are applied—admonishments, make-up work, detentions, apologies. The assumption is that the student will return to compliance with school norms. Most do.

Repeated Difficulties

The student attempts acts similar to the initial one, perhaps repeatedly, until caught again.

Consequences—Questioning Likelihood of Improvement

Stronger consequences are applied. Irritation with the student is expressed. The likelihood of improvement is privately or publicly questioned. Sterner warnings are issued. Privileges are withdrawn by parents. Teachers question the student's behavior on a regular basis.

Stalemate

The student seeks support from peers or concerned adults, usually expressing resentment and hostility toward the punishers or perceived controllers. For the short term, the student becomes more careful and avoids trouble. But the opportunity to repeat or extend the problem behavior eventually presents itself and is taken. The student becomes known informally as a troublemaker or a poor student and is invited by other students with similar status to be an accomplice. Often, wary relations between the school and the individual stabilize in a counterproductive stalemate at this stage. It is still possible for tension either to mount or to dissipate.

Crisis—Formal Stigma

An incident occurs in which the student's problem behavior can be clearly documented as extreme. A crisis is reached. Formal action is taken to stigmatize the difficult student, usually accomplished in a "degradation ceremony" (Garfinkel 1956:420–424). For example, a teacher may shame the pupil in front of the class in an angry scene. An administrator may suspend the student for a period of time so it is obvious to others that punishment has occurred. The shock value of this treatment, and the alarmed or disappointed reactions of parents and guardians, can often help the student to redirect behavior in an effort to shed the stigma.

Trying on the Marginal Role

Sometimes the problem intensifies. Rather than fight the stigma, the marginal learner accepts it, seeking peer support from others similarly labeled. Simultaneously, the student takes steps to avoid the painful source of the stigma. Avoidance behavior (tardiness, class cutting, leaving school grounds) is common. A few students drop out or transfer. Substance abuse often increases. But many students turn to a teacher or principal to complain about the way they have been treated (their way of seeking help). Parents may call the school to do the same. Intervention can still be successful.

Confirming Experiences

At worst, the school, the family, the peer group, and the individual accept the student's marginal social status. The student adjusts to a new role, striving to fulfill expectations for deviance. Parental and school incentive to help tends to decrease because of repeated rejection and lack of progress. Failing grades or continuing behavior problems become expected and tolerated. Rebellious behavior can be the student's final attempt to draw attention to his or her extreme position or to punish the people and places that have rejected him. These incidents "radicalize" the student, who feels a surge of power from temporary "successes" or hardens his or her attitude from the rejection that results. Expulsion from either home or school may be a culminating event that confirms for the student the fact that a serious problem exists.

If the agenda moves more toward compelling the student to "fit in," the conflict between the learner and the school will mount. Sometimes, as the school responds with increasing severity to deviant behavior, the student becomes less willing to meet demands for compliance. In these cases, it is easier for the student to connect with life on the margins, where there is acceptance of the behaviors the school cannot condone. The distance between the learner and the school widens as positions harden. The way to close the gap is unclear, especially if the school is forced by events to focus on minimum expectations and does not explore ways to create or extend possibilities for productive connections.

Principals, teachers, and parents often bend over backwards to find ways to short-circuit this series of events. Students who are becoming marginal receive a great deal of attention and account for a large proportion of administrator and counselor workload (Gulyas 1979).[2] These professionals "let go" only after the failure of many opportunities to foster improvement. Yet, the dynamics of these interactions suggest that successful intervention at each ascending level of seriousness can take place to alter the path that will take the student from minor disconnection to serious alienation.

LEVELS OF SERIOUSNESS

The marginal behavior of students can be considered at four levels of intensity, termed Innovation, Ritualism, Retreatism, and Rebellion (Merton 1938: 672–682). Table 9-1 represents the relationship between these levels and the

TABLE 9-1. BECOMING MARGINAL: EVENTS AND LEVELS OF
SERIOUSNESS

Levels of seriousness	Events
Innovation	First Deviations Consequences—Assuming Improvement Repeated Difficulties
Ritualism	Consequences—Questioning the Likelihood of Improvement Stalemate
Retreatism	Crisis—Formal Stigma Trying on the Marginal Role
Rebellion	Confirming Experiences

sequence of events involved in becoming marginal. The associations proposed here show the match between events and greater severity of disconnection.

As students move from the initial stages of marginality toward more severe alienation, it becomes more difficult to bring them back into the life of the school. Those who observe student behavior at various levels can determine the degree of marginality and the form of intervention necessary to reestablish a constructive relationship between the learner and the educational conditions in the school.

Innovation

It is not uncommon to experience temporary disconnection. The desire to do well often prompts students to take a shortcut and then worry about being caught. This is Innovative behavior, the least serious level of temporary marginality, but still a cause for concern. Innovators desire to accomplish goals valued in the school environment but see their path blocked by "legitimate" means. In response, they stretch the truth, search for an exception to justify their approach, or interpret closely the letter of the law to provide a thin cover for what they have done. Actually, a certain degree of brinkmanship is considered an appropriate way to test limits. For this reason, students who employ parental pressure to have special privileges granted, or who "brown nose" to curry favor can be viewed as negotiating limits to create conditions more favorable to their success.

Innovative behavior is more serious when individuals temporarily use illegitimate means, arguing that their end justifies these means. For example, students who cheat for a grade, copy homework, forge a note from home, purchase term papers, or deliberately plagiarize are expressing doubts over their ability to succeed in sanctioned ways. They represent as their own something that is not—the first split in adjusted identity, their first admission of a potentially serious conflict between individual and environment. Thus, those who clearly and repeatedly break rather than bend the accepted norms are considered to have a bigger problem. Their action cannot be dismissed as a normal outgrowth of independence-seeking behavior during adolescence. Nor can it be summarily squelched. At the Innovative level, some value is placed upon the creativity of marginal people in actually improving institutions. Yet, Innovation can also be the level where unethical professional tendencies are developed. In this zone of behavior, near the fringes of an environment, a fine line separates productive from destructive approaches. Still, the opportunity exists to teach principled action and encourage Innovators to practice it.

Ritualism

Ritualistic behavior is adopted by those who do not see school goals as realistically attainable or as meaningful to them, but who elect nonetheless to accept and follow prescribed means as the path of least resistance. These are the students who simply go through the motions with little expectation of success. They sit for tests but do not finish them; they regularly appear in class, without participating very much; they go to the teacher for help when forced to but seldom ask questions.

Ritualism is the realm of repression, a time when a false front of behavior is maintained because the cost of authentic behavior is seen as prohibitive. Ritualistic behavior occurs on two levels, superficial and deep. Since their overt behavior is institutionally permitted, their implicit doubting or rejection of school goals is accepted as an internal decision. Usually little intervention occurs to assist in connecting the pupil's real interests with school. Labeled underachieving or alienated, these learners are often treated with a casual indifference or "benign neglect," which confirms their attitude of passive endurance or their sense of the absurdity of the educational enterprise. These are the student satisfied with middling grades, especially if comparable to their friends' performance. They annoy their parents because they do not aspire for more and cannot say what they want to study or become. Indeed, because their deeper interests are not expressed and explored, they really do not know.

Many adolescents must work through this reluctance to engage. It takes time to develop confidence in one's competence to accomplish in the accepted way. Those who look upon themselves as nonconformists shun the skill-oriented, group-regulated school environment, which seems to allow only conventional opportunities for connecting surface and depth behavior. Yet, these adolescents find that the best way to be left alone is to conform by going along to the minimum degree permitted.

Ritualists are at a turning point. Prompted by consideration of college or work plans after high school, they may concentrate and improve in school—late bloomers, as it were. Sometimes, they endure until graduation with tolerable results. Later progress is likely. Others invest their attention in outside interests. For them, school is almost a cover they maintain while pursuing their interests.

Finally, some react against their own in authenticity, embrace as valid the way in which they feel different, then act to change or avoid the circumstances that are thwarting them. Once engaged, these can be the most thoughtful and penetrating students—or the ones most likely to enter the next level of marginality.

Retreatism

Retreating students are reluctant to maintain a charade of acceptable behavior. When they can, they reject not only the school's goals but also the means for learning available. The truant, the selective class cutter, the chronically tardy, the pupils caught smoking in bathrooms or hanging out behind the stairs—these young people withdraw to the margins of situations seen as increasingly absurd or hopeless. Their perceptions are generally confirmed when parents or school officials stigmatize and punish them without providing avenues of productive participation. They hold fiercely to their peers as preservers in a turbulent, threatening scene.

Parents and educators must concern themselves with students in retreat. Gradually, these individuals reorganize individual identity around the reasons for being deviant and can therefore become permanently marginal. Evidence of this change is found in the symbolic appurtenances of new roles—in clothes, speech, posture, and mannerisms that heighten social visibility and serve as signals to attract further confirming treatment either by peers who support or others who condemn. For these students, the way they feel themselves to be different becomes the most important element of their public identity, a kind of "master status" (Becker 1963:31–35). around which all other social expectations revolve. If labeled or stigmatized by the community, the students tend to be treated as marginal before other traits and strengths are recognized. Thus, their problem has a contaminating effect on their personality and life (Goffman 1963:2–9). Indeed, assignment to a marginal role can provoke in an individual a process of "retrospective interpretation," in which elements of a person's past are reinterpreted in light of the problem behavior (Schur, 1971:52–56). At this stage, the conflict between student and school has moved inward and becomes inaccessible to those involved in institutional, as opposed to personal, relationships with the student. It is critical, then, that steps are taken to create a more personalized setting if those in Retreat are to learn.

Rebellion

While spontaneous acts of defiance can briefly erupt and subside among discontented adolescents, rebellion as a level of marginality refers to situations in which students not only reject existing goals and means but create opposing goals and means. These sustained or planned efforts to strike back are often expressed in school-directed violence (vandalism), interpersonal violence (assaults), and repeated classroom outbursts. Since it involves considerable risk deliberately and flagrantly to challenge the school, rarely do Rebellious students act without a small support group of co-conspirators. Use of or dealing in drugs and alcohol on school property, political protests, arson or damage to school property, or assaults on teachers and students can usually be understood in the context of Rebellion.

Except in confirmed cases, the marginal individual needs group encouragement to overcome personal fears or feelings of revulsion and guilt involved in these acts. When avenues of participation in conventional activities are subtly or officially closed to marginal learners, subgroups bend to develop their own rigid code and standards of behavior. Group members feel pressured to repeat or extend the antisocial behavior that drew them together on the fringes of school. The danger is that an individual's behavior, self-view, peer relations, and formal treatment will all contribute to a mutually acknowledged, terribly constrained relationship with the school (Schur 1971:69–71).

TOWARD CONSTRUCTIVE INTERVENTION

Just as a wrong answer in class may be a clue that a student is confused and needs assistance, marginal behavior is a warning signal that alerts teachers and parents of the need to intervene. When a student is on the wrong track, it is not enough to provide the same learning opportunities as those provided for successful students. Nor is it enough for administrators to mete out punishment as the dispassionate and calibrated consequence of certain behaviors. Marginal behavior should not be read only on its surface. Nor should it be taken personally by parents or teachers. Instead, the behavior should be interpreted as a distress signal, a call for help from a troubled young person reacting to school conditions that are not working.

It is easier to hear the student's call for help amid expressed anger or rejection when the listener is aware of various forces of conflict and patterns of behavior associated with marginality. For example, understanding that a pattern exists, an observer recognizes cues that mark marginal behavior and begins intervention efforts with a sense of direction.

As parents and educators know, marginality does not dissolve in one conference or one confrontation. When educators recognize marginality as the product of a sequence of interactions to which their past efforts at control and their interpretations of behavior may have contributed, their perspective shifts. Marginal learners can be seen as people in difficulty who are reacting to unfavorable school conditions. They are young people making self-defeating efforts to form a stable connection between themselves and the educational setting. These learners, however, have adopted from their environment a set of limiting self-views that prevent their full participation in school. By rejecting, resisting, avoiding, or passively enduring school, they are searching for accommodation in an institution where they have not been successful or accepted.

The scenarios and sequences of events we have described do not have to occur. Intervention by concerned teachers, parents, and principals can break the cycle. Yet, the form of intervention must vary in accordance with the degree of marginality. Table 9-2 suggests guidelines for appropriate intervention at each level of marginality. The purpose of these guidelines is not to give a prescription for successful intervention but rather to suggest some ways for educators to engage with students who are not realizing their potential. Not intended to be all-inclusive, the guidelines are a way to get started when matching interventions with levels of marginal behavior.

Students who are Innovators should be encouraged to feel that they can accomplish what they want at school through reasonable means. When their criticisms are elicited, these students serve as appropriate data sources for considering adjustments in the way the school operates. Their concerns should be channeled into productive means of expression through which their ideas can be tested for their merit when applied to other groups and individuals.

For Ritualists, the key issue is to reawaken in individuals a sense of commitment to school and to themselves by building on strong concerns and interests. To develop confidence in their own competence, they require a series of protected opportunities for success. Adherence to minimal group standards (e.g., "just enough credit to graduate") should be challenged by expectations for developing a personal code of constructive behavior and individual standards of excellence.

Those in Retreat must receive direct attention so that they can resolve conflict at school. These students require clear limits and defined expectations. In addition, they need adults who will act as advocates and teach them ways to accomplish meaningful goals within the school context. The goals can include changing conditions in school that hinder progress. Trust relationships must be developed before marginality can be reduced.

Those coping with Rebels require forbearance and patience. They must be able to shift the scene of conflict by initiating "negotiations"; they should provide opportunities for expressing alternative points of view. Rebellion sometimes fades when personal goals can be accommodated at school, such as when constructive alternative projects are defined and accepted for credit in a classroom. Appropriate consequences for lack of compliance with necessary school rules can be stressed without responding to every symbolic act of provocation.

Schools and families are often judged by their ability to respond to deviations of students. In this sense, effectiveness is directly related to the ability of the school to intervene with marginal learners. Schools that best identify sources of conflict and levels of marginality are the ones most likely to intervene appropriately and reduce marginal behavior. That students are in the process of becoming marginal does not imply that they are locked in unproductive events. Awareness of what it is like to become marginal is the starting point for those who want to

TABLE 9-2.   INTERVENTION GUIDELINES AT VARIOUS LEVELS OF MARGINALITY

Levels	Intervention guidelines
Innovation	Stress common goals.
	Encourage ways to identify with the traditions and mission of the school.
	Clarify procedures and methods for requesting exceptions.
	Enlist innovators in projects to study or improve conditions.
	Formalize opportunities to work together for change.
	Offer carefully considered extracurricular leadership roles.
	Channel criticisms to constructive academic expression.
Ritualism	Set higher expectations and communicate a belief in the possibility of their attainment.
	Do not accept compliance behavior. Allow anger and conflict situations to develop when someone respected by the student is present to mediate.
	Connect student with an advocate at school who will learn student's real interests and strengths.
	Create opportunities to explore outside interests.
	Encourage long-range planning by constructing a plan of studies to complete high school, by visiting college, or by taking part-time work.
	Encourage private or personal ways to be successful. Do not force public displays of competence unless there is a high likelihood of success.
	Accept the student's concern to differentiate him- or herself from standards used with others, but probe to help the student develop his or her own code of authentic behavior.
Retreatism	Do not transfer the problem to a new setting. Change the environment by altering conditions to permit greater involvement.
	Provide formal and informal opportunities for counseling.
	Establish and enforce clear outside limits for behavior.
	Identify new programs or courses for the near future as something to look forward to once current responsibilities are fulfilled.
	Legitimatize outside interests and relate them to school.
	Monitor class and school attendance closely.
	Define off-limits and acceptable congregating areas on the school campus.
	Limit troubling peer relations by monitoring phone contact and socializing with certain individuals.
	Discipline in ways that continue to offer opportunities for involvement.
	Permit the development of surrogate parent relationships with teachers, physicians, or other adults.

(Continued)

TABLE 9-2. (*Continued*)

Levels	Intervention guidelines
Rebellion	Deal with the reference group as a whole through efforts to communicate with spokespersons. Trying to divide group loyalty only stiffens it.
	Punish acts, not people.
	Create ways for students to reenter once they have been suspended.
	Limit the spread of stigma by discouraging gossip and by restricting information about problem behavior to that essential for safety and security.
	Separate academic placement and evaluation from attitude and discipline problems.

reverse the cycle leading to permanent estrangement of many individuals from the institution designed for their learning.

NOTES

1. For an analysis of the sequence of interactions leading to marginality by a sociologist concerned with deviance, see Lemert (1951:77).

2. In Gulyas's study, 80 percent of those detained received detention more than once; 27 percent of those suspended were suspended more than once, accounting for 40 percent of the cumulative days out due to suspension; and, about 2 percent of the student body were habitual disrupters; yet, they accounted for more than half of the administrative case load.

CHAPTER 10

Social and Communicative Aspects of Language Proficiency in Low-Achieving Language Minority Students[1]

Robert Rueda

INTRODUCTION

One variable that has received a great deal of research attention related to the lowered achievement of minority students is language proficiency. As a result of this research, various investigators have developed theoretical models that attempt to link language and cognitive development in students who speak or are exposed to more than one language. In general, however, this work has failed to consider the possible effects of bilingualism on cognitive development in low-achieving students with identified learning problems. Further, theoretical formulations to this point have tended to narrowly conceptualize language proficiency and to ignore the social and communicative aspects of language. The purpose of the present chapter is to briefly examine current models attempting to link language and cognition in bilinguals in order to assess the potential for generalization, to low-achieving (mildly handicapped) students who have identified learning problems. Further, an argument is made for a broader conceptualization of language proficiency in research on bilingualism and cognitive development, and to suggest potentially fruitful areas for investigation.

The first part of the chapter briefly outlines general considerations regarding the relationship between language and cognition, and the following section briefly summarizes the results of the research that has been conducted. Finally, the implications of this work for bilingual children with cognitive deficits are considered, and a reconceptualization of bilingual language proficiency is proposed.

185

LANGUAGE AND COGNITION IN THE TWO-LANGUAGE SETTING

A Working Definition of Cognition

Since as far back as the 1920s researchers have been interested in evaluating the effects of speaking two languages on cognitive development and cognitive functioning (Mead 1927; Rigg 1928; Smith 1923; Yoshioka 1929). In that body of research, which has attempted to relate bilingual status to cognition, the dependent variable of interest most often has been performance on some measure of cognitive functioning. A logical starting point, therefore, is to specify what cognition entails. Although by no means is there consensus regarding the definition of cognition, a useful description, which will be adopted here for heuristic purposes, has been provided by Neisser (1967):

> Cognition refers to all the processes by which sensory input is transformed, reduced, elaborated, stored, recovered, and used. Further, cognitive structures supply the background ingredients for these processes: When we first perceive or imagine something, the process of construction is not limited to the object itself. We generally build or (rebuild) a spatial, temporal, and conceptual framework as well . . . In general, a cognitive structure may be defined as a non-specific but organized representation of prior experiences. The cognitive approach emphasized that recall and problem-solving are constructive acts, based on information remaining from earlier acts. That information is, in turn, organized to the structure of those earlier acts, though its utilization depends also on present circumstances and present constructive skill. (286)

As these structures are organized in the mind, they are transformed in some fashion and become experiences. One can see a direct parallel between this definition of cognition and more recent work, which has stressed the active role of the person as well as the role of schema in cognitive activity (Schank and Ableson 1977). It should be noted, however, that a major limitation on the attempt to examine either cognitive structures or cognitive processes is that they are not directly observable and are inferred based upon what people say and do under varying conditions.

Language as a Mediator of Cognitive Organization

Before considering the general findings of research on bilingualism and cognition, we will briefly discuss the role of language in cognitive activity. Early but useful descriptions of the specific mechanisms through which language may mediate or organize cognitive functioning has been provided by Jensen (1968) and Cazden (1972). These may include, for example, associations among words in a person's verbal network, the use of mental elaboration as a way of easing the cognitive demands of a task, or verbal cues supplied by someone else (instructions) or by oneself (self-speech) to guide one's action by focusing attention on a particular aspect of a complex problem. In addition, language plays an important role in more recent theoretical statements in the field of cognitive psychology (Schank and Abelson 1977; Lachman, Lachman, and Butterfield 1979).

A careful examination of the voluminous research literature that has accumulated in these areas leads one to the inescapable conclusion that, indeed, language plays a critical role in the cognitive processes involved in transforming sensory input, reducing sensory input once transformed, elaborating and storing this input, and finally recovering and using such input in the service of a problem-solving activity. It is the exact nature of that relationship, however, that has generated a variety of opinions. As Bates, Benigni, Bretherton, and Volterra (1977) point out, theorists in the fields of linguistics, psychology, education, and other areas, have provided different models for considering the role of language and cognition in human cognitive functioning.

It should be clear that there are many complex issues that must be considered in research on language and cognition. These become even more difficult when bilingualism is an additional consideration. The next section briefly considers the outcomes of the research that has attempted to look at the role that language plays in cognitive activity with bilingual children.

Research on Bilingualism and Cognition

The attempt to examine the role that the ability to speak two languages might play in cognitive activity has a long history in psychological research. Early reviews of the area suggested that bilingualism constitutes a form of mental handicap and appears to have detrimental effects on intellectual functioning (Darcy 1953, 1963; Jensen 1962; Peal and Lambert 1962), at least on verbal tests of intelligence. These and later studies suggested that this handicap might extend and generalize to other areas of cognitive functioning as well, such as academic performance (Darcy 1946), semantic tasks (Yela 1975), and Piagetian tasks (Brown, Fournier, and Moyer 1977).

The majority of these early studies have been criticized for methodological errors, especially the lack of control of variables, which could contribute to selection bias and render incomparable the groups under study. Commonly, groups were not matched on age, socioeconomic status, educational background, or level of language competency. In addition, instrumentation bias is evident in almost all of this research. The problems involved in selecting valid and reliable measures of cognitive activity in groups from various linguistic and cultural backgrounds has been discussed in detail by Cole et al. (1971) and by Cole and

Scribner (1974). Although the methodological and conceptual problems created by instrumentation and selection bias are formidable by themselves, the research on bilingualism and cognition is particularly susceptible to the interaction of these variables.

In contrast to the body of research suggesting negative effects on cognition as a result of bilingualism, more recent research has supported a modification of this conclusion (Diaz 1983). These effects had been suggested as early as in the work of Leopold (1939–1949) who used a naturalistic case-study approach to follow the development of his German-English speaking child. He suggested that the mental flexibility that he found in his child was due to the fact that the bilingual child has available alternative ways of perceiving objects and events. Theoretically, the child who has available more than one label for objects and events is able to perceive that the label is separated from the object or event and this, in turn, leads to the realization that language is an arbitrary and abstract tool that can be manipulated. A number of subsequent studies have supported the theoretical notions of Leopold with respect to improved cognitive flexibility of bilingual children (see Diaz 1983 for a review of this work).

In spite of the fact that there are some discrepancies in the findings of those studies indicating cognitive advantages, the majority of the studies suggest that in selected areas of cognitive functioning, bilingualism may have beneficial effects. As a result of this work, various theoretical formulations have been developed to explain this observed relationship. One is based on cognitive factors and is found in the "Metaset" theory proposed by DeAvila and Duncan (1981). The other theoretical formulation relies much more heavily on linguistic factors and is found in the work of Cummins (1979), which has focused on the need for tighter linguistic control over the ways that bilingual and monolingual groups are defined and constituted for research purposes. These will be discussed briefly in the following section.

BILINGUALISM AND COGNITIVE FUNCTIONING

A Cognitive Theory: The Metaset Hypothesis

In examining the relationship between bilingualism and cognition from a neo-Piagetian framework, DeAvila and Duncan (1981) have discussed the notion of conceptual disequilibrium as leading to the integration of schemes within the bilingual child's repertoire. This, in turn, is seen as the basis for cognitive development. As DeAvila and Duncan state, ". . . it is this capacity to integrate schemes to produce novel acts that defines intelligence or capacity" (DeAvila and Duncan 1981:341). This process has been closely linked to the notion of metacognition and metalinguistic awareness by the authors in their presentation and discussions of a "Metaset" theory of cognitive development.

This Metaset formulation is important because it represents the first systematic and comprehensive attempt to specify the characteristics of the bilingual experience which might account for specific differences. It must be kept in mind, however, that Vygotsky's (1962, 1978) theoretical model, which intricately links language (and social interaction) and cognition, provides a firm basis for predicting cognitive advantages for bilinguals. Nevertheless, the Metaset formulation was developed specifically with the bilingual in mind.

The Threshold Hypothesis and Proficiency

In an attempt to identify more specifically the relationship between cognition and bilingualism, Cummins (1979) has proposed an interactive theoretical framework. Specifically, children who achieve "balanced proficiency" in two languages (but who are immersed in a bilingual environment) are cognitively disadvantaged in comparison to monolingual and balanced proficient bilinguals. As Cummins stated, ". . . there may be threshold levels of linguistic competency which a bilingual child must attain, both in order to avoid cognitive disadvantages and to allow the potentially beneficial aspects of bilingualism to influence his cognitive and academic functioning" (Cummins 1978:1). "In this framework, there are minimal levels of linguistic competence, in both a child's home language and in his second language . . . which bilingual children must attain in order to avoid cognitive deficits in their cognitive growth" (Cummins 1979:222).

This formulation quite clearly presents most directly the shift away from a disadvantaged perspective (Darcy 1953, 1963) to an advantaged perspective while at the same time continuing to consider the potential negative influence of bilingualism (unbalanced). This interaction position attempts to account for the success of Canadian-French-immersion bilingual programs for English-speaking children and the failure of English-immersion programs for Spanish-speaking children in the United States.

It should be noted that Cummins's theoretical framework has drawn criticism due to its linguistically questionable use of the notion of "semilingualism," which is equated with the lower threshold levels of linguistic competence (Baral, 1980). It has also been challenged on logical grounds by McNab (1979), who has argued that the increased cognitive performance of proficient bilinguals is due to the possibility that the more intelligent bilinguals are those who become proficient. In spite of these criticisms, the need for tighter linguistic control in studies of bilingualism and cognition is evident, and, in fact, lack of attention to this variable may account for some of the discrepancies in the research literature.

Although Cummins's hypothesis has proved very useful in the interpretation of discrepancies in the research and has drawn attention to the role of relative language proficiency, it has not gone without challenge. For example, based upon data from kindergarten and first grade children just beginning to learn a second language, Diaz (1984) has suggested that the degree of bilingualism is related to variability in cognitive performance only *before* a certain threshold of proficiency is attained and not after, as suggested by Cummins. At any rate, both Cummins's formulation and the Metaset theory have influenced research and educational practice; more important, there are important implications for bilingual low-achieving or mildly handicapped children, as will be seen shortly.

In sum, current theory proposes that certain features of the bilingual environment (notably those involved with fostering cognitive disequilibrium) may tend to accrue positive cognitive effects for the bilingual child. Further, it is suggested that a threshold level of language proficiency is necessary for the attainment of these cognitive outcomes. Largely unexamined in the literature is the language-cognition relationship in bilingual children when anomalous cognitive development may be involved. Further, the conceptualization of proficiency in the preceding models has tended to be narrow. Based upon the analysis of the research and theoretical positions just reviewed, these issues will be considered in the following paragraphs.

Bilingualism and Cognition in Mildly Handicapped Children

As a review of the literature indicates, there are few if any reports of empirical research with exceptional children which have attempted to examine the issue of bilingualism. There are even fewer that have attempted to link linguistic and cognitive behavior in this population. One set of early studies has examined the success of early French immersion programs for language-disabled children (Bruck, Rabinovich, and Oates 1975; Bruck 1978). In the earlier study, children with and without language problems were identified in English and in French immersion kindergarten classes and were closely monitored to the end of grade three. Although the language-delayed children experienced slightly more difficulties in grade two (possibly due to the introduction of English reading), by the end of grade three they were achieving at expected levels and suffered no harmful effects.

In the second study, Bruck monitored another group of students from kindergarten through third grade in the areas of second-language skills, cognitive development, and academic achievement. Language of instruction and presence of handicap were crossed to constitute the four groups for study. Even though the language-disordered children experienced delays, those language-disordered children who were in an immersion setting progressed academically comparably to a control group.

Although the previous study is important as an early attempt to study bilingual exceptional students, only subjects without obvious intellectual problems were included. For this reason the potential for generalization, of results became more difficult. As presently structured, there exists a large number of handicapping conditions within the realm of special education research. In this regard, Rondal (in press), for example, has discussed the need to consider mildly handicapped students separately from those more impaired. In support of this recommendation, there is general consensus regarding the similarity and overlap among those students commonly referred to as mildly handicapped (e.g., mildly mentally retarded and learning disabled). However, even with respect to this relatively homogenous grouping, some have asserted that there are distinguishable cognitive processing differences (e.g., Hall 1980:101). Until more specific information is available, therefore, the interpretation of research such as this, especially with respect to possible generalization, needs to be guided by caution. Keeping this point in mind, we find that an examination of the literature dealing with bilingual children leads to an interesting paradox in the case of mildly handicapped children with cognitive and learning difficulties. This issue will be briefly discussed in the following section.

Bilingualism and Cognitive Deficits

As has been seen earlier, bilinguals might be expected to have a headstart in certain cognitive areas such as an understanding of the arbitrary uses of language, cognitive flexibility, and so forth. As DeAvila and Duncan (1981) suggest, this is a key aspect of metacognition. Mildly handicapped children who are also bilingual represent a theoretically interesting population for study with regard to this last point.

It has been demonstrated that one area of particular difficulty for mentally retarded and other mildly handicapped learners is the appropriate use of strategic behavior (Hallahan 1980). It has been suggested that this deficit is related to metacognitive awareness and skills (Campione and Brown 1977). However, in the case of bilinguals, it has also been suggested, from a separate body of research, that improved cognitive awareness and understanding might be expected. Although this represents an apparent contradiction, it has received little attention thus far.

One recent study examined the cognitive performance (on a metalinguistic measure and a Piagetian measure) of mildly retarded children with moderate levels of language proficiency in Spanish and English in comparison to a matched group of monolingual children (Rueda 1983). In spite of the limitations of the study (small sample sizes, only moderate proficiency on the part of the bilingual subjects, and no independent measure of the language skills of the monolingual sample), it was found that the bilingual group did not suffer any harmful effects as a result of being bilingual. In fact, there were differences in favor of the bilingual group on some of the metalinguistic items. However, the differences on the Piagetian measure were not significant.

Although recent authors have called for more empirical studies in this area (Baca and Cervantes 1984; Omark and Erickson 1983; Cummins 1984), it is evident that a comprehensive research base is lacking. Therefore, the final section of this study will address the implications of the research that has been discussed to this point and will then move on to suggest directions for future research.

IMPLICATIONS FOR MILDLY HANDICAPPED LEARNERS

The Language of Instruction

At the simplest level, it is possible to speculate from the available research with bilingual children who are nonhandicapped, that if all other factors are equal, mildly handicapped bilinguals might experience some cognitive advantages in comparison to monolingual peers. This possibility raises a host of educationally relevant questions. For example, should bilingual education be considered an alternative for mentally retarded children? Is it possible to argue that mentally retarded children have a difficult enough time acquiring and thinking in one language, and, therefore, that such programs should not be considered? On the other hand, if indeed there are cognitive advantages to be gained from exposure to two languages, perhaps students in this group should have available the option of this potentially remedial tool in conjunction with other interventions.

A quote from a recent paper by Rondal (in press) has highlighted some of the issues involved:

> Several questions may be asked: When bilingualism is not imposed by the living conditions of the family is it advisable to engage mentally handicapped children in second language learning? Could they benefit cognitively from a prolonged bilingual exposure? In those situations where bilingualism is a fact of life, how should one proceed with the retarded child? When it is preferable to start second language learning and exposure, how much of the second language is the handicapped child capable to learn? How much can he take in at a time? What about possible negative interferences between first and second language learning, and so forth?

With reference to the issue of second language training with the mentally retarded, Rondal draws as a basis the threshold competence level proposition of Cummins and notes that most immersion programs begin at around five years of age. The rationale behind this, as he notes, is that most normally developing children by about age five reach the level in first language development where they are able to make rapid progress in second language learning at minimal cost to their native language and to benefit cognitively and academically from an immersion program. Reasoning that this same developmental level transposed with mildly mentally retarded children would equal a chronological age of eight or nine, he recommends this as an acceptable age to begin second language training with this group of students. It should be noted that an important assumption behind this recommendation is the equivalence of speech and language development in mentally retarded and other mildly handicapped) children and normally achieving children, that is, that the process is similar but delayed.

This last point makes problematic the same recommendation for the more severely retarded and others who may not develop the language skills of normally achieving children until late adolescence, if at all. Of course, it must be recognized that some children are exposed to two languages by necessity as a normal course of their daily environments. In such cases, Rondal suggests teaching a limited number of functional vocabulary items and simple idiomatic structures. This appears to be consistent with recent approaches to second language instruction which emphasize language as a functional, communicative system (e.g., Krashen 1982a; Krashen, Long, and Scarcella 1982).

It should be clear that there are wide gaps in the empirical research as well as in the norms of educational practice. Further definitive statements on the applicability of current theoretical and educational models must be deferred until a more comprehensive literature exists.

Contextual Variability of Behavior

In analyzing the research that has attempted to link the domains of language and cognition in bilinguals, we find that it is evident that up to this point little attention has been paid to examining the effects of contextual variation on the behaviors measured. Nevertheless, there are important theoretical and methodological reasons for doing so. For example, there is evidence from both the cognitive domains (Cole et al. 1971; Mercer 1973) and the linguistic domains (Labov 1972b) that minority children exhibit surprising differences in school-like or test-like situations as opposed to less constrained everyday contexts. In a recent paper, Rueda and Mehan (in press) discuss the strategic behavior of a learning disabled child in out-of-school settings in his attempts to disguise an inability to read. In spite of this, virtually all of the cognitive research on bilinguals and handicapped students is either laboratory-based or based on constrained laboratory-type tasks. Failure to take this diversity into account may lead to inaccurate judgments about the ability levels of a given child if they are the only or primary data sources. The potential impact of inaccurate judgments at this level on both the development of theory and educational practice need to be seriously considered (cf. Erickson 1984, who has reviewed these same issues with respect to school literacy).

The Complexity of Language Proficiency

An important development within the domain of language research is the increased attention on the functional aspects and naturalistic uses of language in diverse settings (Briere 1979; Rivera 1983; Simich-Dudgeon and Rivera 1983; Wallat 1984). The recognition of language as a complex, functional system is illustrated in a model proposed by Canale and Swain (1980) which includes the following:

1. *Grammatical competence:* mastery of the language code (verbal or non-verbal), thus concerned with such features as lexical items and rules of sentence formation, pronunciation, and literal meaning.
2. *Sociolinguistic competence:* mastery of appropriate language use in different sociolinguistic contexts, with emphasis on appropriateness of meanings and appropriateness of forms.
3. *Discourse competence:* mastery of how to combine and interpret forms and meanings to achieve a unified spoken or written text in different genres.
4. *Strategic competence:* mastery of verbal and nonverbal strategies to compensate for breakdowns in communication and to enhance the effectiveness of communication.

Similar attempts to consider various components of language proficiency are found in Cummins (1980), where a distinction is proposed between Cognitive Academic Linguistic Proficiency (CALP) and Basic Interpersonal Communication Skills (BICS) as separate aspects of language proficiency.

It should be noted that the model proposed by Cummins, although useful from both a theoretical and practical perspective, has not been free of criticism (see for example, Rivera 1984a, in which this issue is addressed). At any rate, this conceptualization is useful from a research perspective since it takes into account situational factors and task-related factors.

It appears that at present the majority of data available on bilingual children is based on performance on standardized language-assessment and intellectual-assessment instruments, which are primarily context-reduced, cognitively demanding tasks. More important, virtually no information exists on the functional language behavior in naturalistic contexts of bilingual children with handicapping conditions. Although most of the theory and research thus far has taken place in the "context reduced" and "cognitively demanding" types of contexts, recent research has begun to emphasize communicative competence, or language as a social tool to accomplish everyday needs (Gumperz and Hymes 1972; Shatz and Gelman 1973; D'Anglejan and Tucker 1973; Erickson and Omark 1981; Seidner 1981; Rivera 1983, 1984a, 1984b; Ramirez 1984). Currently, however, little is known about the various aspects of linguistic proficiency, especially with respect to how they relate to cognitive development, learning, and school achievement.

Cognitive Consequences of Bilingualism

Major developmental theorists such as Piaget and Vygotsky, as well as other researchers (Cole, Dore, Hall, and Dowley 1978; Halliday 1975, 1978; Hymes

1974), have emphasized language as a critical social repertoire. The social roots of language carry special importance for the bilingual child where social tasks include tasks such as choice of language for interaction or the need to differentially employ linguistic codes determined by the social attributes of the speaking contexts (Philips 1972). An important hypothesis regarding this aspect of bilingualism is the general notion that the bilingual environment is qualitatively different from the monolingual environment.

One unexplored avenue of investigation with respect to this last point centers on the link between functional and social aspects of the communication skills of bilingual handicapped children and various cognitive outcomes. An unanswered but important theoretical question is the contribution of communicative and social competence (in contrast with competence in the structural aspects of the language) to cognitive development. For example, it is possible for students to be proficient in the social skills inherent in bilingual environments while not having mastered "correct" form (somewhat the opposite of adults learning a foreign language in another country). That is, a child might display communicative competence without having mastered all the structural aspects of a language, such as grammar, sentence structure, and so forth. Such a child could code-switch appropriately, take into account audience, topic, setting, and so forth, and still score low on a measure of language proficiency.[2] Although no empirical data are available, it is possible that many handicapped bilinguals fall into this category.

As an earlier part of the study suggested, one of the central theoretical notions used to explain the positive effects of bilingualism has been based on the fact that the child has access to more than one linguistic code. For example, he or she learns that there is more than one word for the same object and comes to the realization that language is an arbitrary tool that can be manipulated, leading to metalinguistic awareness and cognitive flexibility. Additionally, the disequilibrium experienced by the bilingual child in his or her environment, and the resulting formation of new schemata has been hypothesized to lead to improved cognitive performance. It can be argued that competence in the social and communicative aspects of bilingual interaction, even in the absence of well-developed grammatical competence, might facilitate the same effects. A child in this situation might be considered nonproficient based on standardized assessment data, but should still experience the type of disequilibrium hypothesized to lead to certain cognitive effects.

Although the relationship between the various types of language proficiency and achievement remains largely unexplored, the issue is receiving increasing attention (Canale 1984). One recent attempt to separate linguistic competence ("mastery of the sound system, semantics and basic structural patterns of a language") from communicative competence ("ability to adapt the totality of one's communicative resources, both linguistic and functional, to a given situation") and to relate each to achievement was reported by Ramirez (1984). A discrete-point language assessment measure was employed to assess linguistic competence (the BOLT, or Bahia Oral Language Test). This test is a twenty-item measure designed to assess certain specific linguistic structures at various levels of complexity. The assessment of communicative competence included the domains of Active Communicative Competence (transmitting information, giving directions, giving instructions, and giving descriptions), Receptive Communicative Competence (following directions on a map, filling out a standardized form, and following instructions by underlining and circling words in a written text), and Sociolinguistic Competence (the ability to recognize speech acts as part of a discrete-item word test). Finally, the measures of achievement used in the study were standardized achievement test scores (California Achievement Test [CAT] or Comprehensive Test of Basic Skills [CTBS]) or the number of district-based competencies passed before graduation. Although the results varied by the ages of the students and by school site, there were interesting positive relationships between the measures of communicative proficiency and academic functioning.

In sum, the theoretical explanations that have been used to account for the positive effects of bilingualism on cognitive development can be used to predict similar outcomes for the child who is communicatively competent though not "proficient." This is important in light of the fact that "balanced" bilinguals are rare in practice and are most likely even rarer among handicapped students. The preceding study at least suggests that this issue requires more systematic attention than it has been given in the past. Especially in light of the negative political, social, and educational implications that are equated with terms such as "semilingual," "disadvantaged," "language impoverished," and so forth, it is important to sort out the independent effects of various aspects of bilingualism on cognitive functioning.

CONCLUSION

The emphasis on the social and communicative aspects in the conceptualization of bilingualism makes it apparent that many previous investigators have failed to differentiate these aspects as dimensions of bilingual skill separate from linguistic proficiency. For example, the ways in which bilingual subjects are selected most often are based only on measures of structural linguistic proficiency, with no separate consideration of communicative competence as an integral part of the relationship between language and cognition. In addition, the research suggests that little is known about the specific mechanisms through which bilingual experiences influence cognition.

Durán (1983) has discussed the potentially valuable contribution of an information-processing theory in attempting to examine these questions. Additionally, the theoretical notions embodied in the work of certain Soviet learning theorists, such as L. Vygotsky, A.N. Leontiev, and A. Luria are particularly relevant (Wertsch 1981). Within this neo-Vygotskian framework, social interaction and learning (cognitive development) are intimately linked in ways that often are not considered by Western psychologists, who often view and study these as separate developmental areas. Coles (1982, 1983) has discussed the potential importance of the type of interactional perspective found in Soviet psychology on the conceptualization, assessment, and remediation of learning disabilities. Although the neo-Vygotskian development of Soviet psychology is much more complex than can be addressed here, it provides a potentially very useful theoretical framework for examining the issues raised here. As an example, the emphasis on the social and interactional aspects of bilingualism which form an important part of current thinking about communicative competence comprises an important part of the Soviet theory. The neo-Vygotskian theory attempts to relate these interactional aspects of human activity to cognition and learning in a systematic and principled fashion. This will become increasingly important as this line of investigation extends to handicapped children.

The preceding discussion suggests that the social, interactional, and functional nature of language needs to be considered both theoretically and methodologically in future studies of language and cognition in bilinguals. Indeed, there are a host of complex and unanswered theoretical questions on this topic when the influence of cognitive and other learning-related deficits are considered. Nevertheless, equally important are the practical questions related to the day-to-day instruction of limited English proficient handicapped students who must be educated in public school settings. At this point, the influence(s) of bilingualism on cognitive development, academic achievement, and social development among bilingual handicapped children remains largely unexplored. As the relative numbers of students with this unique set of characteristics increases, significant resources will need to be committed to explore ways of insuring maximum educational outcomes.

NOTES

1. Portions of this work were supported through federal funds from the U.S. Department of Education to the Southwest Regional Laboratory under contract number 300-83-0273. Additional support was provided through the Special Education Research Laboratory at the University of California, Santa Barbara.

2. Although bilingual code-shifts may not be "correct" from a strictly grammatical framework or in the traditional linguistic sense (Mackey 1968), such language use is rule-governed and logical (Gonzalez and Maez 1980). Additionally, the use of words such as "puchar" (to push) or "colorear" (to color) may not be correct translations on a language proficiency exam, but the fact that they represent separate codes remains (this argument might be extended to the use of Black English as well).

References

Alvirez, D. 1981. Socioeconomic patterns and diversity among Hispanics. *Hispanic Research Center: Research Bulletin* 4 (2–3), April–June.

Amastae, J., and L. Elías-Olivares. 1982. *Spanish in the United States: Sociolinquistic Aspects.* Cambridge: Cambridge University Press.

Anastasi, A. 1949. *Testing Problems in Perspective.* Washington, DC: American Council on Education.

Apple, M. 1982. *Cultural and Economic Reproduction in Education.* London: Routlege, Kegan Paul.

Appleton, N. 1983. *Cultural Pluralism in Education.* New York: Longman, Inc.

ASPIRA of America. 1976. *Social Factors in Educational Attainment among Puerto Ricans in U.S. Metropolitan Areas, 1970.* New York.

Au, K. H. 1980. On participation structures in reading lessons. *Anthropology and Education Quarterly* 9(2): 91–115.

Au, K., and C. Jordan. 1981. Teaching reading to Hawaiian children: Finding a culturally appropriate solution. In H. Trueba, G. Guthrie, and K. Au (eds.) *Culture and the Bilingual Classroom.* Rowley, MA: Newbury House.

Baca, L., and H. Cervantes. 1984. *The Bilingual Social Education Interface.* St. Louis: Mosby Publishing Co.

Baral, P. D. 1980. The effects of home-school language shifts: The linguistic explanations. In R. V. Padilla (ed.), *Ethnoperspectives in Bilingual Education Research: Theory in Bilingual Education.* 136–147 Ypsilanti, MI: Bilingual Programs, Eastern Michigan University.

Bartel, N. R., and D. N. Bryen. 1978. Problems in language development. In D. D. Hamill and N. R. Bartel (eds.), *Children with Learning and Behavior Problems.* Boston: Allyn and Bacon.

Bates, E., L. Benigni, I. Bretherton, and V. Volterra. 1977. From gesture to the first word: On cognitive and social prerequisites. In M. L. Lewis and L. A. Rosenblum (eds.), *Interaction, Conversation and the Development of Language.* New York: John Wiley and Sons.

Bauman, R. 1982. Ethnography of children's folklore. In P. Gilmore and A. A. Glatthorn (eds.), *Children in and out of School: Ethnography and Education* 172–186. Washington, DC: Center for Applied Linguistics.

Becker, H. S. 1963. *The Outsiders,* 31–35. New York: The Free Press.

Benitez, M. A., and L. G. Villareal. 1979. *The Education of the Mexican American: A Selected Bibliography.* Austin, TX: National Clearinghouse for Bilingual Education.

Benton, R. A. 1978. Problems and prospects for indigenous languages and bilingual education in New Zealand and Oceania. In B. Spolsky and R. L. Cooper (eds.), *Case Studies in Bilingual Education.* Rowley, MA: Newbury House.

Blom, J. P., and J. J. Gumperz. 1972. Social meaning in linguistic structures: Code switching in Norway. In J. J. Gumperz and D. Hymes (eds.), *Directions in Sociolinguistics: The Ethnography of Communication.* (407–432) New York: Holt, Rinehart and Winston.

Bloom, B., A. Davis, and R. Hess. 1965. *Compensatory Education for Cultural Deprivation.* New York: Holt, Rinehart, and Winston.

Bloom, L., and M. Lahey. 1978. *Language Development and Language Disorders.* New York: John Wiley and Sons.

Boggs, S. 1972. The meaning of questions and narratives to Hawaiian children. In C. Cazden, D. Hymes, and P. John (eds.), *Functions of Language in the Classroom,* 299–327. New York: Teachers College Press.

Bowles, S., and H. Gintis. 1976. *Schooling in Capitalist America.* New York: Basic Books.

Briere, E. 1979. Testing communicative language proficiency. In R. Silverstein (ed.), *Occasional Papers on Linguistics 6: Proceedings of the Third International Conference on Frontiers in Language Proficiency Testing,* 254–275. Carbondale, IL: Southern Illinois University.

Brown, A., E. Campione, M. Cole, P. Griffin, H. Mehan, and M. Riel. 1982. A model system for the study of learning difficulties. *The Quarterly Newsletter of the Laboratory of Comparative Human Cognition* 4(3): 39–55.

Brown, F., and M. D. Stent. 1977. *Minorities in U.S. Institutions of Higher Education.* New York: Praeger Publishers.

Brown, G. H., N. L. Rosen, S. T. Hill, and M. Olivas. 1980. The condition of education for Hispanic Americans. Washington, D. C.: United States Department of Education, National Center for Educational Statistics.

Brown, R. L., J. F. Fournier, and R. H. Moyer. 1977. A cross-cultural study of Piagetian concrete reasoning and science concepts among rural fifth-grade Mexican- and Anglo-American students. *Journal of Research in Science Teaching* 14: 329–334.

Bruck, M. 1978. The suitability of early French immersion programs for the language-disabled child. *Canadian Journal of Education* 3(4): 51–73.

Bruck, M., M. S. Rabinovich, and M. Oates. 1975. The effect of French immersion programs on children with language disabilities-a preliminary report. *Working Papers in Bilingualism* 5: 47–86.

Bryen, D. N. 1975. Issues and activities in language. Unpublished manuscript. Philadelphia: Temple University.

Burns, M., W. Gerace, J. Mestre, and H. Robinson. 1982. The current status of Hispanic technical professionals: How can we improve recruitment and retention. *Integrated Education* 20 (1–2): 49–55.

Campione, J. C., and A. L. Brown. 1977. Memory and meta-memory development in educable mentally retarded children. In R. V. Kail and J. W. Hagen (eds.), *Perspective on the Development of Memory and Cognition.* Hillsdale, NJ: Erlbaum Associates.

Canale, M. 1984. A communicative approach to language proficiency assessment in a minority setting. In C. Rivera (ed.), *Communicative Competence Approaches to Language Proficiency Assessment: Research and Application.* Clevedon, Avon, England: Multilingual Matters.

Canale, M., and M. Swain. 1980. Theoretical bases of communicative approaches to second language teaching and testing. *Applied Linguistics* 1: 1–47.

Cardenas, B., and J. A. Cardenas. 1972. The theory of incompatibilities. *Today's Education,* February.

Carter, T. P. 1970. *Mexican Americans in School: A History of Educational Neglect.* New York: College Entrance Examination Board.

Carter, T. P., and R. D. Segura. 1979. *Mexican Americans in School: A Decade of Change.* New York: College Entrance Examination Board.

Cazden, C. B. 1972. The roles of language in cognition. In C. B. Cazden (Ed.), *Child Language and Education,* 217–235. New York: Holt, Rinehart & Winston.

Cazden, C. B. 1986. Classroom discourse. In M. C. Wittrock (ed.), *Handbook of Research on Teaching,* 432–463 New York: MacMillan.

Cazden, C. B., and E. L. Leggett. 1981. Culturally responsive education: Recommendations for achieving Lau Remedies II. In H. T. Trueba, G. P. Guthrie, and K. H. Au (eds.), *Culture and the Bilingual Classroom: Studies in Classroom Ethnography.* 69–86 Rowley, MA: Newbury House.

Cheng, L. L. 1983. An ethnographic study of language-impaired preschoolers. Unpublished doctoral dissertation, Claremont Graduate School, Claremont, CA.

Clark, R. M. 1983. *Family Life and School Achievement. Why Poor Black Children Succeed or Fail.* Chicago: University of Chicago Press.

Cohen, R. A. 1969. Conceptual styles, cultural conflict, and nonverbal tests of intelligence. *American Anthropologists* 71: 828–856.

Cole, M. 1975. Culture, cognition and I. Q. testing. *The National Elementary Principal* 54: 49–52.

Cole, M., and R. D'Andrade. 1982. The influence of schooling on concept formation: Some preliminary conclusions. *The Quarterly Newsletter of the Laboratory of Comparative Human Cognition* 4(2): 19–26.

Cole, M., J. Dore, W. Hall, and G. Dowley. 1978. Situation and task in young children's talk. *Discourse Processes* 1: 119–126.

Cole, M., J. Gay, J. Glick, and D. Sharp. 1971. *The Cultural Context of Learning and Thinking.* New York: Basic Books.

Cole, M., and P. Griffin. 1983. A socio-historical approach to re-mediation. *The Quarterly Newsletter of the Laboratory of Comparative Human Cognition* 5(4): 69–74.

Cole, M., and S. Scribner. (1974). *Culture and Thought: A Psychological Introduction.* New York: John Wiley and Sons.

Coleman, J. 1961. *The Adolescent Society: The Social Life of The Teenager and Its Impact on Education.* New York: The Free Press.

Coleman, J. S., E. G. Campbell, C. J. Hobson, J. Partland, A. M. Mood, F. B. Weinfeld, and R. L. York. 1966. *Equality of Education Opportunity.* Washington, DC: U. S. Department of Health, Education, and Welfare.

Coles, G. S. 1982. Learning disabilities theory and Soviet psychology: A comparison of basic assumptions. *Journal of Clinical Neuropsychology* 4(3): 269–283.

Coles, G. S. 1983. The use of Soviet psychological theory in understanding learning dysfunctions. *American Journal of Orthopsychiatry* 53(4): 619–628.

Collier, J. 1973. *Alaskan Eskimo Education: A Film Analysis of Cultural Confrontation in the Schools.* New York: Holt, Rinehart and Winston.

Cook-Gumperz, J. and J. Gumperz. 1979. Beyond ethnography: Some uses of sociolinguistics for understanding classroom environments. Paper presented April, 1979 at the American Educational Research Association Conference. San Francisco.

Corsaro, W. A. 1979. "We're friends, right?": Children's use of access rituals in a nursery school. *Language in Society* 8: 315–336.

Cortes, C. E. 1986. The education of language minority students: A contextual interaction model. In *Beyond Language: Social and Cultural Factors in Schooling Language Minority Students,* 3–33. Sacramento, CA: Bilingual Education Office.

Cummins, J. 1976. The influence of bilingualism on cognitive growth: A synthesis of research findings and explanatory hypotheses. *Working Papers on Bilingualism* 9: 1–43.

Cummins, J. 1978. Bilingualism and the development of metalinguistic awareness. *Journal of Cross-Cultural Psychology* 9(2): 131–149.

Cummins, J. 1979. Linguistic interdependence and the educational development of bilingual children. *Review of Educational Research* 49: 222–251.

Cummins, J. 1980. The cross-lingual dimensions of language proficiency: Implications for bilingual education and the optimal age issue. *TESOL Quarterly* 14(2): 175–187.

Cummins, J. 1981. The entry and exit fallacy in bilingual education. *National Association for Bilingual Education Journal* 4(3): 26–60.

Cummins, J. 1983. The role of primary language development in promoting educational success for language minority students. In *Schooling and Language Minority Students: A Theoretical Framework.* Sacramento: California State Department of Education.

Cummins, J. 1984. Language proficiency, bilingualism and academic achievement. In J. Cummins (ed.), *Bilingualism and Special Education: Issues in Assessment and Pedagogy.* Clevedon, Avon, England: Multilingual Matters, Ltd.

Cummins, J. 1985. Disabling minority students: Power, programs and pedagogy. Unpublished manuscript, Ontario Institute for Studies in Education.

Cummins, J. 1986. Empowering minority students: A framework for intervention. *Harvard Educational Review* 56(1): 18–35.

D'Andrade, R. G. 1984. Cultural meaning systems. In R. A. Shweder and R. A. LeVine (eds.), *Culture Theory,* 88–119. Cambridge: Cambridge University Press.

D'Anglejan, A., and G. R. Tucker. 1973. Communicating across cultures: An empirical investigation. *Journal of Cross-Cultural Psychology* 4(1): 121–130.

Darcy, N. T. 1946. The effects of bilingualism upon the measurement of the intelligence of children of preschool age. *The Journal of Educational Psychology* 37(1): 21–43.

Darcy, N. T. 1953. A review of the literature on the effects of bilingualism upon the measurement of intelligence. *The Journal of Genetic Psychology* 82: 21–57.

Darcy, N. T. 1963. Bilingualism and the measurement of intelligence: Review of a decade of research. *The Journal of Genetic Psychology* 103: 259–282.

Davis, C., C. Haub, and J. Willette. 1983. U. S. Hispanics: Changing the face of America. *Population Bulletin* 38(3), 1–44.

DeAvila, E. 1976. Mainstreaming ethnically and linguistically different children: An exercise in paradox or a new approach. In R.L. Jones (ed.) *Mainstreaming and the Minority Child.* 93–108. Reston, Va.: The Council for Exceptional Children.

DeAvila, E. 1984. Science and math: A natural context for language development. December Conference Proceedings: Delivering Academic Excellence to Culturally Diverse Populations, New Jersey.

DeAvila, E. A., R. A. Cervantes, and S. E. Duncan. 1978. Bilingual program exit criteria. *CABE Research Journal* 1: 23–39.

DeAvila, E. A., and S. E. Duncan. 1981. Bilingualism and the metaset. In R. Durán (ed.), *Latino Language and Communicative Behavior,* 337–354. Norwood, NJ: Ablex.

DeAvila, E. A., and B. Havassy. 1974. The testing of minority children—a neo-Piagetian approach. *Today's Education* 63: 72–75.

DeAvila, E. A., B. Havassy, J. Pascual-Leone. (1976). *Mexican American School Children: A Neopiagetian Analysis.* Washington, DC: Georgetown University Press.

Delgado-Gaitan, C. 1983. Learning how: Rules for knowing and doing for Mexican children at home, play and school. Doctoral dissertation, Stanford University, CA.

Deutsch, M. 1963. The disadvantaged child and the learning process. In Passow (ed.), *Education in Depressed Areas.* New York: Columbia University Teachers College.

DeVos, G. A. 1978. Selective permeability and reference group sanctioning: Psychocultural continuities in role degradation. In J. M. Yinger (ed.), *Major Social Issues,* 7–24. New York: The Free Press.

DeVos, G. A. 1980. Ethnic adaptation and minority status. *Journal of Cross-Cultural Psychology* 11: 101–124.

DeVos, G. A. 1982. Adaptive strategies in U. S. minorities. In E. E. Jones and S. J. Korchin (eds.), *Minority Mental Health,* 74–112. New York: Praeger.

DeVos, G. A. 1983. Ethnic identity and minority status: Some psycho-cultural considerations. In A. Jacobson-Widding (ed.), *Identity: Personal and Socio-Cultural,* 90–113. Upsala: Almquist and Wiksell Tryckeri AB.

DeVos, G. A. 1984. Ethnic persistence and role degradation: An illustration from Japan. Paper read April, 1984 at the American-Soviet Symposium on Contemporary Ethnic Processes in the USA and the USSR. New Orleans, Louisiana.

Deyhle, D. 1980. Fieldwork notes. Unpublished manuscript.

Deyhle, D. 1983. Between games and failure: A microethnographic study of Navajo students and testing. *Curriculum Inquiry* 13: 347–376.

Deyhle, D. 1985. Testing among Navajo and Anglo students: Another consideration of cultural bias. *Journal of Educational Equity and Leadership* 5(2): 119–131.

Deyhle, D. In press. Success and failure: A microethnographic comparison of Navajo and Anglo students' perceptions of testing. *Curriculum Inquiry* 16(4).

Diaz, R. 1983. Thought and two languages: The impact of bilingualism on cognitive development. In E. W. Gordon (ed.), *Review of Research in Education* 10. Washington, D.C.: American Educational Research Association.

Diaz, R. (1984). *Bilingual cognitive development: Addressing gaps in current research.* Unpublished manuscript.

Diaz, S., L. C. Moll, and H. Mehan. 1986. Sociocultural resources in instruction: A context-specific approach. In *Beyond Language: Social and Cultural Factors in Schooling Language Minority Students,* 187–230. Sacramento, CA: Bilingual Education Office, California State Dept. of Education.

Diebold, R. A. 1964. Incipient bilingualism. In D. Hymes (ed.), *Language, Culture, and Society.* New York: Harper and Row.

Diskin, M. 1983. *Trouble in Our Backyard: Central America and the United States in the Eighties.* New York: Pantheon Books.

Durán, R. 1981. *Latino Language and Communicative Behavior.* Norwood, NJ: Ablex.

Durán, R. 1983. *Hispanics' Education and Background: Predictors of College Achievement.* New York: College Entrance Examination Board.

Durán, R. 1985. Influences of language skills on bilingual's problem solving. In S. Chipman, J. Sigel, and R. Glaser (eds.), *Thinking and Learning Skills, vol. 2: Current Research and Open Questions.* 187–207. Hillsdale, NJ: Erlbaum Associates.

Erickson, F. 1977. Some approaches to inquiry in school-community ethnography. *Anthropology and Education Quarterly* 8(2): 58–69.

Erickson, F. 1978. On standards of descriptive validity in studies of classroom activities. Paper presented March, 1978 at the American Educational Research Association Meetings, Conference, Toronto, Canada.

Erickson, F. 1979. Talking down: Some cultural sources of miscommunication in interracial interviews. In A. Wolfgang (ed.), *Nonverbal Behavior,* 99–126. New York: Academic Press.

Erickson, F. 1982. Classroom discourse as improvisation: Relationships between academic task structure and social participation structure in lessons. In L. C. Wilkinson (ed.), *Communicating in the Classroom,* 153–181. New York: Academic Press.

Erickson, F. 1984. School literacy, reasoning, and civility: An anthropologist's perspective. *Review of Educational Research* 54(4): 525–544.

Erickson, F., and G. Mohatt. 1982. Cultural organization of participation structures in two classrooms of Indian students. In G. Spindler (ed.), *Doing the Ethnography of Schooling: Educational Anthropology in Action.* 132–174. New York: Holt, Rinehart and Winston.

Erickson, F., and J. Shultz. 1982. *The Counselor as Gatekeeper: Social Interaction in Interviews.* New York: Academic Press.

Erickson, J., and D. Omark. 1981. *Communication Assessment of the Bilingual Child: Issues and Guidelines.* Baltimore: University Park Press.

Fernandez, C., and E. Marenco. 1980. *Group Conflict, Education and Mexican Americans: A Discussion Paper.* San Francisco: Mexican American Legal Defense and Educational Fund, Inc.

Ford Foundation. 1984. *Hispanics: Challenges and Opportunities.* New York: Ford Foundation.

Fortes, M. 1970. Social and psychological aspects of education in Taleland. In J. Middleton (ed.), *From Child to Adult,* 14–74. Austin: University of Texas Press.

Frake, C. 1964. Notes on queries in ethnography. *American Anthropologist* 66(3): 132–145.

Gallagher, T., and C. Prutting. 1983. *Pragmatic Assessment and Intervention Issues in Language.* San Diego: College Hill Press.

Garfinkel, H. 1956. Conditions of successful degradation ceremonies. *The American Journal of Sociology* 61: 420–424.

Garnica, O. 1981. Social dominance and conversational interaction: The omega child in the classroom. In J. Green and C. Wallat (eds.), *Ethnography and Language in Educational Settings.* Norwood, NJ: Ablex Publishing.

Garvey, C. 1984. *Children's Talk.* Cambridge: Harvard University Press.

Gay, G., and R. D. Abrahams. 1973. Does the pot melt, boil, or brew? Black children and white assessment procedures. *Journal of School Psychology* 11: 330–340.

Geertz, C. 1973. *The Interpretation of Cultures.* New York: Basic Books.

Gerry, M. H. 1973. Cultural myopia: The need for corrective lens. *Journal of School Psychology* 11: 307–315.

Giles, H. 1977. *Language, Ethnicity, and Intergroup Relations.* New York: Academic Press.

Gilmore, P. 1983. Ethnographic approaches to the study of child language. *Volta Review* 85(5): 29–43.

Gilmore, P., and A. A. Glatthorn 1982. *Children in and out of School: Ethnography for Education.* Washington, D. C.: Center for Applied Linguistics.

Goffman, E. 1963. *Stigma: Notes on the Management of Spoiled Identity,* 2–9. Englewood Cliffs, NJ: Prentice-Hall.

Goho, T., and D. Smith. 1973. *A College Degree: Does It Substantially Enhance the Economic Achievement of Chicanos?* Las Cruces: New Mexico State University. Center for Business Services Occasional Paper No. 503.

Goldberg, M. L. 1971. Socio-psychological issues in the education of the disadvantaged. In A. Passow (ed.), *Urban Education in the 1970's.* 61–93. New York: Teachers College.

Gonzalez, G., and L. Maez. 1980. To switch or not to switch: The role of code-switching in the elementary bilingual classroom. In R. V. Padilla (ed.), *Ethnoperspectives in bilingual education, vol. 2: Theory in bilingual education.* 125–135. Ypsilanti, MI: Eastern Michigan University.

Gonzales-Orellana, C. 1970. *Historia de la educacion en Guatemala.* Guatemala: Editorial José Pineda de Ibarra.

Gordon, E. W., and D. A. Wilkerson. 1966. *Compensatory Education for the Disadvantaged. Programs and Practices: Preschool through College.* New York: College Entrance Examination Board.

Gossen, G. H. 1974. To speak with heated heart: Chamula canons of style and good performance. In R. Bauman and J. Scherzer (eds.), *Explorations in the Ethnography of Speaking.* Cambridge: Cambridge University Press.

Green, J., and C. Wallet. 1981. *Ethnography and Language in Educational Settings.* Norwood, NJ: Ablex.

Greenfield, P. M., and J. H. Smith. 1976. *Communication and the Beginning of Language: The Development of Syntactic Structure in One-Word Speech and Beyond.* New York: Academic Press.

Griffin, P., D. Newman, and M. Cole. 1981. Activities, actions and formal operations: A Vygotskian Analysis of a Piagetian task. Unpublished manuscript. Laboratory of Comparative Human Cognition, University of California, San Diego.

Guerra, M. H. 1970. The Mexican-American child: Problems or talents? In H. S. Johnson and W. J. Hernandez (eds.), *Educating the Mexican-American.* Valley Forge, PA: Judson Press.

Gulyas, P. A. 1979. *Improving the behavior of habitually disruptive high school students.* (ERIC Access #180075.) Unpublished manuscript, Nova University, Fort Lauderdale, FL.

Gumperz, J. 1981. Conversational inference and classroom learning. In J. L. Green and C. Wallat (eds.), *Ethnography and Language in Educational Settings,* 3–23. Norwood, NJ: Ablex.

Gumperz, J. 1982. *Discourse Strategies.* Cambridge: Cambridge University Press.

Gumperz, J., and D. Hymes. 1964. The ethnography of communication. *American Anthropologists* 66(6).

Gumperz, J., and D. Hymes. 1972. *Directions in Socio-Linguistics: The Ethnography of Communication.* New York: Holt, Rinehart and Winston.

Hall, E. T. 1973. *The Silent Language.* Garden City, NY: Anchor Press.

Hall, R. 1980. An information-processing approach to the study of exceptional children. In B. K. Keogh (ed.), *Advances in Special Education.* Vol. 2. 79–110. Greenwich, CT: JAI Press.

Hallahan, D. P. (ed.). 1980. Teaching exceptional children to use cognitive strategies. *Exceptional Education Quarterly* 1(1).

Halliday, M. A. 1975. *Explorations in the Functions of Language.* London: Edward Arnold Publishers.

Halliday, M. A. 1978. *Language as a Social Semiotic: The Social Interpretation of Language and Meaning.* Baltimore: University Park Press.

Harris, J. J. 1976. Cultural differences: An analysis of factors influencing educational success. *Clearing House* 50: 39–43.

Harris, M. 1968. *The Rise of Anthropological Theory.* New York: Thomas Y. Crowell Company.

Hatch, E. 1978. Discourse analysis and second language acquisition. In E. Hatch (ed.), *Second Language Acquisition: A book of readings,* 401–435. Rowley, MA: Newbury House.

Hatch, E. 1980. Discourse analysis: What's that? In Larsen-Freeman (ed.), *Discourse Analysis in Second Language Research,* 1–40. Rowley, MA: Newbury House.

Hawkins, J. 1984. *Inverse Images: The Meaning of Culture, Ethnicity, and Family in Postcolonial Guatemala.* Albuquerque: University of New Mexico Press.

Heath, S. B. 1972. *Telling Tongues: Language Policy in Mexico, Colony to Nation.* New York: Teachers College Press.

Heath, S. B. 1982. Questioning at home and at school: A comparative study. In G. Spindler (ed.), *Doing the Ethnography of Schooling: Educational Anthropology in Action.* New York: Holt, Rinehart and Winston.

Heath, S. B. 1983. *Ways with Words.* Cambridge, MA: Cambridge University Press.

Heath, S. B. 1984a. Language contact and language change. *Annual Review of Anthropology* 13: 367–384.

Heath, S. B. 1984b. Linguistics and education. *Annual Review of Anthropology, 13,* 251–272.

Heath, S. B. 1984c. Second language acquisition. Paper presented April, 1984 at the American Speech and Hearing Association Conference, San Francisco, CA.

Heath, S. B. 1986. Sociocultural contexts of language development. In *Beyond Language: Social and Cultural Factors in Schooling Language Minority Students,* 143–186. Sacramento, CA: Bilingual Education Office, California State Dept. of Education.

Heller, C. 1966. *Mexican American Youth: Forgotten Youth at the Crossroads.* New York: Random House.

Hernandez, N. G. 1973. Variables affecting achievement of middle school Mexican-American students. *Review of Educational Research* 43: 1–39.

Hernandez, J., L. Estrada, and D. Alvirez. 1973. Census data and the problem of conceptually defining the Mexican American population. *Social Science Quarterly* 53: 671–687.

Hilliard, A. G. 1979. Standardized testing and African-Americans: Building assessor competence in systematic assessment. In R. Tyler and S. H. White (eds.), *Testing, Teaching and Learning.* 204–218. Report of a conference on research on testing, National Institute of Education, Washington, DC.

Hirano-Nakanishi, M. N.d. *Hispanic School Dropouts: The Extent and Relevance of Pre-High School Attrition and Delayed Education.* Los Alamitos, California: National Center for Bilingual Research.

Hispanic Administrators for Quality Education. 1984. *Symposium on School Dropouts. Summary of Recommendations for Dropouts in California.* San Diego: National Origin Desegregation Lau Center.

Hispanic Policy Development Project. 1984. Make something happen. *Hispanics and Urban High School Reform* I & II. New York: The Hispanic Policy Development Project, Inc.

Holtzman, W. H., R. Diaz-Guerrero, and J. D. Swartz. 1975. *Personality Development in Two Cultures: A Cross-Cultural Longitudinal Study of School Children in Mexico and the United States.* Austin: University of Texas Press.

Hymes, D. 1974. *Foundations in Sociolinguistics.* Philadelphia: University of Pennsylvania Press.

Hymes, D. 1981. Ethnographic monitoring. In H. T. Trueba, G. P. Guthrie, and K. Au (eds.), *Culture and the Bilingual Classroom.* Rowley, MA: Newbury House.

Ingle, D. J. 1970. Possible genetic basis of social problem: A reply to Ashley Montagu. *Midway* 10: 105–121.

It's your turn in the sun. *Time* Oct. 1978: 48.

Jencks, C., M. Smith, H. Aclard, J. J. Bane, D. Cohen, H. Gintis, B. Heyrs, and S. Michaelson. 1972. *Inequality: A Reassessment of the Effects of Family and Schooling in America.* New York: Basic Books.

Jensen, A. R. 1968. *Social Class, Race, and Psychological Development.* New York: Holt, Rinehart and Winston.

Jensen, A. R. 1971. *The I. Q. Argument.* New York: Library Press.

Jensen, A. R. 1973. *Educability and Group Differences.* New York: Harper and Row.

Jensen, J. V. 1962. Effects of childhood bilingualism. *Elementary English* 39: 132–143.

John, V. P. 1972. Styles of learning—styles of teaching: Reflections on the education of Navajo children. In C. Cazden, D. Hymes, and V. P. John (eds.), *Functions of Language in the Classroom.* New York: Teachers College Press.

Johnson, H. S., and W. J. Hernandez. 1970. *Educating the Mexican American.* Valley Forge, PA: Judson Press.

Kagan, S., and R. Buriel. 1977. Field dependence-independence and Mexican American culture and education. In J. L. Martinez (ed.), *Chicano Psychology.* New York: Academic Press.

Kahl, J. 1968. *The Measurement of Modernism: A Study of Values in Brazil and Mexico.* Austin: University of Texas Press.

Kaufman, T. 1976. *Proyecto de alfabetos.* Guatemala: Editorial Pineda Ibarra.

Keller-Cohen, D. 1980. Systematicity and variation in the non-native child's acquisition of conversational skills. *Language Learning* 29(1).

Knowlton, C. S. 1979. Some demographic, economic, and educational considerations on Mexican American youth. Paper read at the South-Western Sociological Association Meeting, Fort Worth, TX.

Krashen, S. 1978. The monitor model for second language acquisition. In R. Gingras (ed.), *Second Language Acquisition and Foreign Language Learning.* 1–26. Washington, DC: Center for Applied Linguistics.

Krashen, S. 1980. The theoretical and practical relevance of simple codes in second language acquisition. In R. C. Scarcella and S. D. Krashen (eds.), *Research in Second Language Acquisition.* Rowley, MA: Newbury House.

Krashen, S. (1981). *Second Language Acquisition and Second Language Learning.* Oxford: Pergamon Press.

Krashen, S. 1982a. Accounting for child-adult differences in second language rate and attainment. In S. D. Krashen, R. C. Scarcella, and M. H. Long (eds.), *Child-Adult Differences in Second Language Acquisition.* 202–226. Rowley, MA: Newbury House.

Krashen, S. 1982b. *Principles and Practice in Second Language Acquisition.* Oxford: Pergamon Press.

Krashen, S., M. H. Long, and R. C. Scarcella. 1982. Age, rate, and eventual attainment in second language acquisition. In S. D. Krashen, R. C. Scarcella and M. H. Long (eds.), *Child-Adult Differences in Second Language Acquisition.* Rowley, MA: Newbury House.

Krashen, S., and R. Scarcella. 1979. On routines and patterns in language acquisition. *Language Learning* 28(2): 151–167.

Labov, W. 1972a. *Language in the Inner City: Studies in the Black English Vernacular.* Philadelphia: University of Pennsylvania Press.

Labov, W. 1972b. The study of language on its social context. In P. Gigplioli (ed.), *Language and Social Context.* Harmondsworth: Penguin Publishing Co.

Lachman, R., J. L. Lachman, and E. Butterfield. 1979. *Cognitive Psychology and Information Processing.* Hillsdale, NJ: Erlbaum Associates.

La Feber, W. 1984. *Inevitable Revolutions: The United States in Central America.* New York: W.W. Norton & Co.

Laosa, L. M. 1978a. Maternal teaching strategies and field dependent-independent cognitive styles in Chicano families. *Educational Testing Service Research Bulletin* RB-78-12, September.

Laosa, L. M. 1978b. Maternal teaching strategies in Chicano families of varied educational and socio-economic levels. *Child Development,* 49: 1129–1135.

Laosa, L. M. 1981. Maternal behavior: Sociocultural diversity in modes of family interaction. In R. W. Henderson (ed.), *Parent-Child Interaction: Theory, Research, and Prospects.* New York: Academic Press.

Laosa, L. M. 1982. School, occupation, culture and family: The impact of parental schooling on the parent-child relationship. *Journal of Educational Psychology* 74(6):791–827.

Lefkowitz, B. 1985. Renegotiating society's contract with public schools: The national commission on secondary education for Hispanics and the national board of inquiry into schools. *Carnegie Quarterly* 29(4): 2–11.

Leighton, D., and C. Kluckhohn. 1948. *Children of the People.* Cambridge: Harvard University Press.

Lemert, E. W. 1951. *Social Pathology: A Systematic Approach to the Theory of Sociopathic Behavior,* 77. New York: McGraw-Hill Book Company.

Leonard, L. B., J. A. Perrozzi, C. A. Prutting, and R. K. Berkeley. 1978. Nonstandardized approaches to the assessment of language behaviors. *ASHA* 20: 371–379.

Leopold, W. F. 1939–1949. *Speech Development of a Bilingual Child: A Linguist's Record.* 4 Vol. Evanston, IL: Northwestern University Press.

LeVine, M. 1976. Academic achievement test: Its historical context and social function. *American Psychologist* 31: 228–238.

Longstreet, E. 1978. *Aspects of Ethnicity.* New York: Teachers College Press.

Ludwig, M. 1981. Structuring classroom participation: The use of metaphrasing by black and white eighth grade students. In H. Trueba, G. Guthrie, and K. Au (eds.), *Culture and the Bilingual Classroom: Studies in Classroom Ethrography.* 196–211. Rowley, MA: Newbury House.

Lund, N. J. and J. F. Duchan. 1983. *Assessing Children's Language in Naturalistic Contexts.* Englewood Cliffs, NJ: Prentice-Hall.

Mackey, W. F. 1968. The description of bilingualism. In J. Fishman (ed.), *Reading in the Sociology of Language.* The Hague: Mouton and Company.

Madaus, G. F. 1985. Test scores as administrative mechanism in educational policy. *Phi Delta Kappa* May, 611–617.

Madsen, W. 1964. *The Mexican-Americans of South Texas.* New York: Holt, Rinehart and Winston.

Maehr, M. L. 1974. Culture and achievement motivation. *American Psychologist* 29: 887–896.

Maestas, L. C. 1981. Ethnicity and high school student achievement across rural and urban districts. *Educational Research Quarterly* 6: 32–42.

Manuel, H. T. 1930. *The Education of Mexican and Spanish-Speaking Children in Texas.* Austin: The University of Texas Press.

Manuel, H. T. 1965. *Spanish-Speaking children of the Southwest.* Austin: University of Texas Press.

Martinez-Peláez, S. 1979. *La patria del criollo.* San José, Costa Rica: Editorial Universitaria Centroamericana.

Matute-Bianchi, M. E. 1985. Chicano and the oppositional process: The historical creation of a collective identity. Paper presented May–June, 1985 at the University of California Linguistic Minority Research Conference, Tahoe City, California.

McCollum, P. 1981. Attention-getting of Anglo American and Puerto Rican Students: A microethnographic analysis. Doctoral dissertation. University of Illinois, Champaign-Urbana.

McCollum, P., and C. L. Walker. In press. The assessment of bilingual students: A sorting mechanism. *Issues of Language Assessment,* 3. Illinois State Board of Education.

McDermott, R. 1974. Achieving school failure: An anthropological approach to illiteracy and social stratification. In G. Spindler (ed.), *Education and Cultural Process,* 82–117 New York: Holt, Rinehart and Winston.

McDermott, R. 1982. Stages in the ethnography of school failure, 1960–1980: From the rhetoric of schooling through the problems of our children to a confrontation with the system. Paper presented March, 1982 to the Third Annual Ethnography in Education Research Forum, University of Pennsylvania, Philadelphia.

McDermott, R., and K. Gospodinoff. 1981. Social contexts for ethnic borders and school failure. In H. T. Trueba, G. Guthrie, and K. Au (eds.), *Culture and the Bilingual Classroom,* 212–230. Rowley, MA: Newbury House.

McKay, R. 1974. Conceptions of children and models of socialization. In R. Turner (ed.), *Ethnomethodology,* 180–193. Middlesex: Penguin Education.

McNab, G. L. 1979. Cognition and bilingualism: A reanalysis of studies. *Linguistics* 17: 231–255.

Mead, M. 1927. Educational research and statistics: Group intelligence tests and linguistic disability among Italian children. *School and Society* 25(642): 465–468.

Mecham, M. J., J. L. Jex, and J. D. Jones. 1977. *Utah Test of Language Development.* Salt Lake City: Communication Research Associates.

Mehan, H. 1978. Structuring school structure. *Harvard Educational Review* 45(1): 311–338.

Mehan, H. 1979. *Learning Lessons: Social Organization in the Classroom.* Cambridge: Harvard University Press.

Mehan, H. 1981. Ethnography of bilingual education. In H. Trueba, G. Guthrie, and K. Au (eds.), *Culture and the Bilingual Classroom: Studies in Classroom Ethnography.* 36–55. Rowley, MA: Newbury House.

Mercer, J. 1972a. IQ: The lethal label. *Psychology Today* 6, 44: 46–47; 95–96.

Mercer, J. 1972b. Current retardation procedures and the psychological and social implications on the Mexican American. Paper presented June, 1972 at a workshop on testing and career counseling of minority students, Las Vegas, New Mexico.

Mercer, J. 1973. *Labeling the Mentally Retarded.* Berkeley: University of California Press.

Mercer, J. 1974. A policy statement on assessment procedures and the rights of children. *Harvard Educational Review* 44(1): 125–141.

Merton, R. 1938. Social structure and anomie. *American Sociological Review* 3(5), 672–682.

Mexican-American Advisory Committee to Wilson Riles 1981. A summary of school-related factors associated with the achievement of Mexican-American children. Unpublished manuscript, Sacramento, California.

Mohatt, G., and F. Erickson. 1981. Cultural differences in teaching styles in an Odawa school: A sociolinguistic approach. In H. Trueba, G. Guthrie and K. Au (eds.), *Culture and the Bilingual Classroom: Studies in Classroom Ethnography.* 105–119. Rowley, MA: Newbury House.

Mohn, S. L. 1983. Central American refugees: The search for appropriate responses. *World Refugee Survey. 25th Anniversary Issue:* 42–47.

Moore, A. 1973. *Life Cycles in Achalan: The Diverse Careers of Certain Guatemalans.* New York: Teachers College Press.

Morgan, T. B. 1983. The latinization of America. *Esquire* 47.

Moynihan, D. 1967. *The Negro Family.* Cambridge, MA: Massachusetts Institute of Technology Press.

National Center for Education Statistics. 1975. *National Longitudinal Study of the High School Class of 1972.* Washington, D. C.: U. S. Department of Health, Education, and Welfare.

National Center for Education Statistics. 1976. *Survey of Income and Education.* Washington, DC: U. S. Department of Health, Education, and Welfare.

National Center for Education Statistics 1982. *Hispanic students in American high schools: Background characteristics and achievement.* Washington, D.C.: US. Department of Health, Education, and Welfare.

National Commission on Secondary Schooling for Hispanics. 1984. *Make Something Happen: Hispanics and Urban High School Reform.* I and II. Washington, D. C.: Hispanic Policy Development Project.

National Council of La Raza. 1982. *Hispanic Statistics Summary: A Compendium of Data on Hispanic Americans.* Washington, D. C.: National Council of La Raza.

National Puerto Rican Forum. 1970. A Study of Poverty Conditions in the New York Puerto Rican Community. New York.

Neisser, U. 1967. *Cognitive Psychology.* New York: Appleton.

Nielsen, F., and R. M. Fernandez. 1981. *Achievement of Hispanic Students in American High Schools: Background Characteristics and Achievement.* ERIC Document Reproduction Service No. ED 218 036).

Ogbu, J. 1974. *The Next Generation: An Ethnography of Education in an Urban Neighborhood.* New York: Academic Press.

Ogbu, J. 1977. Racial stratification and education. The case of Stockton, California. *IRCD Bulletin* 12(3). Institute for Urban and Minority Education, Columbia University Teachers College.

Ogbu, J. 1978. *Minority Education and Caste: The American System in Cross-Cultural Perspective.* New York: Academic Press.

Ogbu, J. 1981a. Origins of human competence: A cultural-ecological perspective. *Child Development* 52: 413–429.

Ogbu, J. 1981b. Societal forces as a context of ghetto children's school failure. In L. Feagans and D. Clark (eds), *The Language of Children Reared in Poverty: Implications for Evaluation and Intervention.* New York: Academic Press.

Ogbu, J. 1982. Cultural discontinuities and schooling. *Anthropology and Education Quarterly* 13(4): 290–307.

Ogbu, J. 1983a. Minority status and schooling in plural societies. *Comparative Education Review* 27(2): 168–190.

Ogbu, J. 1983b, November. Indigenous and immigrant minority education: A comparative perspective. Paper presented at 82d Annual Meeting of the American Anthropological Association, Chicago, IL.

Ogbu, J., and M. E. Matute-Bianchi. 1986. Understanding sociocultural factors: Knowledge, identity and school adjustment. In *Beyond Language: Social and Cultural Factors in Schooling Language Minority Students,* 73–142. Sacramento, CA: Bilingual Education Office.

O'Malley, J. M. 1981. *Children's English and Services Study: Language Minority Children with Limited English Proficiency in the United States.* Rosslyn, VA: National Clearinghouse for Bilingual Education.

Omark, D. R., and J. G. Erickson. 1983. *The Bilingual Exceptional Child.* San Diego: College-Hill Press.

Padilla, A. M. 1979. Critical factors in the testing of Hispanic Americans: A review and some suggestions for the future. In R. Tyler and S. H. White (eds.) *Testing, Teaching and Learning.* 219–243. Report of a conference on research on testing, National Institute of Education, Washington, D. C.

Park, M., R. Cambra, and D. Klopf. 1979. Characteristics of Korean oral communication patterns. *Korea Journal* 19(7): 4–8.

Paulston, C. B. 1974. Linguistic and communicative competence. *TESOL Quarterly,* 8(4): 347–362.

Peal, E., and W. E. Lambert. 1962. The relation of bilingualism to intelligence. *Psychological Monographs: General and Applied* 76: 1–23.

Peck, S. 1978. Child-child discourse in second language acquisition. In Hatch (ed.), *Second Language Acquisition.* Rowley, MA: Newbury House.

Peters, A. 1977. Language learning strategies: Does the whole equal the sum of the parts? *Language* 53: 560–573.

Peters, A. 1983. *The Units of Language Acquisition.* Cambridge: Cambridge University Press.

Philips, S. 1972. Participant structures and communicative competence: Warm Springs children in community and classroom. In C. Cazden, D. Hymes, and V. John (eds.), *Functions of Language in the Classroom.* 370–394. New York: Teachers College Press.

Philips, S. 1983. *The invisible culture: Communication in the Classroom and on the Warm Springs Indian reservation.* New York: Longman, Inc.

Piaget, J. 1930. *The Child's Conception of Physical Casuality.* London: Kegan Paul, Trench, Trubner & Co. Ltd.

Piaget, J., and B. Inhelder. 1969. *The Psychology of the Child.* New York: Basic Books.

Piersel, W. G. 1977. Further examination of motivational influences on disadvantaged minority group children's intelligence test performances. *Child Development* 48: 1142–1145.

Pike, K. 1954. Emic and etic standpoints for the description of behavior. In his *Language in Relation to a Unified Theory of the Structure of Human Behavior,* 8–28. Glendale, CA: Summer Institute of Linguistics.

Rakow, S. J., and C. L. Walker. 1985. The status of Hispanic American students in science: Achievement and exposure. *Science Education* 69(4): 557–565.

Ramirez, A. 1984. Pupil characteristics and performance on linguistic and communicative language measures. In C. Rivera (ed.), *Communicative Competence Approaches to Language Proficiency Assessment: Research and Application.* 82–106. Clevedon, Avon, England: Multilingual Matters.

Ramirez, M., and A. Castañeda. 1974. *Cultural Democracy, Bicognitive Development and Education.* New York: Academic Press.

Rigg, M. 1928. Some further data on the language handicap. *Journal of Educational Psychology* 19: 252–256.

Rist, R. C. 1970. Student social class and teacher expectations: The self-fulfilling prophecy in ghetto education. *Harvard Educational Review* 40: 411–451.

Rist, R. C. 1978. *The Invisible Children—School Integration in American Society.* Cambridge: Harvard University Press.

Rivera, C. 1983. *An Ethnographic/Sociolinguistic Approach to Language Proficiency Assessment.* Clevedon, Avon, England: Multilingual Matters.

Rivera, C. 1984a. *Communicative Competence Approaches to Language Proficiency Assessment: Research and Application.* Clevedon, Avon, England: Multilingual Matters.

Rivera, C. 1984b. *Language Proficiency and Academic Achievement.* Clevedon, Avon, England: Multilingual Matters.

Robinson, H., W. J. Gerace, and J. P. Mestre. 1980. Factors influencing the performance of bilingual Hispanic students in math and science related area areas. *Integrated Education,* 18(5–6): 38–42.

Rodriguez, R. C., and R. L. Gallegos. 1981. *Hispanics, Engineering and the Sciences: A Counselling Guide.* ERIC Clearinghouse on Rural Education and Small Schools, Las Cruces, New Mexico: New Mexico State University.

Roemer, D. 1983. Children's verbal folklore. *Volta Review* 85(5): 55–71.

Rohwer, W. D. 1971. Learning, race and school success. *Review of Education Research* 41: 191–210.

Romo, H. 1984. The Mexican origin population's differing perceptions of their children's schooling. *Social Science Quarterly* 65: 635–649.

Rondal, J. A. In press. Bilingualism and mental handicap: Some prospective views. In Y. Lebrun and M. Paradis (eds.), *Early Bilingualism and Child Development.* Amsterdam: Swets and Zeitlinger.

Rueda, R. 1983. Metalinguistic awareness in monolingual and bilingual mildly retarded children. *National Association for Bilingual Education Journal* 8(1): 55–68.

Rueda, R., and H. Mehan. 1986. Metacognition and passing: Strategic interactions in the lives of students with learning disabilities. *Anthropology and Education Quarterly.* 17(3), 145–165.

Samora, J. 1963. The education of the Spanish-speaking in the Southwest: An analysis of the 1960 census materials. Paper presented January, 1963 at the Mexican American Workshop, Occidental College, Los Angeles, CA.

Sanchez, G. I. 1932. *The Age-Grade Status of the Rural Child in New Mexico, 1931–1932.* Santa Fe, NM: State Department of Education.

Savignon, S. 1972. *Communicative Competence: An Experiment in Foreign Language Teaching.* Philadelphia: Center for Curriculum Development.

Savignon, S. 1983. *Communicative Competence: Theory and Classroom Practice.* Reading, MA: Addison-Wesley.

Saville-Troike, M. 1982a. Communicative tactics in children's second acquisition. Paper presented at the University of Wisconsin Symposium on Universals of Second Language.

Saville-Troike, M. 1982b. *The Ethnography of Communication: An Introduction.* Baltimore, MD: University Park Press.

Saville-Troike, M. 1984. What *really* matters in second language learning for academic achievement? *Teaching English to Speakers of Other Languages,* 18(2): 199–219.

Schank, R. C., and R. P. Ableson. 1977. *Scripts, Plans, Goals and Understandings.* Hillsdale, NJ: Erlbaum Associates.

Schumann, J. 1976. Second language acquisition research: Getting a more global look at the learner. H. Brown (ed.), Papers in second language acquisition [special issue]. *Language Learning* 4.

Schur, E. M. 1971. *Labelling Deviant Behavior,* 52–56; 69–71. New York: Harper and Row.

Schwartzman, H. B. 1976. The anthropological study of children's play. *Annual Review of Anthropology* 5: 289–328.

Scollon, R. 1974. One child's language from one to two: The origins of construction. Unpublished doctoral dissertation, University of Hawaii.

Scribner, S., and M. Cole. 1981. *The Psychology of Literacy.* Cambridge: Harvard University Press.

Seidner, S. 1981. *Issues of Language Assessment: Foundations and Research.* Proceedings of the First Annual Language Assessment Institute. Illinois State Board of Education.

Selinker, L. 1972. Interlanguage. *International Review of Applied Linguistics* 10: 201–231.

Shatz, M., and R. Gelman. 1973. The development of communication skills: Modifications in the speech of young children as a function of listener. *Monographs of the Society for Research in Child Development* 38(5).

Shultz, J. 1984. I'm going to take a long time: The three-year old as a social being. Unpublished manuscript, University of Cincinnati.

Shultz, J., S. Florio, and F. Erickson. 1982. Where's the floor? Aspects of the cultural organization of social relations in communication at home and in school. In P. Gilmore and A. Glatthorn (eds.), *Children in and out of School,* Vol. 2. Washington, D. C.: Center for Applied Linguistics, Language and Ethnography Series.

Shweder, R. A., and R. A. LeVine (eds.). 1984. *Culture Theory: Essays on Mind, Self, and Emotion.* Cambridge: Cambridge University Press.

Simich-Dudgeon, C., and C. Rivera. 1983. Teacher training and ethnographic/sociolinguistic issues in the assessment of bilingual students' language proficiency. In C. Rivera (ed.), *An Ethnographic/Sociolinguistic Approach to Language Proficiency Assessment.* 106–130. Clevedon, Avon, England: Multilingual Matters.

Simon, C. 1979. *Communicative Competence: A Functional-Pragmatic Approach to Language Therapy.* Tucson, AZ: Communication Skill Builders.

Skutnabb-Kangas, T. 1981. *Bilingualism or Not. The Education of Minorities.* Clevedon, England: Multilingual Matters, Ltd.

Smart, C. 1977. Manners private and public. *Korean Journal* 17(12).

Smith, F. 1923. Bilingualism and mental development. *British Journal of Psychology* 13: 270–280.

Smith, F. 1982. How children learn. *Interdisciplinary Voice No. 1.* Austin: Society for Learning Disabilities and Remedial Education.

Smith, T. W. 1980. Ethnic measurement and identification. *Ethnicity* 7: 78–95.

Southern California's Latino Community. 1983. A series of articles reprinted from the Los Angeles *Times.*

Spindler, G. 1955. *Anthropology and Education.* Stanford, CA: Stanford University Press.

Spindler, G. 1974. *Education and Cultural Process: Toward an Anthropology of Education.* New York: Holt, Rinehart and Winston.

Spindler, G. 1982. *Doing the Ethnography of Schooling.* New York: Holt, Rinehart and Winston.

Stavenhagen, R. 1970. Classes, colonialism, and acculturation. In I. Horowitz (ed.), *Masses in Latin America.* New York: Oxford University Press.

Steinberg, L., P. L. Blinde, and K. S. Chan. 1984. *Dropping Out among Language Minority Youth: A Review of the Literature.* Los Alamitos, CA: National Center for Bilingual Research.

Stewart, S. O. 1981. Language in Guatemala: Planning and prospects. *The Linguistic Reporter* 23: 6–7.

Suarez-Orozco, M. M. 1985. Opportunity, family dynamics and achievement: The sociocultural context of motivation among recent immigrants from Central America. Paper read at the University of California Symposium on Linguistic Minorities and Education, Tahoe City, California, May 30–June 1, 1985.

Suarez-Orozco, M. M. 1986. In Pursuit of a dream: New Hispanic immigrants in American schools. Unpublished doctoral dissertation. University of California, Berkeley.

Suarez-Orozco, M. M. In press. Transformation in perception of self and social environment in Mexican immigrants. In S. Morgan and E. Colson (eds.), *People in Upheaval.* Stanton Island, NY: Center for Migration Studies.

Sue, S., and A. Padilla. 1986. Ethnic minority issues in the United States: Challenges for the educational system. In *Beyond Language: Social and Cultural Factors in Schooling Language Minority Students.* 35–72. Sacramento, CA: Bilingual Education Office.

Swain, M., and M. Canale. 1981. The role of grammar in a communicative approach to second language teaching and testing. In S. S. Seidner (ed.), *Issues of Language Assessment: Foundations and Research.* Springfield, IL: Illinois State Department of Education.

Tax, S. 1937. The "municipios" of the midwestern highlands of Guatemala. *American Anthropologist* 39: 423–444.

Troike, R. 1978. Research evidence for the effectiveness of bilingual education. *National Association for Bilingual Education Journal* 3(1): 13–24.

Trueba, H. 1974. Bilingual bicultural education for Chicanos in the Southwest. *Council on Anthropology and Education Quarterly* 5(3): 8–15.

Trueba, H. 1983. Adjustment problems of Mexican American children: An anthropological study. *Learning Disabilities Quarterly* 6(4): 395–415.

Trueba, H. In press. Organizing classroom instruction in specific sociocultural contexts: Teaching Mexican youth to write in English. In S. Goldman and H. Trueba (eds.), *Becoming Literate in English as a Second Language: Advances in Research and Theory.* Norwood, NJ: Ablex.

Trueba, H., and P. Wright. 1980–81. On ethnographic studies and multicultural education. *Journal of the National Association for Bilingual Education* 5(2): 29–56.

Trueba, H., G. Guthrie, and K. Au (eds.). 1981. *Culture and the Bilingual Classroom.* Rowley, MA: Newbury House.

Trueba, H., L. Moll, S. Diaz, and R. Diaz. 1984. *Improving the Functional Writing of Bilingual Secondary School Students.* (Contract No. 400-81-0023). Washington, DC: National Institute of Education. ERIC, Clearinghouse on Languages and Linguistics, ED 240: 862.

Tyler, R. W. 1979. Educational objectives and educational testing: Problems now faced. In R. Tyler and S. H. White (eds.), *Testing, Teaching and Learning.* 36–51. Report of a conference on research on testing, National Institute of Education, Washington, D. C.

Ulibarri, D. 1982. *Limited-English Proficient Students: A Review of National Estimates.* National Center for Bilingual Research, November.

Ulibarri, D., M. L. Spencer, and G. A. Rivas. 1981. Language proficiency and academic achievement: Relationship to school ratings as predictors of academic achievement. *National Association for Bilingual Education Journal* 5(3): 47–80.

Underwood, H. 1977. Foundations of thought and values: How we differ. *Korean Journal* 17(12).

U. S. Bureau of the Census. 1973. *1970 U.S. Census. Puerto Ricans in the United States.* PC(2)-1E, June.

U. S. Bureau of the Census 1981. Persons of Spanish origin in the United States. *Current Population Reports* Series P-20, No. 361.

U. S. Commission on Civil Rights. 1972. *The Excluded Student. Educational Practices Affecting Mexican Americans in the Southwest.* Mexican-American Education Study, Report III. Washington, D. C.: U. S. Government Printing Office.

U. S. Commission on Civil Rights. 1976. *Puerto Ricans in the Continental United States: An Uncertain Future.* Washington, D. C.

U. S. Congress. Senate. 1976. *Equal Educational Opportunity for Puerto Rican Children.* Hearings before select committee on equal educational opportunity. 91st Congress, 2nd session, Part 8, 3683–3973.

U. S. Department of Labor. 1970. *Labor Force Experience of the Puerto Rican Worker.* Bureau of Labor Statistics, Regional Report No. 9, June, 1968. Washington, D. C.

VanNess, H. 1981. Social control and social organization in an Alaskan Athabaskan classroom: A microethnography of "getting ready" for reading. In H. Trueba, G. Guthrie and K. Au (eds.), *Culture and the Bilingual Classroom: Studies in Classroom Ethnography.* Rowley, MA: Newbury House.

Vygotsky, L. S. 1962. *Thought and Language.* Cambridge: MIT Press.

Vygotsky, L. S. 1978. *Mind in Society: The Development of Higher Psychological Processes.* M. Cole, V. John-Teiner, S. Scribner, and E. Souberman (eds.). Cambridge: Harvard University Press.

Walker, C. L. 1980. Locus of control and attribution responses of bilingual Spanish-English children. Unpublished doctoral dissertation, University of Illinois, Urbana-Champaign.

Walker, C. L., and S. J. Rakow. 1985. The status of Hispanic American students in science: Attitudes. *Hispanic Journal of Behavioral Sciences* 7(3): 225–245.

Wallat, C. 1984. An overview of communicative competence. In C. Rivera (ed.), *Communicative Competence Approaches to Language Proficiency Assessment: Research and Application.* Clevedon, Avon, England: Multilingual Matters.

Waller, W. 1932. *The Sociology of Teaching.* New York: John Wiley and Sons.

Warren, K. B. (1978). *The Symbolism of Subordination.* Austin: University of Texas Press.

Wax, R. 1976. Oglala Sioux dropouts and their problems with educators. In J. Roberts and S. K. Akinsanya (eds.), *Schooling in the Cultural Context.* 216–226. New York: David McKay Company, Inc.

Werner, O., and K. Begishe. 1968, August. Styles of learning: The·evidence from Navajo. Paper presented for conference on styles of learning in American Indian children, Stanford University, Stanford, California.

Wertsch, J. V. 1981. *The Concept of Activity in Soviet Psychology.* New York: M. E. Sharpe, Inc.

Wertsch, J. V. 1985. *Vygotsky and the Social Formation of the Mind.* Cambridge: Harvard University Press.

White, S. H. 1973. *Federal Programs for Young Children: Review and Recommendations,* Vol. I. Goals and Standards of Public Programs for Children. Washington, D. C.: Government Printing Office.

Whorf, B. L. 1964. *Language, Thought and Reality.* J. B. Carroll, (ed.). Cambridge: M.I.T. Press.

Wilcox, K. 1982. Ethnography as a methodology and its applications to the study of schooling: A review. In G. Spindler (ed.), *Doing the Ethnography of Schooling: Educational Anthropology in Action,* 456–488. New York: Holt, Rinehart and Winston.

Willett, J. Forthcoming. An ethnographic study of children acquiring a second-language in an academic context. Unpublished doctoral dissertation, Stanford University. Stanford, CA.

Wolf, E. 1957. Closed corporate peasant communities in Mesoamerica and Java. *Southwestern Journal of Anthropology* 13(1): 1–18.

Wong-Fillmore, L. 1976. The second time around: Cognitive and social strategies in second language acquisition. Unpublished doctoral dissertation, Stanford University.

Wong-Fillmore, L. 1982a. Instructional language as linguistic input: Second language learning in classrooms. In L. Wilkinson (ed.), *Communicating in Classrooms,* 283–296. New York: Academic Press.

Wong-Fillmore, L. 1982b. Language minority students and school participation: What kind of English is needed? *Journal of Education* 164: 143–156.

Wong-Fillmore, L. 1984. Variations in second language acquisitions: What is normal and what is not? Paper presented April, 1984 at the American Speech and Hearing Association Conference, San Francisco, CA.

Wong-Fillmore, L., P. Ammon, and B. McLaughlin. 1985. *Learning English through Bilingual Instruction.* Final Report. National Clearinghouse for Bilingual Education.

Yela, M. 1975. Comprensión verbal y bilingualismo. *Revista de Psicologia General y Aplicada* 30: 1045.

Yoshioka, J. G. 1929. A study of bilingualism. *Journal of Genetic Psychology* 36: 473–479.

Zerubavel, E. 1981. *Hidden Rhythms: Schedules and Calendars in Social Life.* Chicago: University of Chicago Press.

Zimmerman, I., V. Steiner and R. E. Pond. 1979. *Preschool Language Scale.* Columbus: Charles E. Merrill Publishing Co.

Zintz, M. V. 1963. *Education across Cultures.* Chicago: Holt, Rinehart and Winston.